More praise for *Walking Ghosts*

"Steve Dudley has visited more of Colombia's harsh venues, and sat patiently in them longer than any other foreign journalist, to understand the forces that have propelled Colombia's conflict for decades and decades. What he has produced is a passionate narrative, rich with the characters and landscape of a remarkable country, that explains why Colombia's confounding war continues to resist all attempts to stop it."
—Scott Wilson, Andean bureau chief of *The Washington Post*

"With compassion, insight, and a nose for detail, Dudley presents the definitive tale of the political drama behind Colombia's seemingly endless violence. Meticulously reported, *Walking Ghosts* is an intense, hair-raising account of a complex conflict that leaves the reader on the edge of his seat. More than any other reporter before him, Dudley has brought to life the brave, the innocent, the murderous, and the evil who have been thrown together in the cauldron of Latin America's longest-running civil war."
—Juan Forero, Andean regional bureau chief for *The New York Times*

"Steven Dudley's haunting account of the rise and blood-soaked fall of Colombia's Patriotic Union (Union Patriotica) party is essential reading for anyone who wants to fully understand the causes of Latin America's longest-running civil war. A brave and unflinching book."
—Joseph Contreras, Latin America Regional Editor, *Newsweek*

"With verve and compassion, Dudley tells the riveting story of a political genocide that has cost Colombia thousands of lives. No one else has written this history so well and with so much first-hand access to its protagonists. It is a painful, complex, funny, and provocative read, and goes to the heart of how modern Colombia really works."
—Robin Kirk, Senior Researcher, Human Rights Watch-Americas Division and author of *More Terrible Than Death: Massacres, Drugs, and America's War in Colombia*

"Dudley brilliantly captures the political complexity and moral ambiguity of the country's ongoing internal war. His tale is not one of heroes in white hats with clean hands fighting the just fight against the dark forces of unvarnished evil. It is a story of intrigue and betrayal, of torture and murder, of bloody sacrifice and loss on all sides of Colombia's fratricidal violence. It has no false happy ending. It is the tragic story of Colombia today."
—Bruce Bagley, Department of International Studies, *University of Miami*

WALKING
GHOSTS

WALKING GHOSTS

MURDER AND GUERRILLA POLITICS IN COLOMBIA

STEVEN DUDLEY

Routledge
Taylor & Francis Group
New York London

First Routledge hardcover edition, copyright © 2003 by Taylor and Francis Books, Inc.
First Routledge paperback edition, copyright © 2006 by Taylor & Francis Group, LLC

Published in 2006 by
Routledge
Taylor & Francis Group
270 Madison Avenue
New York, NY 10016

Published in Great Britain by
Routledge
Taylor & Francis Group
2 Park Square
Milton Park, Abingdon
Oxon OX14 4RN

© 2006 by Taylor & Francis Group, LLC
Routledge is an imprint of Taylor & Francis Group

Printed in the United States of America on acid-free paper
10 9 8 7 6 5 4 3 2 1

International Standard Book Number-10: 0-415-93304-8 (Softcover)
International Standard Book Number-13: 978-0-415-93304-9 (Softcover)
Library of Congress Card Number 2003012445

Library of Congress Cataloging-in-Publication Data

Dudley, Steven S.
  Walking ghosts : murder and guerilla politics in Colombia / by Steven Dudley.
      p. cm.
  Includes bibliographical references and index.
  ISBN 0-415-93303-X (hbk.) - ISBN 0-415-93304-8 (pbk)
  1. Colombia--Politics and government--1974- 2. Unión Patriótica (Colombia) 3. Fuerzas Armadas Revolucionarias de Colombia. 4. Insurgency--Colombia--History. 5. Political violence--Colombia--History. 6. State-sponsored terrorism--Colombia--History. I. Title.

F2279.D83 2004
986.106'35-dc21   2003012445

Taylor & Francis Group
is the Academic Division of Informa plc.

Visit the Taylor & Francis Web site at
http://www.taylorandfrancis.com

and the Routledge Web site at
http://www.routledge-ny.com

TO MY POLITICAL GODFATHER, ALBERTO ROJAS PUYO

CONTENTS

x

Colombia is 440,000 square miles, roughly three times the size of Iraq and four times the size of Vietnam. Three vast mountain ranges split the country into several distinct regions that vary widely in climate, population, and economy. The cattle and coca-growing Eastern Plains encompasses nearly one-third of the territory but just a small percentage of Colombia's forty million residents. The Middle Magdalena Valley is the heart of the country's oil industry and holds part of its illegal drug economy. Urabá is known for its banana plantations and arms and drug trafficking routes. Throughout Colombia, infrastructure is neglected and roads are in disrepair. Along with the war, these obstacles make it hard to unify the country.

Manuel "Sureshot"
Marulanda
FARC Leader

Jacobo Arenas
FARC Leader

Alfonso Cano
FARC Leader

Braulio Herrera
FARC/UP Leader

Álvaro Salazar
FARC/UP Leader

Alberto Rojas Puyo
UP Leader

Jaime Pardo Leal
UP Leader

1948
Gaitán
assassinated;
La Violencia
begins

1957–58
Rojas Pinilla ousted;
"National Front" begins

1966
Communist Party
forms FARC under
M. Marulanda,
J. Arenas

1982
FARC holds
historic
VII Conference
under J. Arenas
leadership

1983
Communist envoy
A. Rojas Puyo
meets with
FARC to
discuss UP

1984
FARC/Govn.
sign La Uribe
ceasefire
agreement

1986
First UP presidential
candidate, J. Pardo
gets 328,752 votes

1985
FARC launches
UP under leadership of
B. Herrera, J. Pardo

1953
Gen. Rojas Pinilla
takes power

1964
Colombian and US
attack Communist
"Independent Republics";
La Violencia ends,
modern war begins

1960
US Govn.
sends aid to help
fight against
Colombian insurgency

1981
FARC kills
Jesús Castaño;
Castaño's sons form
paramilitary group

1982
Belisario Betancur
elected Colombian President;
Gen. Landazábal
becomes Colombian
Defense Minister

1982
First paramilitary
meetings in
Puerto Boyacá

1985
Black Vladimir joins
paramilitaries
in Puerto Boyacá

1986
Virgilio Barco
elected Colombian
President

1985
J. Rodríguez Gacha,
Henry Pérez,
and others
forge paramilitary
alliance

TIMELINE 1948–2003

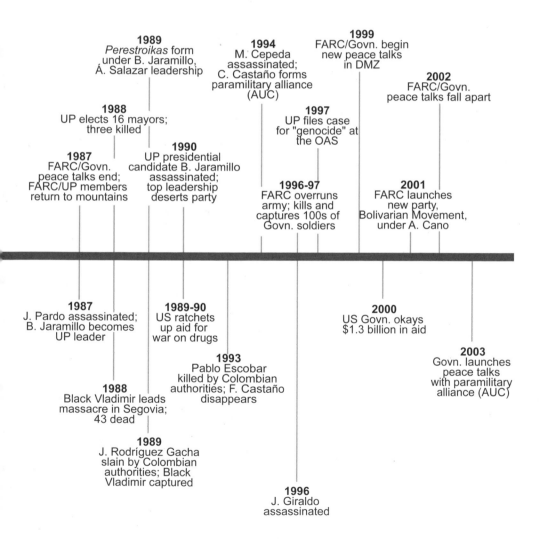

Bernardo Jaramillo
UP Leader

Josué Giraldo
UP Leader

Gen. Fernando Landazábal
Colombian Defense Minister

Fidel Castaño
Paramilitary Leader

Carlos Castaño
Paramilitary Leader

Black Vladimir
Paramilitary Commander

José Rodríguez Gacha
Drug Trafficker/
Paramilitary Leader

1989
Perestroikas form
under B. Jaramillo,
Á. Salazar leadership

1988
UP elects 16 mayors;
three killed

1987
FARC/Govn.
peace talks end;
FARC/UP members
return to mountains

1990
UP presidential
candidate B. Jaramillo
assassinated;
top leadership
deserts party

1994
M. Cepeda
assassinated;
C. Castaño forms
paramilitary alliance
(AUC)

1997
UP files case
for "genocide" at
the OAS

1996-97
FARC overruns
army; kills and
captures 100s of
Govn. soldiers

1999
FARC/Govn. begin
new peace talks
in DMZ

2002
FARC/Govn.
peace talks fall apart

2001
FARC launches
new party,
Bolivarian Movement,
under A. Cano

1987
J. Pardo assassinated;
B. Jaramillo becomes
UP leader

1989-90
US ratchets
up aid for
war on drugs

1993
Pablo Escobar
killed by Colombian
authorities; F. Castaño
disappears

1988
Black Vladimir leads
massacre in Segovia;
43 dead

1989
J. Rodríguez Gacha
slain by Colombian
authorities; Black
Vladimir captured

1996
J. Giraldo
assassinated

2000
US Govn. okays
$1.3 billion in aid

2003
Govn. launches
peace talks
with paramilitary
alliance (AUC)

ACKNOWLEDGMENTS

This type of book can only be researched and written when people take long hours out of their days to speak with you at length about painful subjects. Countless former and active militants of the UP, the Communist Party, and the FARC took the time to answer my questions and help me understand the events that led to the destruction of their political party. Among these people, Álvaro Salazar, Alberto Rojas Puyo, Medófilo Medina, and Mariella Barragán met with me on numerous occasions and helped me establish links to other protagonists in the story. Special mention should also go to the Communist Party weekly, *Voz*, whose editor, Carlos Lozano, gave me access to its archives and photos. Several of the party's enemies were also generous enough to talk to me about why they destroyed the UP, including Carlos Castaño and some of his cohorts in the paramilitaries.

Human rights groups like *Justicia y Paz* and their data collectors at the *Banco de Datos* also greatly contributed to this effort. Lawyers' groups like the *Colectivo de Abogados* and the *Comisión Colombiana de Juristas* gave me guidance and stacks of information. The *Colectivo* also provided me with documents concerning Manuel Cepeda's and Wilson Borja's cases. Javier Cruz, the director of the archives at *Semana* magazine, provided me with hundreds of articles. Judges like Julio Ballén gave me access to sensitive judicial cases. And professors like Gonzalo Sánchez, Alejandro Reyes Posada, Medófilo Medina, and Henry Dietz gave me historical and political perspective.

I would like to thank my colleagues at Peace Brigades International—who taught me that Colombia is ambiguity and ambiguity is Colombia—and friends who work for Amnesty International and Human Rights Watch. I'm also grateful to my journalist colleagues who showed me a new world. For every "thousand pockets," "lunchbox legend," and "cyclops," there is a Martin

Hodgson, a Karl Penhaul, a Kirk Semple, and a Scott Wilson. Martin, Karl, and Kirk also read early drafts of the book and gave me invaluable advice.

My assistant, Andrea Domínguez, pulled together the final pieces of this book in record time, and my photographer friends—freelancers Marcelo Salinas and Carlos Villalón, and Richard Emblin at *El Tiempo*—helped me gather the precious photos. Susan Dreyer, a friend and confidant, read and commented intelligently on early drafts of the book. Michael Evans at the National Security Archives provided me with all the declassified U.S. documents he could get his hands on. Scott Wilson and Dita Smith of the *Washington Post* paved the way for Laris Karklis to draw the country map.

I would like to give special thanks to Eyal Press, my good friend and ad-hoc agent, and Eric Nelson, my editor at Routledge. Eric and Routledge took a chance on this young, unagented freelance writer, then Routledge's Angela Chnapko and Nicole Ellis made sure it all came together.

Most of all, I would like to thank my friends and family. My sister, Deborah Dudley, made the timeline at the beginning of the book and helped lay out the photos in the middle. My mother, Shirley Dudley, and a friend, Victor Cruz, helped proofread the galleys. Many others commented on early drafts. All of them resisted the temptation to pull me out of the country even when they didn't hear from me for weeks at a time. Their unwavering support for this project is what ultimately made it a reality.

May 2003

PREFACE

I began writing this book when I realized that I had to leave Colombia. This is not a book that will sit well with anyone actively involved in that country's four-decade-old civil war. Any one of them might want to kill me for writing this story. I wish I were exaggerating. But I know from talking to them personally that none of them wants this story to be told in its entirety. Each draws different conclusions from the same results. Each seeks to use the story to justify their ongoing wars against one another. Each hates when people contradict them. This is why I had to leave Colombia before this book was published, and this is why I may have a hard time returning while the war continues.

This book is the result of years of research and soul-searching, investigation and self-examination. I didn't write these words or come to these conclusions easily. The story is painful to tell. I wish Colombia were more black and white. I wish there were clear-cut good guys and clear-cut bad guys. But Colombia isn't a story of good guys and bad guys. Colombia is much more than that, which is why it's difficult to ignore. It's raw: humans at their best and worst.

I first went to Colombia as a human rights observer in 1995. I worked with Peace Brigades International. Peace Brigades International is made up of volunteers who accompany the politically persecuted and document the human rights situation. While I was with Peace Brigades, I began to meet the people who would form the core of this story. Human rights are a dangerous endeavor, in part because they are enveloped by politics. More than ever, human rights are playing a critical role in determining relationships between citizens and nations. In some parts of the world, working in human rights is noble. In Colombia working in human rights has come to be associated with supporting the rebels. This is not unfounded, but the broad generalizations the enemies of human rights workers make have cost hundreds of innocent people their lives and have only served to prolong the conflict.

As a human rights observer, I traveled to and worked in some of the most notoriously dangerous places in the country. For eight months in 1996, I lived in a blue-collar town in Colombia named Barrancabermeja. Barranca, as Colombians call it, is an oil town in the Middle Magdalena Valley, an extensive plain that separates two striking mountain ranges in the heart of the country. When I lived there, Barranca was a guerrilla stronghold. Rebel graffiti adorned the walls, a pro-guerrilla oil union and peasant syndicate dominated the popular movement, and the city served as Colombia's unofficial anti-gringo headquarters. During the May Day parade I watched people drag a papier-mâché dummy of the then–U.S. ambassador down the street and burn it in effigy in front of the union headquarters.

Living in Barranca was like getting a master's degree in Guerrilla Science. We often had our meetings amid background music to drown out our voices because we were worried about bugs and the nosy neighbors we suspected were listening. We also wouldn't talk about anything political in cafés, taxis, or supermarkets for fear of being overheard by one side or the other. We spoke in our own code over the phone. On the street, I was told to look at people's shoes, their motorcycles, and their style of dress in order to tell if they were rebels or undercover policemen. I couldn't go into certain neighborhoods without an escort because I might be kidnapped.

Needless to say, it was difficult to distinguish friend from foe. Without even knowing it, I had become part of the larger political game. I could never really tell whom I was speaking to or why they were speaking to me. I got invited to so many "cookouts" I started to think that maybe it was code for something else; and I still do. On the flip side, army and navy commanders would frequently lecture me about guerrilla politics and manipulation. And I was only just beginning to understand the multiplicity of motives behind the violence. The civil war was but one reason why people died. Illegal drug trafficking, contraband of liquor and cigarettes, gasoline theft, adultery, and lottery ticket scams all left bodies in the streets.

Nevertheless, I thought I knew what was right, and I stuck to my beliefs. I was particularly taken by political murder of left-wing sympathizers. The government and its proxy allies, the right-wing paramilitary groups, killed hundreds of suspected guerrilla collaborators. The victims didn't have trials or defense lawyers. The killers didn't need lawyers either. They assassinated with impunity. While I was in Barranca, the paramilitaries were slowly encroaching on the city. They worked in teams of fifteen or twenty men who acted more like death squads than any military force I had known. They attacked one town at a time and killed suspected rebels wherever they found them. In what turned out to be a prelude of things to come, dead bodies were beginning to appear in ditches and along the roads near Barranca. It was only a matter of time before Barranca would succumb to the dirty war politics of the state.

In this context I began looking at one particular case of political persecution that would eventually become this book. As I shifted from being a human rights observer to being a master's candidate at the University of Texas at Austin, I started studying the *Unión Patriótica*, or Patriotic Union. The UP, as it was known, was the brainchild of the country's largest guerrilla group, the Fuerzas Armadas Revolucionarios de Colombia, the Revolutionary Armed Forces of Colombia or, as it was known by its Spanish acronym, FARC. The FARC launched the new party in 1985 as part of a peace process it was carrying out with the government. But from there, the party's story got complicated, so I break it down into three parts.

The first part of the book covers the period during which the FARC created its political party. The UP was the equivalent of Sinn Fein, the Irish Republican Army's political wing, and the Palestine Liberation Organization (PLO). As with Sinn Fein in Ireland and the PLO in the Middle East, the UP was the voice of the insurgents, a means through which the FARC could test their ideas at the polls. It was also supposed to be part of a pathway to peace, a way for the Colombian rebels to enter the political mainstream and leave their guns behind. In reality, it was neither, but the FARC spent a huge amount of energy and effort establishing its party.

Even while the rebels were creating the UP, their enemies were developing a strategy to combat the party. For the same reasons that Sinn Fein and the PLO represent a threat, the UP scared many Colombians. Over time, the UP became the focus of the dirty war, a lightning rod for the FARC's enemies to channel their anger. Soon after it formed, UP members were murdered in huge numbers. During the six-year period I study in this book, thousands were killed. How many died remains unknown, but the killing extinguished the party and the peace process along with it. The second part of the book covers this physical extermination of the UP.

The last part of the book is a postmortem look at the party. The UP still plays a role in Colombia's conflict. The FARC uses the extermination to justify its never ending war against the government. The paramilitaries point to it as an example of guerrilla treachery. Those in between, the majority of Colombians, see it as another sad reason why peace is still so far away.

At first, the story of the UP seemed like such a simple tale to tell: a small, well-meaning political party crushed by its foes in the government, the paramilitaries, and the oligarchy. But with time and investigation, these stories begin to take on the shades of gray that so characterize Colombia. As political analysts and journalists have repeatedly pointed out, Colombia does not easily fit into stereotypes. Luckily, I had an advantage: I wasn't Colombian, and this gave me access I would not have gotten had my subjects felt I was tainted by living there my whole life. As a graduate student and then later as a journalist for National Public Radio and the *Washington Post*, I found the doors open to me on all sides.

During my four-year investigation into the destruction of the UP, I had the opportunity to interview the party's creators and its killers, its champions and its critics. I tell this story through these people because it was from these sources that I discovered the strategy behind the party and the strategy of how to destroy it. And it was because of what these sources told me that I began to doubt my convictions and beliefs about the war in Colombia.

Throughout my investigation I tried to maintain a level, objective mind. It wasn't easy. The people enmeshed in this endless war treated me well. The union members in Barrancabermeja gave me an unforgettable drunken send-off. The paramilitaries took me on a private plane to see their top commander. The guerrillas gave me beds and mosquito netting to sleep under in their jungle camps. Current and former Communist Party and UP members took me into their homes and told me stories they'd kept to themselves for years. Judges gave me access to investigations normally kept under lock and key. Analysts took time from their busy schedules to share with me their documents, maps, and insights.

That's not to say there weren't problems. Rebels stuck guns in my face. Paramilitaries confused me for a CIA agent. The Colombian military "detained" me for several hours. But these were the exceptions. The doors were opened for me, and I took advantage. Now I'm afraid they will think that I've betrayed their trust and come after me. This was, after all, an impossible story to tell without injecting my own opinion, my own analysis, and my own sad conclusions. For that, I may never be able to return to a place that embraced me.

Miami, Florida
May 2003

PROLOGUE

THE MARTYRS

In Colombia there are walking ghosts, people who have crossed death's frontier. They're still alive, but many of them wish they were dead. Living, as it stands, is a burden. They're not suicidal. They're just suffering because their enemies have them cornered. The time they have left is short, and they know it. They're surrounded by threats and bodyguards. Not only is death beckoning but guilt. These walking ghosts live in a world of wakes and funerals. They have survived when so many others have perished. What's left of them is often used to hasten the end, to take that final step into the other world. While some search for safety, most of them search for a perch where they can die with dignity. They would rather be considered martyrs than cowards.

I met one such walking ghost in 1995, early in my stay in Colombia. His name was Josué Giraldo. Josué was an inconspicuous person, Colombian in so many ways. He had dark, wavy brown hair, which was neatly trimmed, and a light, European-*mestizo* colored skin. The first and only time we met, he was clean shaven and wearing a pressed shirt and pants. He was compact and strong. He reminded me of the wrestlers I had known in high school. His friends later told me that Josué played basketball and soccer, and jogged regularly.

But Josué's cool look couldn't hide his anxiety. He was noticeably nervous. His movements were jerky, and he had a rigid handshake. We exchanged names and a few pleasantries that day but little else. Words came quickly out of his mouth, and I had a hard time understanding him because I was still getting used to Colombian Spanish.

Josué lived in a world I was only beginning to comprehend. His main job was in human rights. He worked with a Catholic nongovernmental organization, *Justicia y Paz*, in Bogotá and the local human rights committee in the city of Villavicencio, the capital of the province of Meta and the beginning of the vast Eastern Plains that cover nearly a third of Colombia's territory. But Josué was also

1

a member of the Communist Party and one of the few remaining active militants of a leftist political party known as the *Unión Patriótica* or Patriotic Union, which people referred to by its Spanish acronym, UP. In human rights and politics, Josué could not have chosen two more dangerous professions in Colombia.

The day we met, Josué had driven four hours from his home in Villavicencio through the steep mountain pass to Bogotá. He was going to be a panelist at a human rights conference. Two bodyguards were with him, and he was carrying a little pistol that he tucked beneath his belt. I was working with an international human rights organization at the time and was accompanying him to the panel as an added measure of protection. Despite the guns and guards, I was as jittery as he was as we set off toward the conference in his armored car. I had been in Colombia for about two weeks, and I was terrified. I thought it would be like other countries I had visited, where fear of the unknown wears off quickly once you arrive. Instead, I found myself just waiting for something bad to happen.

The Colombia I had known up until then was mostly from the few English-language books on the country. They compare Colombia's civil war to others around the world. And at its roots, Colombia's war is like most. Close to half of the population is in poverty. There is a severe shortage of schools and health facilities. About 15 percent of the population is illiterate, and a quarter lack basic public services like electricity and water. The richest ten percent of the population control more than half of the wealth. Four percent of the ranches and farms occupy three-quarters of the arable land. The inequalities lead to unrest, which leads to protest, which leads to war.

The books highlight the civil strife by giving horrible figures: nearly 30,000 murders per year (15 times that of the United States); 75 political assassinations a week; 10 people kidnapped per day. There are over 20,000 leftist guerrilla soldiers fighting 250,000 government soldiers and police. There are another 10,000 of the government's proxies, the right-wing paramilitaries, who fight the rebels and assassinate anyone they suspect aids the guerrillas. Most of these armed men are hidden in army barracks, distant jungles, and mountainside hideouts. Still, to a newcomer like myself, the numbers were overwhelming. In my first few weeks, everyone was a potential assailant, and every situation had become a dangerous one. The abstract left me with an utter sense of dread, especially when I spent time with people, like Josué, who had received death threats.

Raindrops slid down the car windows as Josué, his bodyguards, and I wove through the Bogotá traffic that day. The moisture blurred the lights of the other cars that jostled for position between the lanes. Impatient drivers honked furiously at the traffic cops, other cars, the rain, and anything else that was in their way. Downtown Bogotá looks like a modern city—tall buildings, fancy apartments, bright neon signs—covered with a layer of soot. When it rains, the mud simply deepens and the traffic becomes unbearable. I didn't like being stationary for long periods of time that day, but the cars were stacked in a seemingly impossible knot.

Inside our car, there was little noise: no radio, no talking, just an occasional *clink* when the bodyguards' machine guns tapped the windows as the car jerked into motion again. Josué and I sat in the backseat together. We didn't speak about him, his human rights work, or the UP; I didn't really know too much about the political party that would later become my obsession, just that it was a major target of the paramilitary groups flourishing around the country. And I was too unsettled by the guns to speak in complete sentences.

After forty-five minutes in the Bogotá rain, we finally reached the conference. The auditorium was half full. We removed our jackets and shook off the water. I settled into my seat. Josué made his way to the front to greet the other panelists. Then I noticed something odd, the first indication that Josué was special: The others on the panel stood up to greet him and shook his hand gently; he spoke collegially to them while they simply smiled at him, talked to him slowly, and then stepped out of the way as he moved to sit down. None of this would have been so strange except that Josué was only thirty-six at the time, younger than all of them. Yet they treated him like he was an old, withering soldier. The gestures didn't seem so much out of pity as reverence. It soon became obvious that Josué was a hero to many of them, a survivor from a lost era.

The panel began. And although Josué sat next to them, the other panelists referred to him as if he weren't even there.

Colombia's democracy is lauded as one of the oldest in the region. Democratic elections were interrupted only once, during the mid-1950s by a brief military dictatorship. There's a thriving party system, albeit with most of the activity limited to the two traditional parties, the Liberals and the Conservatives. The two parties have been running the country since the early nineteenth century. They've alternated power in democratic and less than democratic ways. More importantly, they've sown the seeds of loyalty so deep that it's been impossible to unseat them from their throne. For over a hundred years, Colombians have been either Liberal or Conservative. It was in their blood, it was said, as much as the tradition of voting. Even when military dictators took over many other Latin American countries for long stretches in the 1960s and 1970s, the two parties survived and the country remained a democracy. What's more, Colombia's leading politicians condemned the repression throughout the region.

But it was as ingenuous as it was hypocritical for the Colombians to take the moral high ground during the dictatorships. Violence has always surrounded Colombian politics, and most of it has been administered by these two ruling parties. There have been countless civil wars, the most famous of which have daunting names like "The War of a Thousand Days," or the "War of the Supremes." One historian counted fifty-nine "local revolutions" in the nineteenth century alone. Political violence is almost as common as elections. Still, Colombia has a way of propping itself up as a beacon of development and first world values even while politicians are being assassinated in staggering numbers.

Such was the case with Josué Giraldo's party, the UP. The UP was a tiny leftist party, a marginal player compared with the Liberals and Conservatives. At its height in the mid-1980s, the UP garnered a small percentage of the vote. Its impact was largely symbolic. Despite the UP's size and scant representation, it had given the country a startling number of martyrs, which I had read about before coming to Colombia. For me, these dead were largely a faceless group—another figure to throw into the mix along with the number of murders per year, political assassinations per week, and kidnappings per day. But then, on that rainy day in Bogotá, I went with Josué to that conference, and he did something that none of the books I had read could have: He stood up between his admiring colleagues and gave the UP victims shape and meaning.

They were unionists, teachers, students, housewives, and children. Some made the speeches, Josué said, and others organized the crowds; the majority simply attended the rallies and voted. Many of them were rejoining politics after a long absence, he explained. They had given up on the democratic process as long as the Liberals and Conservatives dominated the government. Before the UP was launched in 1985, they had believed all politicians were corrupt, and voting didn't seem to change this fact. But for a brief time the UP had given them hope, and many of them had returned to politics with a renewed vigor. They all paid for this choice with their lives.

Some UP politicians were murdered in full public view—in front of their homes, their friends, their children, their wives. Other militants were killed as they traveled along dirt roads or played billiards in popular pool halls. UP members died drinking coffee in outdoor cafés, picking up their children from school, or parking their cars. Other UP leaders' lives were torn apart by threats or assassination attempts that forced them into exile.

The party's killers used automatic weapons and pistols, Josué said. Very often men riding double on motorcycles or leaning out of cars with tinted windows fired the guns. These men didn't hide their faces. But few of them have ever gone to jail for these murders, he lamented. The investigations sat in stacks in the attorney general's office. Those behind these crimes didn't hide either, he added. Many of them were rival politicians in the Liberal and Conservative Parties who publicly vilified the UP at every turn and paved the way for the hitmen to kill even more of them.

In all, perhaps as many as three thousand UP leaders and supporters had been killed. Josué called it a "political genocide." Many relatives and friends of the victims didn't seek redress in the cases of their loved ones because they feared for their lives and saw justice as a remote possibility. Less than a dozen paramilitary assassins and low-level army personnel had ever served time for killing UP militants. The party, Josué concluded, had been destroyed on every level, and the democratic left was still recovering from what was a deciding blow to its belief that the region's oldest and most celebrated democracy really could genuinely be a democracy.

Josué had probably given the talk at dozens of conferences, but for me it was a turning point. For the first time, I could see the front lines in Colombia's war. They weren't made up of rivers and mountains where the guerrillas and paramilitaries had their camps. They were made up of houses, parks, cafés, and armored cars driving through traffic jams in Bogotá. And the frontline soldiers weren't carrying Kalashnikovs and Galils, and marching toward army barracks and jungle hideouts. They were carrying notebooks and participating in these human rights conferences.

The war that killed three thousand members of the UP began long before Josué even joined the party. It was as much political as it was economic, and it would devour the entire country. While much of the world was consumed by the Cold War, Colombia had its own internal war known as *La Violencia* or "The Violence." The origins of *La Violencia* dated back to the 1930s. Large farmers—particularly those in the coffee belt in central Colombia, which dominated the country's economy—were industrializing their holdings. They wanted to be able to compete in the emerging global coffee market. But small farmers who wanted to keep their plots intact were resisting change. The fights turned bloody in the mid-1940s. The large landowners, which included members of both the Liberal and Conservative Parties, got help from the police in subduing the peasants and expanding their properties. The peasants sought political help to fight off the onslaught. They found it in a charismatic Liberal Party peasant organizer named Jorge Eliécer Gaitán.

Gaitán was a city boy, well educated and from the upper echelons of the Liberal Party. He had even gone to school in France. But the injustices and repression in the countryside pushed him to turn on his mentors and create a peasant syndicate to fight the large landowners. His mastery of the language of agitation and dissent appealed to these peasant farmers. Gaitán also got support from the small shop owners and unionists who were disgusted with the favoritism among the political elite. Gaitán's message was simple: Protect the weak from the strong. And he delivered it with passion before the hungry *pueblo*. Grainy black-and-white photos of Gaitán with his mouth open and arm raised to the sky are draped in the hallways of Colombia's libraries and universities. He remains one of the few indisputable heroes who virtually everyone has since claimed for their own political benefit.

In the 1940s, however, Gaitán was the enemy of powerful Conservative and Liberal leaders. He threatened their hold on power, and so both parties launched public smear campaigns. The ones who were afraid of him called him "the wolf." The ones who were insecure called him "the idiot." Both parties' leaders likened him to a communist, a thinly veiled attempt to pull the United States to their side. U.S. officials believed Gaitán's opposition. Gaitán has the same supporters as the communists, a 1946 cable from the U.S. embassy to Washington read, and is an equally effective "agitator." Despite the opposition, Gaitán's popularity and Colombian's spirits continued to rise. This was their president, they were saying, and this was their time to rule.

But it was not to be. There were too many political obstacles, too many enemies, and already too many guns. On April 9, 1948, a so-called madman shot Gaitán as he left his Bogotá office for lunch. A crowd mauled the shooter, killing him on the spot and destroying any chances of uncovering the identities of his senders; Gaitán's death remains an unsolved mystery. The list of suspects—which includes leaders of the Liberal and Conservative Parties, U.S. spies, and the Communist Party—remains as long as the day Gaitán was shot.

With Gaitán's death, Bogotá erupted. *Gaitanistas* overran police and looted stores. The army was called in but couldn't corral the angry mobs. Gunfights and fires broke out. The resulting chaos left hundreds dead and half of the historic downtown in ruins. Eventually, the fury spread to the countryside and provided the impetus for the current war. It was, as historian Eric Hobsbawm put it, "the only known nationwide revolution by spontaneous combustion." *La Violencia* had begun.

Initially, the fight was along party lines: "Blue" Conservatives versus "Red" Liberals, the same two parties that had fought the "local revolutions" during the previous century and had jockeyed for political power for over a century. Both parties organized armed groups to protect their interests. The Conservatives used the police and death squads known by names such as *pájaros* or "birds" to swoop into Liberal strongholds. Paramilitaries like "Tarzan" and "Captain Vengeance" tore through villages with a fervor befitting their names. The massacres that followed pushed the Liberals to organize armed groups of their own: "bandits," "goons," and "guerrillas." As time passed, in-party fighting began, and soon there were Liberal guerrillas fighting both Liberal and Conservative Parties' death squads. *La Violencia* also opened the way for people to settle vendettas against unruly neighbors, cheating husbands, ruthless landlords, and uncompromising bosses.

Historian Gonzalo Sánchez Gómez calls the era "a monster of a thousand heads." He says the goal wasn't just to kill the enemy but to wipe it from the earth completely, to destroy the idea that it had ever existed. To this end, paramilitaries chopped Liberal Party supporters to bits with machetes, skinned Liberals with knives, raped Liberal women, burned and looted the Liberals' houses. Babies were bayoneted, men's genitalia wrapped around their necks. Liberal guerrillas often responded with a similarly bewildering barbarity. "There is this ceremonial display of murder," Sánchez writes of *La Violencia*, "expressed in an almost studied perversion like cutting out the tongues (the words of the other), goring pregnant women (eliminating the possibility of the other reproducing), crucifixion, castration and many other things that are directed not only at eliminating 200,000 people or more during that period (1948–1964), but at leaving an indelible mark on the millions of Colombians who remained."

But the efforts at destroying the other didn't work, and the scale and brutality of the murders have only made it more difficult for Colombia to climb from the abyss. The fight tore families apart, destroyed villages, and split the country into pieces. What's left are the memories. There isn't a Colombian who doesn't have a story of mutilation, massacre, or flight to tell—and with these stories come the reasons to keep fighting.

La Violencia forms the backdrop to this and every other tale of war in Colombia. It also shaped people's form of resistance and struggle. During *La Violencia*, each party began to take on the patterns that would characterize its fighting for years to come. The Conservatives used paramilitary death squads. The Liberals used guerrilla groups. The Communist Party just tried to survive with whatever was available.

To fend off the assaults during *La Violencia*, the Communists began organizing what they called "self-defense" groups. Able-bodied men, boys, and even women were called to stand guard. They fanned out into the hills surrounding their farmlands and waited. When opposition groups appeared poised for an assault, the guards would blow bugles. The men would gather their guns and meet in farmhouses and public parks. Then they would get ready for battle.

One of the peasants' favorite weapons was known as the *catalicón*, a metal tube that the fighters soldered on one end and filled with gunpowder, rocks, pieces of metal, and dirt on the other. After preparing a wick, the peasants would fasten the tube to a tree and set it facing the trail where they expected government troops to pass. "For the army, it was a terrifying weapon," one Communist historian wrote, "because it killed everything in its path."

While in the countryside Colombian Communists fought a war, in the cities the Communists rallied support for their political party. Eventually, the strategy of using both war and politics took on a name: *la combinación de todas las formas de lucha*, or "the combination of all forms of struggle." The strategy was simple: The Communists would have politicians, unionists, and student groups acting in their interests in the plazas, the factories, and the classrooms; they would have guerrillas and peasant syndicates defending their interests in the hills, mountains, and jungles. In other words, they would use all the tools, or "forms of struggle" as they said, at their disposal to fight off and eventually topple the government.

Colombian Communists borrowed from the teachings of Vladimir Lenin to justify the *combinación* strategy. To Lenin, all strategy obeyed circumstances. Strategy does not bind "the movement to any one particular form of struggle," he stated. Marxism, he continued, "demands an attentive attitude to the *mass* struggle in progress, which, as the movement develops, as the class-consciousness of the masses grows, as economic and political crises become acute, continually gives rise to new and more varied methods of defense and attack."

The Colombian Communist Party interpreted Lenin's words as meaning it should use all forms of struggle at all times. What's more, the circumstances during *La Violencia* required it. And in the late 1940s, with the country in the throes of the vicious political upheaval that characterized the era, the Colombian Communist Party issued its first public stance on the strategy. "The Communists should proceed to organize self-defense groups in all the regions where reactionary forces may attack them," party leaders boldly wrote.

In the years that followed, the self-defense groups protected Communist followers in several mountainous towns surrounding Bogotá. These groups were small in size and scope, but the strategy was effective; having a gun and organizing armed groups helped the Communists survive. When they were attacked—as they often were by the army, Conservative *pájaros*, and later by the "clean" Liberals—the Communists fought to protect their followers. When they were overrun, they fled in large groups. This "armed colonization," as the escape was later called, would mark these populations for generations to come: Their relationship with the government, the military, and opposition political parties would be one of conflict and struggle; the Communists would be their only defense. There was no "legal" and "illegal" struggle. Only survival mattered.

The battles would continue for years. The government attacked, and the Communists retreated. It's sad to think what Colombia would be today had the government sought peace in those first few years. At the time, communism in Colombia amounted to no more than a few insignificant political posts and some rural strongholds; a bit of land and a secure peace deal would have sufficed. But politicians and military officers seemed blinded by Cold War notions of the world. It was the early 1960s. Fidel Castro had taken over Cuba. Revolutionary movements were emerging in other parts of Latin America. Colombia could be next, the Colombian government and its new progenitor, the U.S. government, concluded hastily.

In many ways—just as the political parties' response to *La Violencia* shaped them for decades—modern U.S.-Colombia relations were shaped by these first years of the Cold War. To combat the communist threat, President Kennedy had launched the Alliance for Progress, an economic development strategy for Latin America. Under the tutelage of the U.S. government, the Colombians were starting their own plan. *Plan Lazo*, or "Plan Unite," was a derivative of the Alliance for Progress. It was designed to rein in the rebel groups and simultaneously provide economic stimulus to poverty-stricken rural areas. "Bullets and beans," as it was known, was the U.S. way of handling communism worldwide; the strategy would change very little as the years passed. The Colombian government embraced this idea, then applied the "bullets" full force. The U.S. government helped.

This first battle between the Communists and the Colombian government culminated in 1964 in the foothills of the Tolima province, 140 miles southwest of the capital city, Bogotá. There the Communist Party loosely controlled five small municipalities where its followers would have happily lived in obscurity with a little livestock, a small wooden shack, and a party banner hanging on their porches. But for the Colombian and U.S. governments, it was five municipalities too many. Debates raged in Colombia's congress over what one prominent Conservative senator began calling the "independent republics." The words provoked consternation from Bogotá to Washington, D.C. The Colombian government responded by choking the "independent republics"—cutting off the roads leading into the region. Then, with the help of the U.S. military, it organized what it hoped would be the last attack on the Communist footholds. In May 1964, the Colombian military sent thousands of troops and dozens of airplanes to the Communist enclaves with mortar bombs and U.S.-supplied napalm. There, forty-two lightly armed men and a smattering of civilians awaited.

By military standards, the government offensive was a success. The "independent republics" were wiped out, and the Communists fled again. But over time, it was clear that the long-term winners were the Communists. No more than a few Communists lost their lives during the offensive. The government attacks simply reinforced their use of the self-defense groups. In the cities, Communist leaders hailed the resistance and praised their strategy, *la combinación de todas las formas de lucha*. In the countryside, the Communist Party put a name to the resisters: "The Southern Tolima Bloc." The bloc would protect their followers in their new home just as they had during their entire journey. The peasants would repay them by forming the backbone of the new organization created in 1966, two years after the attack on the "independent republics": the Revolutionary Armed Forces of Colombia, better known by their Spanish acronym, FARC. Colombia's modern-day war had begun.

For the Communist Party, the attacks on the "independent republics" became the hallmark moment of *La Violencia*. In the years that followed, this David-and-Goliath tale would color everything that the Communist Party and the FARC did. They were always the underdogs who, with their will, could defeat the enemy. It was a mental state as much as a physical prowess that allowed them to survive, they reasoned. In this context, the "self-defense" groups would forever have a place, and the Communist strategy of *la combinación de todas las formas de lucha* would inevitably become the party mantra.

But as time passed, the costs of adhering to this strategy grew. Glorifying the self-defense groups strengthened the guerrilla side of the organization. Inevitably, the self-defense groups replicated themselves, and the FARC grew. The political side, the Communist Party, tried to maintain control, but soon the rebels began taking to the offensive. With military victories came more political power for the FARC. Soon it was clear that the rebels were becoming the leaders of the organization.

Eventually, under the cover of peace talks the guerrillas launched with the government in the early 1980s, the FARC decided to create its own political party, apart from the Communist Party. The guerrillas called it the *Unión Patriótica*, or UP. As a mixture of the Communist Party and the FARC, the UP was the embodiment of *la combinación de todas las formas de lucha*. By then, the *combinación* was part of the way of doing things, as normal as having coffee with breakfast: Communists campaigned in the cities; self-defense groups battled government troops in the countryside. The UP, the FARC decided, would represent and work for both sides of the organization.

However, the FARC underestimated its opposition. From almost the beginning, the UP's enemies dissected the new party's purpose. These enemies didn't wait to hear the UP's platform or understand its motives. They simply equated the UP with the FARC and started shooting. The "political genocide" had begun. Over the next ten years, thousands of UP militants were killed. Hundreds of others went into hiding or fled the country. Even when it was clear that the UP had no more political power, their enemies kept killing them. As it was during *La Violencia*, the goal wasn't just the extermination of the party. It was the extermination of this idea that David could actually fell Goliath.

By the time I met Josué Giraldo, this idea was all the UP had left to fight for. And this is what made Josué a walking ghost. He couldn't win the war. He couldn't even win the battle. Josué's side had lost. Thousands were in the morgue. Hundreds were on the run. Josué and some of his brave UP colleagues were all that was left. Yet there they stood sticking their chests out, waiting for the bullets to hit them. It was sad and inspiring all at once. In a way, I don't blame Josué or the UP for taking this unconventional stance. They were a product of Colombia's violent political history and victims of its unforgiving wrath. For them, the only way to live was to prepare for death. They were the martyrs.

Part of Josué enjoyed this dark fame. He liked being slapped on the back by his colleagues, revered by fellow panelists, and considered a hero in leftist political circles. Josué was a member of both the Communist Party and the UP. He was a revolutionary and as such was a willing soldier in the fight to topple the government through either political or military means. Like the UP, he was the embodiment of *la combinación de todas las formas de lucha*. He embraced the idea that he could contribute to the revolution, which sometimes meant helping the leftist rebels. It was a strategy that confused me—why help the guerrillas and at the same time openly campaign for human and political rights? Even stranger, Josué's status seemed to rise, including his position within the UP, as he became more of a target. Around the time I met him, he was said to have a $30,000 price tag on his head. This left him both scared and proud.

But while he liked the attention he got from surviving, Josué didn't quite know how to handle living, as it was. Through eleven years of politics in the most targeted political party in the country, somehow he'd been spared; many of his closest friends and colleagues had not, and this seemed to eat away at him. He became manic, unpredictable. On some days, Josué could be defiant, daring his enemies to kill him. On other days, he behaved like a frightened puppy dog. Every day, he was paranoid. He had trouble sleeping. He would wake up at night, walk around the house or read. The anxiety mostly made him cautious. He would change his routes, avoid getting into predictable routines, and never go out after dark. He loved sports but limited his activities. He would jog on the road and in the abandoned lot in front of his two-story mini-colonial home where his wife, Mariella, could keep an eye on him. He also occasionally took his two young daughters out on their bicycles.

But the constant threat wore Josué down. He told his wife about his fears, and she urged him to leave the UP. "No," he would reply, "that would be like being a coward." And she wouldn't mention it again. She didn't want to be the bitter one, the one who tore him away from his struggle. But Josué shared some of her feelings as well. He longed to live a normal life: to jog without his wife keeping watch; to be with his two young daughters without fear they might suffer in an attack on him. But like so many UP members before him, Josué found that these two urges—a dedication to the UP and a desire to live a normal life—were polar opposites. Dedication to the UP made leading a normal life impossible, because Josué was on the front lines.

"We don't go to the movies," Josué wrote of his family life. "We don't go out dancing. We don't go to the park. We don't have guests over. We've shut ourselves into a room because of this death sentence. It's like we're in prison. We can't even think about taking a trip, not even in our own city. I don't like going out with the girls because it puts them at risk. I can't even get an ice cream with them. This has helped me stay alive but at a huge cost to my family. We have moments of collective tension because of this prison-like existence when we feel like just exploding; we want to throw ourselves out the window or run away."

On the morning he was finally killed, Josué was trying to be what he couldn't: a playful father. He and his daughters were putting up a tent in the lot in front of their home. As Josué took a machete to the grass to make room for the tent, his friend and colleague Michael Lopez, a lawyer with the human rights group *Justicia y Paz*, and a U.S. citizen who was visiting him that weekend, sat on the front steps reading a book. After clearing the grassy area with a machete, Josué began setting up the tent with Michael's help. The girls played near them and occasionally offered to hold a stake steady while their father gently hammered it into the ground.

Josué's wife, Mariella, was inside the house putting on her makeup for church. In contrast to Mariella, who never missed mass, Josué didn't go to church. His faith, he said, came from helping other people. "I think I'll go to heaven much faster than anyone in church," Josué often told her. And he believed it. His lifetime commitment to the UP, to a party forged with the blood of martyrs, gave him the right to believe a lot of things.

The tent was only partway up when a short, curly-haired man with a thin mustache appeared on the other end of the lot and slowly approached Josué. Since he'd joined the UP eleven years before, Josué had begun noticing strange movements and suspicious characters. He also knew what assassins looked like since they had shot him once already; the only reason he had survived the first attack was because the gunman ran out of bullets before he could finish the job.

But on this day, Josué's guard had fallen. As the assassin slinked through the tall grass feeling for his gun, Josué didn't even notice him. Perhaps he was daydreaming. Perhaps he was wrapped up in his daughters' joy in putting up a tent. Perhaps he was wondering if his friend Michael was enjoying himself. Perhaps he was just trying to be normal and had given up looking over his shoulder, wondering when the bullet was going to come again. He wouldn't have been the first UP member to feel like it was hopeless to keep fighting. For the UP, there seemed to be an endless number of assassins, and they didn't stop until they'd hit their target. Others before him had tired of the chase and taken death head-on. Josué, it appeared, was doing the same. He had left his bodyguards in Bogotá that weekend. He had put his pistol away in the house. He was ready, and it was his turn.

The curly-haired man was only a few feet away when Josué finally saw him. He immediately shouted to his daughters, "Run! Run! Run!" But the gunman was already firing at him. The UP leader sprinted away, zigzagging across the grassy lot. Michael grabbed the girls and ran into the house. Then he turned to see the gunman standing over Josué with the weapon pointed at the back of his friend's head. Michael watched as the gun recoiled and Josué's body jiggled in one last dying spasm. Then the assassin shot a second time and ran to other end of the lot, where he sped off with another man on a motorcycle.

Josué slumped over on his side, spilling blood onto the pavement. His eyes were wide open and looked skyward. His journey was over. Along with his UP colleagues, he had been transformed into a martyr, a dead soldier in the battle for his party.

Josué's death jolted me. If his speech on that rainy day in Bogotá made the UP victims real, then his murder brought the UP dilemma horrifyingly close. It also brought on some questions that went well beyond just trying to resolve the identity of his killers. Who was Josué and how could he accept such a certain fate? What was it that was so worth dying for when he had such a beautiful family? How did he become the person he was: both cowering and defiant, both submissive and combative?

The questions didn't have easy answers, so I began to find out more about Josué and his political party. Over time, I got to a know a man who perplexed me and a political party that enthralled me. Like the UP, Josué was a living contradiction. He was a strange mixture of dedicated father and uncompromising UP militant. He lived for his family but never seemed to truly assess what he meant to them, alive. For he was, it seemed, caught up in a struggle that went against all common sense. This struggle led Josué and the UP to their ends.

I also found out that Josué's martyrdom was just a part of the larger story, as was he. The UP was full of walking ghosts like Josué, but the UP was also once full of energetic and creative people who believed in the party. These people weren't interested in *la combinación de todas las formas de lucha*. They didn't take orders from the FARC or the Communist Party. They weren't trying to become martyrs. They sought to work through democracy. They believed the UP wasn't just a part of the struggle of the masses, it was *the* struggle.

I discovered there was even a time when Josué himself was more hopeful than submissive. When the UP first started, he was a daring young Communist lawyer who joined the party to fight for peace; a tireless organizer who set up art openings, read poetry, and directed plays for the nascent party; a sports lover, a giving son and brother. In those days Josué had life and spirit for his cause. He was afraid, of course, but that fear was mitigated by the incredible possibilities.

As I found out, the story of the UP was less about fear and submission than about boundless hope. When the party started, thousands like the spirited Josué joined the UP to push for an end to the war. As the party's name suggested, they were patriots. They saw Colombia as one of the wealthiest and most educated countries in Latin America. And they saw politics as a means to start a new peaceful era. Events surrounding them made them believe in themselves and their party even more. The government and the FARC were talking peace. Guerrillas were coming down from the mountains and campaigning for political posts. Opposition politicians were supporting the UP's efforts.

Indeed, a story that would end in tragedy began with courage and optimism. And that's where I need to begin.

PART ONE

CHAPTER 1

FIGHTING HISTORY

The story of Josué Giraldo and his party, the *Unión Patriótica* (UP), started with the idea of peace, of settling the long-standing conflict that had ripped the country apart for decades. The new party was a crucial part of a peace process between the government and the FARC guerrillas. It was established as a means to reconcile the two sides: The UP was going to be the conduit through which the FARC—by then one of the country's four guerrilla groups—could drop its guns and pick up its placards, give speeches in the plazas, and slip a ballot into a slot. At least that was the idea.

It was the early 1980s when the notion of the UP began to take shape. Colombia had seen nearly thirty-five years of uninterrupted war, the last of which had been some of the worst. Hundreds of political dissidents and suspected rebel collaborators had been jailed and tortured by government troops. Many had died. The army had also launched attacks on rebel strongholds. Despite the government's resolve, the size of the guerrilla armies had increased fourfold. To many, like presidential candidate Belisario Betancur, it was looking increasingly like a stalemate.

During his presidential campaign in 1982, Betancur promised a "democratic opening" and to seek peace with the rebel groups. The Conservative Party leader was going against the trend in the region. In El Salvador and Guatemala civil wars were heating up, and military governments in those countries were ushering in scorched earth policies to deal with the guerrillas. The United States, under the Reagan administration, supplied these governments with massive military assistance. Colombia could have gone to the United States and argued for the same treatment to deal with its guerrilla problem. But Colombians were tired of war, and Betancur gauged this mood perfectly. His overwhelming support at the polls proved this. He won the elections handily that same year. Betancur would eventually support peace efforts in Central America as well.

When Betancur took office, he moved quickly on his promises to seek peace. "To those who have taken up weapons, I extend my hand so that they might exercise their rights," he told Colombians in his inaugural speech, which was attended by U.S. vice president George Bush. "I raise the white flag of peace and offer it to all my countrymen. I offer peace to my fellow citizens without distinguishing between one another."

Shortly thereafter Betancur sent emissaries to the guerrillas' jungle hideouts to see if the rebel groups were interested in a dialogue. They were, and so the meetings became more frequent and intense. It was a critical moment in Colombian history—the first government effort to forge peace with the country's modern-day rebel forces—and Betancur had decided he would take advantage of the opportunity. The guerrillas would be drawn into a peace process now or continue to flourish, the new president reasoned. He would bet his political career on it.

Betancur was not a typical Conservative Party leader. He was a former political dissident and outspoken journalist. He was once jailed during Colombia's only military dictatorship in the mid-1950s, and in the years that followed, Betancur maintained his distance from the conservative elements of his own party. As the Conservative Party shifted to the right after the dictatorship ended, Betancur stayed in the middle. He advocated for more social spending and less bellicose measures to fight a rising wave of dissent in Colombia, which included the nascent rebel movements. His compassionate conservatism won him the title of "hippie." It also won him the mayoral campaign in Bogotá and eventually the presidency. "I will work day and night, without rest, to help the weak and the poor," the newly elected president said in a victory speech.

Once in office, Betancur had a difficult job. In 1982, there were about four thousand guerrillas, who were split into four major groups. The most popular was the April 19 Movement or M-19, a mostly urban-based cadre of brash ex-Communists and leftist intellectuals. The M-19 was followed closely in popularity by the Ejército Nacional de Liberación, National Liberation Army, or ELN, which adhered to a Fidel Castro line. The ELN had also drawn in some Catholic priests to augment its image. Then came the Ejército Popular de Liberación, Popular Liberation Army, or EPL, a Maoist faction that focused on winning over the peasantry in the countryside. Finally, there was the FARC, the hard-line pro-Soviet Marxist-Leninist group connected to the Communist Party of Colombia in the cities. Of these groups, most considered the M-19 to be the most potent and dangerous. But the shrewd President Betancur sent emissaries to talk with all the rebel groups. The best of these emissaries went to work on what he correctly perceived as the country's biggest guerrilla threat, the FARC.

Betancur's intuition may have been related to his shared history with the FARC and the Communist Party. Both Betancur and the Communist Party had risen in dissent against the military dictatorship of General Gustavo Rojas Pinilla in the mid-1950s. Rojas Pinilla took over Colombia in 1953 when it seemed the bloody intraparty fight known as *La Violencia* was getting out of control. General Rojas Pinilla took a hard line. When some members of the Conservative and Communist Parties openly protested the coup, the general targeted them. Shortly after Rojas Pinilla took office, the army imprisoned Betancur and many of his Conservative colleagues. The general also declared the Communist Party illegal and sought to jail them as well. Dozens of Communist Party leaders were imprisoned. Others went into hiding. Then Rojas Pinilla mounted several large-scale offensives against the Communist Party's "self-defense" groups and their supporters in the countryside. Many more died or had to flee from their homes during this period.

But while Betancur felt he understood the Communists because of their similar experiences, the president knew the government's history of betraying the Communist Party far surpassed what he had experienced during his short stint in jail. Both the FARC and Communist Party leaders had long lost faith in the government's word, and Betancur couldn't blame them. They'd all watched closely, for example, when General Rojas Pinilla signed a truce with the Liberal guerrillas in 1953. Many hoped the truce would end *La Violencia*. But within weeks, several Liberal guerrilla leaders were gunned down by shady and, some believed, government-financed assassins. Other former Liberal guerrillas, some of whom had fought alongside the Communist Party, were allegedly dropped from an airplane as they went to see some land the Rojas Pinilla government had promised them as part of the peace accord. When the Communists sent two delegates to start a negotiation of their own with the government, the army assassinated them as well. As one future FARC leader said about the two Communist messengers, "They gave their lives looking for a way to coexist."

Even after General Rojas Pinilla was ousted and things between Conservatives and Liberals began to calm in the late 1950s, Communist leaders were still getting murdered. To quell the continuing violence, Liberal and Conservative leaders made a pact, known as the National Front, whereby they would rotate the presidency and divide cabinet posts between them. For a time, it looked as if the National Front might bring the country back together and finally put an end to *La Violencia*. Communist leaders hailed the move as a positive step toward peace, and some tried to participate in the new government. But the political elite who had forged the agreement refused to accommodate the Communists. Within a few years, the National Front was targeting the Communists again in the so-called independent republics, which eventually gave way to Colombia's modern-day civil war.

When Betancur won the presidency in 1982, it had been nearly twenty years since the attacks on the "independent republics," but FARC leaders still mistrusted the government. As government envoys and rebel leaders shared coffee and conversation in the guerrillas' jungle hideout, FARC leaders steeled themselves for the worst. The president tried his best to gain their trust by holding the meetings with guerrilla leaders in secret. The details of the meetings were not divulged to the press nor were the results. Betancur would run a discrete peace process, one that didn't need the public's or any other part of the government's approval. His secrecy would later be his undoing. But in those first weeks of making contact with the guerrillas, the government's plan moved swiftly, not least because of the able men Betancur had picked to be his emissaries. Among them, perhaps the most important was an old Communist Party stalwart named Alberto Rojas Puyo. Rojas Puyo would play a key role in both the peace process and the creation of the FARC's political party, the UP.

On several counts, Rojas Puyo was an excellent choice to be a peace emissary. He had lived on two continents, fought against two dictatorships, and worked for the two political parties in question. He was a natural mediator and peace lover. He was also an eternal optimist, if at times naievely so. But he understood his role and sought ways to use his peculiar background to his advantage.

For a Communist, Rojas Puyo had begun his political career in the oddest of places: as a member of the Conservative Party. He had little choice. His parents were Conservatives, and it was the late 1940s, the beginnings of *La Violencia*. During those days, few even dreamed of switching parties, much less to the Communist Party. If "Red" Liberal was grounds for a slogging, then "Red" Communist was grounds for a lynching. But Rojas Puyo had a drive that went beyond politics. His conviction, he said when I met him some years later in his tenth-story apartment in central Bogotá, came from his gut. He was a loyal Conservative, but an even more loyal Catholic. "A part of me was impregnated with the ideals of social justice, which came from my Christian background," he said.

Virtually all Colombians are Catholic and spend much of their time fighting over who is the most Catholic. The Conservative Party, for instance, claims it is more Catholic than the Liberal Party. The Liberals have taken anti-clerical stances, but both parties have priests in their ranks. During *La*

Violencia, some priests not only gave homilies espousing violence against the opposition, but organized the armed thugs to do the deed. Throughout Colombia's civil strife, the Catholic Church has remained a largely conservative institution and has supported the traditional political parties in their efforts to maintain the status quo. The Catholic Church's attitude irked Rojas Puyo, who said the church made a mockery of its mandate. "I took these Christian ideals seriously," he told me stridently.

When I met him, Rojas Puyo looked much the same as he did when Betancur called him in the early 1980s to work with the FARC on a peace deal. He was tall and thin, and impeccably dressed for a Communist. His shoes were shined, and he had buttoned his suit coat to partially cover his paisley tie. The only thing that gave him away as a leftist was his wavy hair. During the Betancur years, he had also had a little white beard pointing from his chin, which he had shaved since.

Rojas Puyo's optimism was constantly on display. Throughout our conversations he smiled and laughed at the difficult times. Pictures of Rojas Puyo grinning alongside FARC leaders were also placed neatly on a coffee table in his living room. He spoke in a soft, scratchy baritone that put me at ease. Still, there was no mistaking his passion, which came from years of dodging bullets.

When General Gustavo Rojas Pinilla took over Colombia in 1953, Rojas Puyo came alive with fury. After all, it was a Conservative president who had been removed to make way for the military government. As the general settled into power, Rojas Puyo and some of his Conservative colleagues started writing for an anti-dictatorship newspaper. He organized protests and petitions as did other Conservatives like future president Belisario Betancur. Rojas Puyo was as passionate a Conservative as Betancur, and both got into trouble for their open political dissent. The army threw Betancur into jail. But Rojas Puyo, with the help of fellow party members and the Spanish embassy, escaped to Spain, where the embassy got him a scholarship to study in Barcelona.

From there, Rojas Puyo continued to write for the anti-dictatorship newspaper in Colombia. But his relationship with the Conservatives didn't last. In Spain, he found a more abhorrent dictatorship in Franco than the one he had known in Colombia and, as he had at home, he joined in anti-dictatorship rallies. Eventually he became part of the anti-Franco movement. Unbeknownst to him, he had taken his first steps away from the Conservative Party and toward the Communist Party. It was a while before he gained the trust of the Spanish anti-dictatorship crowd, but soon they admitted to him they were Communists. Then they invited him to join. Typical of Rojas Puyo, he didn't jump into the new party. He studied it first. He read Marxist books and debated the relative merits of the prevailing economic models with his new friends. His true conversion came only after a history professor invited him for a long Spanish *almuerzo*.

"After lunch, the professor said to me, 'I can see you're searching for something, but you haven't found what you're looking for. But your search is interesting,'" Rojas Puyo slowly recounted for me. The two went to the professor's library, where the professor handed the Colombian student Engel's *The Anti-Dühring*, the classic Marxist response to the German philosopher Eugen Karl Dühring's work. "I went straight to my room, and I read the book without stopping. I didn't even sleep," Rojas Puyo explained to me excitedly. "Suddenly, I could connect political experiences I'd already had in the anti-dictatorship movements with the theory laid out by Engels. . . . This transformed my life. Right then I became a Marxist."

But Rojas Puyo was not like most in the Colombian Communist Party. Almost from the beginning, he questioned the party's strategies, above all the Communist use of political movements in the cities and its guerrilla movement in the countryside, a strategy known popularly as *la combinación de todas las formas de lucha*. He was, he would explain to me, a troublemaker, not a conformist. While some accepted the party's dicta until it cost them their lives, a small number within the Communists' fold expressed skepticism like Rojas Puyo, a skepticism that would later become outright dissent and cost them their party IDs.

In part, Rojas Puyo owed his clarity to the years he had spent abroad. After Spain, Rojas Puyo moved to Paris, where he began writing for communist magazines and communicating regularly with the Communist Party in Colombia. He would tell the party about the latest Marxist theories and communist strategies on the continent. The Colombians would return the favor with material of their own, some of which startled Rojas Puyo. "When I started to get documents from the party, I was surprised to see *la combinación de todas las formas de lucha*," he told me, "and the news that there were armed groups that were called 'self-defense' organizations that were created by the party. The young rebel that I was, though, I was sympathetic to this."

For years, Rojas Puyo stayed loyal to the strategy of the *combinación*. After the Colombian army attacked the "independent republics" in 1964, Rojas Puyo wrote a series of articles for *Le Monde* explaining the party's version of the revolutionary war in Colombia. The heroes in the articles were the Southern Tolima Bloc, later to be called the FARC. The thought of the articles embarrassed Rojas Puyo when I spoke to him. "The Communist Party assured me that these peasants in self-defense groups were part of the struggle of the masses," he said to me. "I told myself, 'Fine, in Colombia, the struggle of the masses includes the armed struggle.' I *believed* what the Communist Party told me. I didn't have any reason not to."

From the information he had received from the Colombian Communist Party, Rojas Puyo also surmised that Colombia was in ruins. He imagined broken-down buildings, potholed roads, and poverty-stricken citizens protesting in front of the president's house. He thought there were massive union and peasant movements marching in the streets and army and police personnel doing their best to repress them with batons and bayonets. He believed the party when it told him that the country was going up in flames, and that the armed insurgency was necessary to fight off the assaults on freedom.

He also imagined a burgeoning Communist Party, one that was acting as the vanguard of anti-government activity, uniting all fronts of the struggle, and fomenting insurrection. The truth was that the party was a marginal player. It had been marginal since the 1930s, when it competed with the popular Liberal Party peasant organizer Jorge Eliécer Gaitán and his peasant supporters for political power and lost. Furious with Gaitán's success (and perhaps their own failure), the Communists allied themselves with Gaitán's opponents at the end of his life and were still recovering from the political fallout that came with his murder. Many people saw the party as a sellout, and who could blame them? During the volatile 1940s, party leaders proclaimed right-wing Liberal candidates as "progressives." These same progressives would later attack the Communist Party.

When Rojas Puyo returned to Colombia in the late 1960s after fifteen years in Europe, he found both a struggling Communist Party and a country that had developed to a level he thought was comparable to Europe's. Roads crisscrossed the coffee region, still Colombia's economic engine. Electricity lit up the countryside. Potable water filled people's kettles. It seemed to him that more and more people were obtaining televisions and telephones. There was a visible middle class buying cars, wearing suits, and taking their children on walks in the parks. The shock had an immediate impact on Rojas Puyo's politics.

"I began to question the whole thing, to question whether armed struggle was really the most appropriate thing for the conditions of Colombia," he told me. But like many others before and after him, Rojas Puyo swallowed hard and did what he was told. "I was a disciplined [party] member," he explained, his face straining from the memory. "Maybe I disagreed more than others, but I was disciplined, and I followed the line." Following the line meant getting involved in the armed struggle. When I asked him to specify what he had done for the rebels, Rojas Puyo smiled and simply said, "I did some things; let's just leave it at that."

Others, however, were more specific. They said they stored guns, medicine, and food for the guerrillas. In Bogotá, for instance, the Communist Party had a Solidarity Committee that would send care packages to the FARC. The committee collected money and supplies like toothbrushes, toothpaste, knapsacks, and shoes. "We always had to show we were with them," one former party member said to me, "It was a romantic concept." The party also idealized rebel leaders in speeches and articles. The Communist Youth, known as the JUCO, carried on the tradition as well. The group's cells would take on names of guerrillas who had heroically given their lives for the cause.

Still, the Communist Party seemed to want it both ways with the rebels. While Communist leaders used the FARC's appeal to draw new militants, they also constantly reminded the young Communists who was running the movement. When someone asked too much about the rebels, the party applied the "rules of compartmentalization" and became quiet about guerrilla operations, then added to the curious neophyte, "Your struggle is with the masses." When JUCO members said they wanted to join the FARC, party leaders tried to talk them out of it and made it clear that armed revolution wasn't their principal form of struggle.

During this whole time, Rojas Puyo's conscience ate away at him. He sought out party leaders who could convince him he was doing the right thing by helping the rebels. But he didn't find any. What's more, he saw the results of the *combinación* strategy up close. "I realized that this was a disaster," he told me. "Wherever the guerrillas appeared, the army came in right after them. And the army finished off everything. They didn't just make the guerrillas run, they also shut down the party's apparatus, which had often brought the guerrillas there in the first place. . . .While the party did some political organizing, everything was fine; while they formed social movements, everything was fine. But when they started to act like guerrillas, it was like when a puppy dog walks into mass; it went horribly for them. . . . In the end, the peasants had to take the brunt of the army's punishment."

"It was the idea," he continued, "that they [the Communists] had to respond to this repression . . . which led them to the wrong conclusion. The adversary made violence its strategy, and the Communists fell right into its trap responding with the same strategy as the enemy—revolutionary violence. They should have tried democracy and organizing the people against this violence . . . not incorporating them into the war. In the war we had no chance. The Communists were always the minority in this country. How did we think we were going to declare war on the state? With what help? With whom?"

But what could Rojas Puyo do? Over time, the *combinación* was a doctrine that had taken on a life of its own, a credo that could not be disavowed under any circumstances. To understand it was to be part of a club of elite Communist Party intellectuals. To practice it was to show absolute devotion to the cause and gain supporters within the Communist command. It was almost like a cult that nurtured its argument with a self-fulfilling prophecy: The more the government opted for a military response, the more justified the armed revolutionary response became. It was an endless spiral that would inevitably convert the once small military wing, the FARC, into the vanguard of the Communist Party and many party militants into ready targets for their right-wing enemies.

Rojas Puyo's experience abroad bolstered his beliefs. Communists around the world thought the *combinación* strategy was ludicrous, as did other communist strains in Colombia. By the late 1970s, Rojas Puyo's doubts turned into fear. He was scared of the political fallout that came with the party's overt connection to the rebels. He was also afraid for his own and others' safety. In 1978, President Julio César Turbay had begun a radical campaign to rid the country of guerrillas and their suspected sympathizers. By 1980, Amnesty International was reporting that there were close to 500 political prisoners in Colombia and 33 "torture centers." On more than one occasion, Rojas Puyo had put himself in danger as well. Finally, he decided he had had enough.

As the party gathered in the early part of the 1980s for a national meeting, Rojas Puyo openly criticized the *combinación* strategy to fellow Communists. But the nature of the organization and party politics made it very difficult for him to present his ideas to the quorum. The party was a decidedly Stalinist organization, which in the simplest terms meant that the leaders were a dogmatic group, believers in the science of socialism. Dissent was tantamount to heresy and, to them, illogical due to the scientific nature of the doctrine. Party leaders were above reproach, and longtime strategies like the *combinación* strategy were not subject to debate.

Like Stalin, the party had also created a hierarchical system that concentrated power in a five-person Executive Committee. Rojas Puyo was not a member of the Executive Committee. Nor was he a member of the larger, but less powerful Central Committee that debated the party's strategies with the Executive Committee. He was an outsider who lost the trust of the inner sanctum the more he pushed his "radical" notions forward. Some members of the Central Committee listened to him. But the Executive Committee quickly squashed his ideas and further marginalized Rojas Puyo from party affairs.

Rojas Puyo didn't take these attacks personally. He was resigned to the fact that the Communist Party leaders might never understand or admit their mistakes. The party was not one for self-criticism. This didn't bother him as much as their intransigence. The duplicity of the Communists was apparent to everyone but themselves, he thought. How could they believe they could get away with it? Everyone knew that the Communists had created the FARC, and that the two maintained a working relationship—that FARC leaders were members of the Central Committee of the Communist Party! They were one and the same, he thought, and while this was romantic in theory, in practice, the result would be the deaths of many, many people.

With all avenues blocked at the Communist Party, Rojas Puyo turned his appeal to the FARC. He had known some of its leaders for years, and they seemed to trust him. That was one of the reasons why his old Conservative Party colleague, now president, Belisario Betancur had called on him to form part of the special peace commission in the early 1980s. He was marginalized from Communist Party affairs, but with his new job, Rojas Puyo was suddenly in a position to exert some influence on party strategy again. In part, this was due to the FARC's increasing autonomy over the Communist Party. In part, this was due to Rojas Puyo's marvelous ability to mediate.

During Betancur's first year in office, Rojas Puyo and the other emissaries gathered several times with FARC leaders in a small shack on the outskirts of a village just south of Bogotá. On occasion, they met deeper in the jungles, where they talked beneath the cover of some rudimentary tents. A few times, the government commission had to avoid the Colombian army so as not to tip it off to the rebel's position. Nevertheless, the secret contacts fostered trust between the sides, in particular between Rojas Puyo and the rebel leaders.

Since Rojas Puyo had initiated regular contact with it, the FARC had frequently sought his advice. The level of trust between him and the leadership was strong and growing stronger with each meeting. Rojas Puyo had even teased them about their uncertain futures. "If we have a cease-fire, what are you guys going to do?" he once asked them, "Are you gonna sit down and sun your bellies or what?" The answer, of course, was for them to create a political party. With Rojas Puyo's assistance, they determined they would call it the *Unión Patriótica* or UP. However, little had been decided beyond the name, and about a year after the secret talks had begun between the government and the rebels, the FARC requested that Rojas Puyo travel to their headquarters to talk further.

As he bounced along the road through the barren mountains just south of Bogotá, Rojas Puyo must have been chuckling at the irony of his fate. He had gone full circle and was back to doing favors for a Conservative leader. His experience as an errand boy for the rebels had turned him against his own party and its strategy, *la combinación de todas las formas de lucha*. Now his only possible saviors were the very ones who were pushing the strategy the most. It was a huge burden to carry. But he was perhaps one of the few people in the country who could bridge the gap between the two worlds that had fought each other for so long and mend his own party at the same time.

On that trip, two FARC sentries met Rojas Puyo in San Juan de Sumapaz, a town about thirty miles south of Bogotá. There they mounted separate horses and began their slow trot toward the guerrillas' base camp. The Sumapaz region had been a rebel stronghold for decades, and it was obvious to Rojas Puyo why. The three men worked their way through steep canyons and gullies, narrow paths, and obligatory transit points. The area was virtually impenetrable, an "ambushers' paradise" and an "attackers' nightmare," one guerrilla would say of it later. "A single rebel gunman could hold an entire army at bay forever," he would add.

After three days of lumbering through the cold mountain pass, Rojas Puyo and the guerrilla sentries arrived at a small, well-constructed mud hut. Several women rebels moved in and out of the house. In the distance, Rojas Puyo could see guerrilla soldiers meandering around some trees. These men were part of the FARC commanders' special guard. Inside the hut, Alfonso Cano and Jacobo Arenas awaited him.

The rebels had designated Cano and Arenas to run the UP's affairs from the mountains. Arenas was a burly man who wore European scarves, bulky coats, and a train conductor's cap. He also had thick, tinted glasses, which he rarely removed because his eyes were very sensitive to light. Cano was twenty years younger than Arenas. He was a skinny, thick-bearded intellectual who dressed in T-shirts and Wellingtons. He also had square-rimmed glasses that looked big on his thin face.

Arenas was part of the FARC's leadership council, the Secretariat. Cano was a top commander. Each had experience in political organizing. Each commanded intellectual respect. Yet these particular commanders also had their insecurities. Both were considered *políticos*; their rise through the guerrillas' ranks was due to their ability to analyze political situations rather than create military strategies. Their comrades in arms, however, didn't always respect this. Some called Cano a *comandante de media-carrera*, or "part-time commander," behind his back. Arenas inspired more trust but was still a long way from the homage paid to the FARC's supreme commander, Manuel "Sureshot" Marulanda. Sureshot had been fighting for over thirty years and had been pronounced dead more than twenty times by government and media outlets.

Simply surviving this many close calls made his political postures irrelevant and relegated his fellow commanders to lifelong secondary roles.

Rojas Puyo sat down with Cano and Arenas in their mud hut and talked political strategy. A fire burned at their side, while the women guerrillas brought them some cognac. Rojas Puyo took his with a little milk on the side. The women rebels made sure it was always warm. It was a gesture that Rojas Puyo remembered with a twinkle in his eye years later as he spoke with me. The talks lasted through the night. The guerrillas didn't know what the shape of the UP would be. They seemed to be improvising. Would it be a movement, a party, or both? Who would lead it? How would we organize it? What were its goals? What about our weapons? Do we have to turn over our guns? The questions seemed to have few answers, but Rojas Puyo tried to calm their nerves.

"Some of them said that I was saying they should demobilize the FARC," he explained to me, leaning forward in his chair. "But I said, 'You're not demobilizing. This is just a new type of revolutionary mobilization, a mobilization through peace and democracy, a political mobilization without the guns.'" But Arenas and Cano protested that the rebels would never give up their weapons. All three men knew the stories of what happened to the guerrillas who had accepted General Rojas Pinilla's amnesty in 1953. "As soon as everyone laid down their arms," Arenas would constantly remind people, "the government failed to honor these promises." Betrayal was as common as battle during the Colombian civil wars, they said; they could never give up their guns.

There was little that Rojas Puyo could do to dissuade the rebel leaders. The FARC had reason to be afraid, he thought to himself. "The lifelong rebel has had to be suspicious of everything," he told me. "And [he] looks to surround himself with the most security possible while he's a soldier and especially once he decides he's going to leave the guns behind and turn to politics because he knows that people don't forget [what he's done]." The only thing Rojas Puyo could do was assure them that the government was serious about hammering out an agreement. The guerrilla leaders were uneasy with this but promised they would consider handing over their weapons, if their new political party, the UP, was a success.

As he scanned the terrain on his way back to Bogotá, Rojas Puyo pondered the possibilities. Where the FARC saw doom, he saw hope. When the rebels backpeddled, he pushed forward. History could change, he thought; under the right circumstances, the country could have peace. He was scared but euphoric nonetheless. They were going to do it, he said to himself, they were really going to start a new political movement or party or whatever. It didn't matter. What was important was that, if things went well, they would stop fighting, hand over their guns, and focus on their new party, the UP. *La combinación de todas las formas de lucha* would end, and the carnage could be avoided. The FARC leaders had assured him of that, and Rojas Puyo believed them.

CHAPTER 2

THE DESERT FOX

The most dangerous enemy the *Unión Patriótica* had never killed a single member of the party. He never raised a gun against the UP and rarely mentioned the party in his speeches. In fact, he was retired by the time the UP formed in 1984. His weapon was a single idea that he espoused over and over again: Communism must be destroyed. He chastised the Marxist guerrillas for decades in print, on the podium, and at the pulpit. In dozens of articles and books, he dissected the Communist Party's duplicitous use of *la combinación de todas las formas de lucha*, the multipronged strategy of combining legal and illegal fights to topple the government. He was accused of hatching numerous plans to eliminate all Communists. His enemies even said he ate children for breakfast.

Yet General Fernando Landazábal was more than just an ardent anticommunist. He was the military's campaigner and its public defender. For years, politicians, academics, and military analysts badmouthed the armed forces, blaming them for not winning the war. Landazábal was the first to counter these critics with whatever tools he had. It wasn't an easy job. The general was a solid military tactician but had a mediocre fighting force, limited resources, and tempered political support. He was like an explorer without a good map.

The situation made Landazábal both overconfident and insolent, frustrated and conniving. The general's hero was Erwin Rommel, the feared Desert Fox who'd led the Nazis campaign in North Africa in World War II. Like Rommel, Landazábal studied his enemy; then, he attacked. But every time he felt he had the enemy cornered, the government would tell him to pull his troops back. He didn't always follow orders though, and his trangressions would later cost him his job. To Landazábal, the important thing was never the job. It was saying things as he saw them, even if others didn't agree.

By the time Landazábal became defense minister under President Belisario Betancur in 1982, he believed he knew exactly what the enemy was thinking: By hinting at peace, the Communist Party and the FARC were making fools of him and the Betancur administration; what they wanted, Landazábal warned his president, was more war. Betancur didn't always listen to his defense minister. Yet Landazábal's campaign against the rebels would eventually have an effect anyway. It wouldn't destroy the Communist Party or the FARC, but it would carry the military to its "final solution" with the UP.

Landazábal did not campaign alone. Betancur's decision to seek peace with the rebels sparked outrage among many in the political and economic elite. By the early 1980s, the guerrillas had increased in size to include close to 4,000 soldiers, but some business leaders and politicians still dismissed the rebels as a nuisance. The guerrillas dominated distant villages, far away from the business deals and political backscratching in Bogotá. The few battles between the rebels and the army occurred in remote jungles and isolated mountain towns. More importantly, Colombia's economy hummed along with few interruptions despite the seemingly endless low-intensity war in the countryside. Beginning in the 1950s, Colombia had steadier economic growth than either Chile or Argentina, which were long considered the European bastions of Latin America. The violence in Colombia seemed to be on the periphery. Besides, the military finally seemed to be making headway against the rebels.

In 1978, Colombian president Julio César Turbay had granted the military unprecedented power to corral the burgeoning rebel threat. The military had taken advantage of these powers to incarcerate, torture, and murder hundreds of guerrillas and suspected guerrilla collaborators. Army personnel had raided safe houses and had ransacked universities where the rebels' urban cells operated. The police had broken up protests and jailed dozens of dissidents. Military tribunals had held spurious trials to make sure the suspects would spend years behind bars. Back then, you were guilty until proven innocent.

Still, some believed the tactics were working, especially against the popular urban guerrilla group, the M-19. "The Colombian army has crippled, if not broken, South America's most famous active guerrilla movement," the *Washington Post* wrote at the time. Two of the M-19's top three leaders were in jail. The other was on the run. "The subversive movement in our country has been minimized by our armed forces," President Turbay said just before leaving office.

But four years after the army's massive crackdown had begun, Betancur won the presidency. The new "hippie" president made it clear from the beginning that he would not continue Turbay's policies. "Conversation is always better than confrontation," Betancur would say. One of Betancur's first acts was to introduce an amnesty bill for the guerrillas. A few months later, while his emissaries were meeting in secret with the rebel leaders, the amnesty bill passed through congress. Hundreds of guerrillas went free. Colombia's political and economic elite seethed, while the military rumbled with frustration.

The army, in particular, felt betrayed by the amnesty. As the point men in the Colombian military's hierarchy, the army's leaders believed they were about to win the war. In spite of the growth of rebel groups, they argued that Turbay's policies had worked. In a way, they were right. The crackdown had hurt the guerrillas. It was the crackdown, for instance, that had spurred the Communist Party stalwart, Alberto Rojas Puyo, to confront party leaders about the danger of using *la combinación de todas las formas de lucha*. Yet military officials were also intransigent. Guerrilla popularity meant nothing to them. They simply saw rebels in jail and counted but a few insignificant armed "bandits" fleeing into the jungles. The sight of guerrillas they had incarcerated walking free again infuriated the old guard, most of all Betancur's new defense minister, General Fernando Landazábal.

Landazábal's ideas weren't particularly illuminating, but he was frank about how he felt. To many people his theories about Marxism came across as simple, almost crass. But his honesty was a welcome change from the Colombian politicians' double-talk. "Everything from communism comes from the *Communist Manifesto*," he explained to me when I met with him in his spacious office in northern Bogotá a number of years after his stint as defense minister. "'The workers of the world unite and we're going to impose communism using *la combinación de todas las formas de lucha*,'" he paraphrased before adding his own interpretation. "This includes violence, assassination, criminal activities, politics, working in government, psychological warfare, indoctrinating the masses; everything that Communists do here."

Landazábal was noticeably fit for a man in his late fifties: about 5' 10", thin around the waist with broad shoulders. Although he was retired and dressed like an old salesman—in a worn, dark blue suit, with shiny black shoes—he still had the look of a general. He had what seemed like a permanent scowl on his face; his small eyes sat neatly behind his square-rimmed glasses; his mouth was tightly closed. During his years as defense minister, cartoonists perfected the scowl: nose elongated, frown extended to his ears, eyes piercing the subject of his disgust. His wife cut out these caricatures and kept them for her amusement.

Behind the cruel veneer, Landazábal was a tireless family man. Although a career military soldier, he didn't keep many friends in the service. He devoted his free time to his wife and seven children. Landazábal's dad died when he was six, and the general was determined to ensure his family would never know the feeling of being in a fatherless home. He was a particular fan of grilling beef on Sunday afternoons, when he could tell his sour jokes to make his wife giggle.

At work, Landazábal was all business. He had learned his trade from the best. The general was a Cold War baby, a perfect product of U.S. training. He got his first lesson about communism while he was fighting with U.S. soldiers in Asia. In 1951, Colombia's president sent a group of "volunteers" to fight in Korea with the United States and the Colombians proved to be brave if overzealous soldiers. A Colombian who fought there told me that during one mission the United States heavily bombed a North Korean unit, then sent the Colombian soldiers to retrieve the wounded and prisoners of war. But many Koreans had survived the bombing, and they ambushed the advancing Colombian troops. The ex-soldier said the Colombians regrouped and killed off the enemy in a brutal display of hand-to-hand combat. "The American commander told us, 'Good job,' when we returned," the old soldier explained. "'But you guys didn't follow orders,' the American said, 'You were supposed to bring them back alive.'"

Korea had a huge impact on Landazábal. When I met with him, the general still had a black-and-white photo prominently displayed on his office wall showing the young soldier in dark fatigues standing with a group of Colombian "volunteers" on Korean soil. After the war ended, he and the others returned to Colombia as heroes. The government pinned them with the highest honors, and they rapidly rose through the ranks. The "Korea Generation," as they became known, also saw a new enemy in the communists and in turn embraced a new friend. "In the last few years, the Colombian army has been the United States' staunchest ally, I mean the staunchest," Landazábal told me. "There's practically been a direct line of communication between the Colombian Army and the United States Army."

Between 1954 and 1964, the United States trained an average of 250 Colombians per year in counterinsurgency, Landazábal included. In 1964, that number increased to 300 per year. After showing me his Korea photos, the general pulled me over to see the half-dozen plaques he had gotten from the U.S. government for being an excellent student and professor at the different U.S. war schools he had attended. Colombians, along with other future generals and leaders of their countries, got U.S. training in Panama, Georgia, Texas, and North Carolina, where they learned everything about communism anyone would want to know: its economic theory, party structure, organization, recruitment, and strategy.

Controlling the communist threat at the time involved what was known then as the National Security Doctrine. The doctrine, however, was as trustworthy as a witches' brew: "geopolitical" scientists' ruminations about the "Red Menace" along with a dash of the Prussian war theorist Karl von Clausewitz stirred into the volatile Cold War atmosphere. Still, the students ate it up. It served their purposes, and it seemed to be true. For the young officers to be, the communist menace was growing and not just on the battle front. Communist Party candidates throughout Latin America were gaining ground in the polls. In Chile in 1947, the Communist Party garnered 17 percent of the vote. In Brazil around the same time, the Communists won 10 percent. Membership in the party reached half a million in the region. The answer to this threat was outlawing the Communist Party. By late 1948, eight countries had made being a communist illegal. The party's numbers began to dwindle, but for some officers like Landazábal, it would never be enough. They were determined to destroy the enemy. The United States provided them the tools to do this.

The U.S.-espoused National Security Doctrine reduced every fight to a struggle between communists and capitalists. Sometimes doctrinaires cast the battle in political terms, other times in religious terms. The enemy, however, was always the communists, and the communists were *everywhere*. "He uses trickery," one Brazilian officer and a National Security Doctrine proponent once wrote. "He adapts to any environment and uses all means, legal and illegal, to obtain his objectives. He dresses up as a priest or a professor, a student or a peasant farmer, a vigilant defender of democracy or an advanced intellectual, a Catholic or an extreme Protestant. He goes to the countryside, to the schools, to the factories and to the churches, to the cathedrals and to congress. He will use whatever uniform or civilian garb is necessary. In conclusion, he will play whatever role that he considers convenient to trick, lie, and trap the good nature of western societies."

Soon, it was easier to find the bad guys than the good, and communism, the doctrine's advocates had you believe, was seeping into Latin America like a virus. It wasn't long before people became closed, guarded, and paranoid. The region's fledgling democracies were particularly vulnerable. "What threatens the West," one doctrinaire wrote, "isn't so much open military aggression as much as the combination of military and political action together—almost more political than military—with the goal of taking advantage of Western civilization and using these weaknesses to destroy the West."

The results of the U.S. war schooling were horrifying, especially for places like Latin America. In the 1960s and early 1970s, military proponents of the doctrine evoked "national security" to overturn democracies in half of the hemisphere. Some of these were U.S.-trained officers who, once in power, tortured and killed thousands of their own citizens to "win the war against communism." In Argentina, Brazil, and Chile alone, at least 40,000 people were "disappeared" or murdered by National Security Doctrine proponents.

The National Security Doctrine also had an immediate impact in Colombia, where its followers included the former military dictator from the 1950s, General Gustavo Rojas Pinilla—who had made the Communist Party illegal—and, of course, Landazábal. "There's nothing more vulnerable in this hidden war than a democracy because a democracy is made from voluntary consensus," Landazábal told his fellow officers prior to becoming joint commander of the Colombian Armed Forces. "If this democracy allows criticism, opposition, freedom of expression, freedom of movement—as it will because this is natural in a democracy—it will be vulnerable because what happens in a war is that there is no starting point and there's no defined boundary from where the war can emerge."

By the time he became defense minister in 1982, Landazábal's frustrations with Colombia's democracy had built up like a volcano. He was one of the most battle-tested officers in the army. He had fought North Koreans, Liberal guerrillas, and Colombian Communists. He later led one unit into the foothills of the Tolima province to battle "bandits" and almost died when his helicopter crashed into the side of a mountain. On several occasions he thought he had the enemy on the run. In the late 1970s and early 1980s, Landazábal headed up the military's crackdown on the rebels under President Turbay. At the time, he thought victory was in his grasp. Hundreds of guerrillas were in prison, the others in hiding. But as had happened in the past, the politicians told him to retreat so they could talk peace. Then they released the rebels he had imprisoned. Landazábal believed it was a pattern that repeated itself one too many times.

Landazábal's—indeed, the army's—anger was also related to overall budget policy. Colombia's politicians had routinely and purposely limited the power of the military. During the 1970s and 1980s, the government allocated between 1.5 and 2.0 percent of the gross domestic product to the military, putting it at the median for Latin American nations. At the same time, Colombia's armed forces had about three soldiers for every 1,000 people. For

its population of 29 million (today, it's 45 million), that made the military one
of the smallest in the region.

The difficult geography and sheer size of Colombia—double that of
France—require more military personnel than your average Latin American
country. Colombia could be five countries instead of one. It has a wide range
of climates and topographical obstacles. It's split by three mountain ranges
and rippled by a number of smaller ranges and rock formations that make for
perfect, self-contained hiding places. For 150 years, guerrillas of all colors
have made use of these hiding places and left their opponents reeling after
repeated ambushes. Colombia also has hundreds of rivers and long, sprawl-
ing marshes. There are impenetrable jungles and impassable swamps. To
make matters worse, in many rural areas there are few roads. The only means
of transport is by boat or on foot. Even with modern equipment, the army
has had trouble with the terrain, losing almost as many helicopters to acci-
dents as it does to battle.

But during Landazábal's time the money for the military to cover this
vast terrain never came; nor did the airplanes, the guns, or the uniforms. And
the army wallowed in mediocrity. Aside from the military's occasionally suc-
cessful offensives, it has a history marred by very public failure. The M-19
guerrillas were particularly adept at embarrassing Landazábal's military,
which made the Betancur amnesty that much more painful for the general.
In 1979, the rebels stole a cache of 4,200 weapons from a Bogotá-based army
outpost by tunneling underneath it. They followed this up by overrunning
the Dominican Republic's embassy during a diplomatic soiree and taking
thirty-two hostages, including the U.S. ambassador to Colombia. They held
the hostages for two months and then brokered a $1 million ransom and an
airplane to Cuba. Just before the rebels boarded the plane, some of their
hostages hugged them in a tearful good-bye.

Ironically, the armed forces' lack of resources was a direct result of the
famed National Security Doctrine. Fearful of the growing presence of the
military in other Latin American countries, Colombian politicians deliberately kept their own armed forces just big enough to keep the guerrillas in
check, but not big enough to threaten their hold on the government. "The
politicians don't let the armed forces grow," Landazábal growled when I met
with him, "because they don't trust them. They're afraid of a coup. And when
things get bad, to save their own asses, they blame the military; they say we
can't win the war."

Such was the military's dichotomy in Colombia: It had an independent
strong-minded officer corps that was faced with a constant shortage of war
materiel. What's more, the politicians used the army as the scapegoat for the

country's problems. The deficit and the humiliation would eventually lead the military into a deadly alliance with a dangerous and unpredictable partner.

But first, Landazábal took his frustrations out by writing. The general was prolific. Before he became defense minister in 1982, he had written four books, all on the guerrillas' military and political tactics. His colleagues were astounded. How do you do it? they would ask. He shrugged it off. He didn't write to impress them; he was on a one-man PR campaign to convince Colombians that a "war without borders" was winnable. He berated the guerrillas and the government alike. But his audience was as small as the defense department's budget, and he didn't get very far.

Still, he kept writing. When I met with him, he had just published what would be his eleventh and last book. He also wrote countless articles. The general was a convincing if not always a good writer; his penmanship and prose had even won him a wife many years earlier. As he headed toward Korea on a U.S. naval ship in the early 1950s, he wrote infamous love letters and poems to his then girlfriend. "Today, I have seen you more beautiful," one poem read, "your beauty . . . grows like an ear of wheat that never stops." His soldier friends were both aghast and delighted at Landazábal's talents. They copied the letters and sent their girlfriends versions of the same messages; the general's writing career had gotten its first big break.

More than anything, Landazábal's books are full of warnings. It's to be expected. He was a military man, a career alarmist. But he also understood his country and his enemy. Where the politicians saw hope, he saw treachery. Where they saw trust, he saw betrayal. When I spoke to him, Landazábal was still disgusted with the "hippie" Betancur for his naivete. "The Betancur administration arrived with the proposition of making peace, to give the guerrillas what they wanted in order to achieve peace," he told me. "But he didn't take into account that when you get involved with the guerrillas, they don't give up; they're going for power. It's a decision they've already made. The guerrillas organize to get rid of the government, and if it takes forty years, then it takes forty years, but until the government is overthrown, it's not over. This is the essence of armed revolution: No one joins the guerrillas to make small social changes, but rather to overthrow whoever is in power."

The Betancur years would be Landazábal's biggest challenge, and the general had prepared himself well. Years earlier he had written in detail exactly what he would do once he had the post. More than anything, Landazábal saw the war as a race: Whoever won over the peasantry first would win. Landazábal knew that the guerrillas had already made strong inroads by organizing "peasant leagues" and community organizations in the countryside. He'd spent years writing about it. The government needed to do the same or risk losing entire portions of the country to guerrilla rule, he argued in his preministerial manifesto.

The document also outlined a complete overhaul of the armed forces. The military, Landazábal argued, was isolated from its mission of helping people. The army should prepare "to be part of the economic development of the country," he wrote echoing the thoughts of his U.S. teachers. It was the old "bullets and beans" concept of the 1960s all over again. He called for the creation of "Engineering Corps and Economic Development Command Centers." These units would work in the areas most affected by the violence; they would lead the country to prosperity once the war had ended.

The laundry list of his military concerns reflected Landazábal's attitude toward Colombian politicians. Like so many generals who preceded him, he thought they had failed. The politicians weren't interested in winning the war, he concluded; with over half of the population wallowing in poverty, it was clear that they had abandoned the peasantry. The politicians were also corrupt and bowed to their local interests. They lacked discipline and were *incumplidos*, or irresponsible, he fumed. "The subversives are stronger today than they were yesterday," he wrote in *Armed Forces Magazine*, "And as patriotic and faithful soldiers, we are going through the worst of times. We are convinced that the army can defeat the guerrillas militarily but also convinced that despite this advantage, the subversives will continue if there aren't changes in the social, political, and economic conditions." The editorial provoked fury and sparked rumors of a Landazábal-led coup. In the end, there was no coup. But a year later, General Landazábal was settling into his new job as defense minister.

Initially, President Betancur implemented some of Landazábal's ideas; the two traveled together to war-torn areas to inaugurate several military "engineering corps," and the president secured more aid for these regions. But as promised, the president also corralled the army and pushed for the amnesty of jailed guerrillas. Landazábal gritted his teeth. The general could scarcely hold back his anger. The amnesty was the ultimate insult, and it sent Landazábal down a destructive path.

While the amnesty debate raged in congress, Landazábal began a public campaign to discredit the nascent peace talks and the "hippie" president. Despite Betancur's attempts to keep them secret, Landazábal had found out about Betancur's negotiations with the guerrillas almost immediately. Naturally, the general was insulted. Talking peace with the guerrillas was the same as admitting defeat, he believed, and he said so. "The government and the Armed Forces aren't going to give a cease-fire," he told a journalist during a one-on-one interview just days before the government and the FARC signed a cease-fire agreement. "The political vacuum, the power vacuum that there would be in the countryside would be filled by the guerrillas. It would be just like giving them an 'independent republic' for each one of their [rebel] columns."

Other public barrages followed. Landazábal's popularity soared as his president's popularity declined. One poll in 1983 placed the general as the third most popular person in Colombia, well ahead of the increasingly unpopular President Betancur. Still, Betancur continued talking peace with the guerrillas, forcing Landazábal to alter his strategy again. This time he did it in a military way he thought befitting of his hero, Erwin Rommel, the Desert Fox.

The plan required encircling the FARC's leadership, the Secretariat. Landazábal believed, perhaps correctly, that cutting off the head of the snake might destroy the rebels' whole body. The general knew where the guerrilla leaders were from intelligence reports seeping out of the southern region where the secret meetings were taking place between the government and the FARC. He also received word that the two sides were planning another meeting in Tolima, the exact province where the general's helicopter had crashed in the early 1960s. Now it was Landazábal's turn to surprise these "bandits."

As Betancur's secret commission prepared to go to Tolima to meet with FARC leaders, Landazábal positioned his troops to strike. The president's commission had had to avoid soldiers in the past, but this time, the army hid thinking it could ambush the rebel leaders. Up until the last minute, the plan seemed as if it might actually work. Landazábal had the meeting surrounded and in his sights. But as he was waiting for the right moment, guerrilla sentries smelled out the army soldiers and informed their leaders. The FARC complained to the government commission, who quickly got word to President Betancur. The president then called Landazábal and asked him to stand down. The general obeyed the order, but the betrayal was too much for him to take. Like his hero Rommel, Landazábal would not subject himself to any more humiliation. Rommel poisoned himself. Landazábal poisoned his own country.

When he realized that he could no longer thwart the president's efforts to talk peace with the guerrillas, General Landazábal focused on a new strategy. Drawing from his U.S. training, Landazábal sought to undermine the FARC and the Communist Party using an old trick of war: polarizing the population. In the 1940s, U.S. war theorist Paul Linebarger wrote, "A people can be converted from one faith to the other if given the choice between conversion and extermination." In the early 1980s, Landazábal wrote, "The armed forces have a firm conviction that they should maintain strong contact with the people. When this is achieved, it will be the final step, in our view, so that the nation as a whole, without distinction of class, of ideas and beliefs, finally chooses between good and evil, between violence and peace, between craziness and sensitivity."

These words were a sign that the dirty war had begun.

At the time, using civilians to fight the guerrillas was legal in Colombia. Following a regional pattern, a 1965 decree had opened the way for authorities to organize citizens into militia groups. Similar legal precedents were established in Peru, Guatemala, and El Salvador. In all three of these countries, the governments, with the help of the U.S. military, used civilians to fight leftist insurgencies. Guatemala's plan was perhaps the boldest of the three. In the early 1980s, the Guatemalan government enlisted close to a million men and boys to serve as "civil patrols." The army regularly employed these "patrols" to butcher their own neighbors in a slash-and-burn campaign that left over 100,000 dead.

The 1965 Colombian decree said that "all Colombians, men and women . . . will be used by the government in activities and work that contribute to the reestablishment of order." The Colombians had drawn up the decree on the recommendation of a U.S. special forces commander who had visited the country just a few years earlier. The decree gave way to a law in 1968, which, fifteen years later, gave way to a flustered general who wanted to use it. As defense minister, Landazábal pushed through a law that forced male peasant farmers to "give service" on weekends. "Our proposal has to be clear, simple, and widely known," the general wrote in *Armed Forces Magazine* at the time, "to work shoulder to shoulder with those in civilian clothes to achieve their security, the continuous progress of the nation, and the establishment of peace in all the territory."

Landazábal picked an economically important region, the Middle Magdalena Valley, to test his plan. Straddled by two towering mountain ranges and split by the shallow, muddy Magdalena River, the valley is considered the heart of Colombia. It's the center of the country's oil industry and home to Colombia's largest refinery. Sputtering oil fields dot the countryside around it, along with a network of pipelines that run through the low hills. Colombia's oil industry isn't large, but it's constant. There are also important gold and nickel deposits buried in the San Lucas mountain range at the western edge of the region and large cattle ranchers spread throughout the lush lands of the valley. As it is in so much of Colombia, the legal straddles the illegal in the Middle Magdalena Valley. The region has thousands of acres of coca fields, the raw material for cocaine. And there's an illegal gasoline trade that relies on local families to puncture the pipelines and siphon fuel into empty milk cartons.

The region's riches lured the country's armed factions to the area. For years, both the FARC and the ELN used money from the drug and illegal gas trade to fund their war against the state. The FARC also kidnapped and extorted the region to death. The abuse made the area ripe for a change. Many locals were unhappy with the FARC's increasing use of extortion and kidnapping and turned to Landazábal's military for help.

In 1981, several of Landazábal's officers began talking with business leaders, middle-class peasants, and shop owners. The local elite and the military proposed forming what they called *autodefensas* or "self-defense" groups to combat the rebels. It was the same name the Communists had used for their first armed groups in the 1950s. The new *autodefensas*, however, would facilitate the army's work. A formal meeting between the military officers and prominent cattle ranchers, large businessmen, and powerful politicians in the small cattle-ranching village of Puerto Boyacá occurred the next year. One of the participants was Texas Petroleum, a subsidiary of Texaco. The hat was passed, money was collected, and the new *autodefensas* were born.

Almost immediately it was clear that these groups were going to do more than just defend themselves. They divided into small units and took on fearsome names like "Death to Kidnappers," "Embryo," "Small Fry," and "Black Faces." Then they began a campaign to terrorize the Middle Magdalena. As it was with their forefathers during *La Violencia*, the goal wasn't just killing the person, it was to kill the entire idea that the enemy could exist. They called it a "cleanup," and its targets were Communist Party members and suspected FARC collaborators. The victims—found in ditches and on the sides of the road, and washed up on river beds—bore the mark of the new dirty war: "Dead because was a Communist" and "Dead because informant for Communists" were just two of the signs left on the murdered.

The carnage was staggering. In 1983, Amnesty International reported more than 800 extrajudicial executions in the Middle Magdalena Valley. The military said that paramilitaries had killed 459 people in the region, which Defense Minister Landazábal attributed to a fight of "subversion against subversion." The deaths even caught the attention of the general's old teachers, the U.S. government, who said that perhaps as many as 500 people had been assassinated in the region. "Puerto Berrío, the community hit the hardest by the violence," a U.S. embassy cable from the time read about one town in the valley, "is almost a ghost town." Schoolteachers, the cable continued, were particularly vulnerable because of their alleged pro-Communist sentiments.

The teachers fled the onslaught and "school enrollment is down a reported 70 percent. . . . What began as a 'clean-up' of Communist guerrillas, their supporters and their sympathizers by the vigilantes reportedly has broadened to include members of the non-violent MOIR [a Maoist political party], criminals, petty malefactors, and homosexuals—everyone in fact who is not acceptable to the vigilantes."

The U.S. government observers had little doubt as to army complicity in the crimes. "The reign of terror has proceeded largely unimpeded because the security forces in the region deliberately have not interfered with the vigilante bands," the cable read.

In fact, the army worked openly with these new paramilitary groups. In 1983, in Puerto Berrío—the same city cited in the U.S. government cable as the focal point of the repression—General Landazábal launched the XIV Brigade. Over the next few years, the brigade would become the epicenter of paramilitary activity providing information and cover for the paramilitary groups that had amassed in the region. These groups may have had different names, but they had one central chain of command. From the XIV Brigade Landazábal's troops could reach into the conflictful provinces of Antioquia and Santander, where the guerrillas and Communist Party had flourished. The general also established two accompanying battalions: one near the mining village of Segovia about sixty miles to the north, the other in the cattle-ranching area of Puerto Boyacá about sixty miles to the south. All worked closely with the paramilitaries.

It was still a full two years before the UP would have its first national convention, but its enemies were already sharpening their knives. The main course was yet to come, and Landazábal was sitting at the head of the table.

CHAPTER 3

THE MASTER PLAN

Civil wars follow strange patterns. When the battle begins, both the government and the guerrillas seek support for their causes. They spend time gathering followers and winning over those on the margins of the war through fighting, propaganda, and civic programs. As the battles become more intense, these people on the margins have less room to maneuver. They are frequently given a choice by those who seek their support: join or die. Eventually, when one or the other side has a clear advantage and wins or when there is a stalemate, the two start to talk. Dialogue frequently coincides with some of the heaviest fighting as both sides jockey for position at the negotiating table. The months leading up to any peace talks are often the bloodiest of all.

This describes Colombia's civil war in the early 1980s. The army was giving the people of the Middle Magdalena Valley the choice of joining its efforts to "clean up" the region or die. But even as the repression of the Communist Party in the Middle Magdalena hit its peak, preliminary peace talks between the government and the FARC continued apace. While dozens of Communist Party militants and suspected FARC guerrillas were being assassinated, Alberto Rojas Puyo, the Communist stalwart and peace envoy, and the other government delegates were meeting with the guerrillas in the rebels' secret hideouts just a few hundred miles to the south. The violence didn't seem to stall the talks at all. It was as if by the 1980s this was an accepted Colombian tradition: peace talks on one side, bloody war on the other.

Just about the only distraction to the talks was Colombia's Desert Fox, Defense Minister General Fernando Landazábal. In 1983, fifty-nine of his soldiers came under government investigation for their involvement with the death squads ripping through the countryside, including several officers in the Middle Magdalena Valley. But the general remained steadfast. He

defended the officers and vilified the investigators. "Every time you attack the
military institutions, you strengthen the guerrillas," he told the magazine
Cromos at the time. "And every time you strengthen the guerrillas, the armed
forces' morale drops. These wars are unwinnable because we've lost the edge."
In late 1983, after Landazábal wrote a scathing critique of the government's
peace plan in *Armed Forces Magazine*, President Belisario Betancur decided
he had had enough. A few weeks after the article appeared, he asked the general to step down. It was the end of Landazábal's public-service career, but he
had left his deadly paramilitary group coiled up like a cobra.

With Landazábal pushed aside, the government and the FARC forged a
historic accord. In April 1984, the government and the FARC announced the
Uribe Agreement. It was the first between the rebel group and the government since the army's attacks on the "independent republics" in 1964. Most
of the population was both surprised and excited. "At noon, activity throughout the country stopped for two minutes," *Time* magazine wrote of the celebration. "People at office windows, on the street, or in buses waved white
handkerchiefs. Car horns blared, church bells pealed, and radio and television
stations broadcast the national anthem. In downtown Bogotá, more than
10,000 people gathered in silence as 1,000 doves were released from the par-
liament building."

Named after the small municipality where it was signed, the Uribe
Agreement paved the way for a cease-fire between the two sides and the
beginning of a peace process. The FARC agreed to condemn and forbid
"kidnapping, blackmail and terrorism in all its forms." President Betancur
told Colombians that the government was willing to "carry out constant
efforts to improve all the educational, health, housing, and employment levels . . . [and] promote, once peace has been restored, and as has happened on
other occasions, initiatives to strengthen the conditions that guarantee fra-
ternal democracy, which requires that we forgive and forget; and to improve
all the Colombian people's economic, political, and social conditions."

The two sides said they would meet on a regular basis in the FARC's
headquarters in La Uribe, known as the *Casa Verde* or "Green House," where
they would work on settling the finer details of the long-standing conflict.
The talks did, however, have an important provision: The FARC would not
relinquish its weapons. That would be a more gradual process, the two sides
decided, facilitated by the creation of the rebels' new party, the *Unión
Patriótica*, or UP. The UP was a critical part of the agreement since it was the
mechanism by which the FARC would enter the political mainstream.
Recognizing the party's importance, the government committed itself to protecting the UP.

"The government, in accordance with the Constitution and the laws, will give the *Unión Patriótica* the guarantees and security it needs so that it can campaign as well as participate in elections in the same way other political parties do," the agreement read. "The government will use all the force of the law against any citizen or authority that inhibits these rights or denies, ignores, or refuses to recognize the rights that they [the members of the new party] have. The government will also guarantee security and liberty to the FARC during the process of incorporating its members into political activity."

For many, the Uribe Agreement was the beginning of the end of the war. Government leaders were particularly pleased. Despite the brouhaha surrounding Landazábal's resignation, President Betancur was ecstatic. He had fulfilled part of his promise in pulling the FARC from the jungles to the negotiating table. Now he looked to seal a peace agreement with the rebel group, and by doing so, pressure the other guerrilla groups—the M-19, the ELN, and the EPL—into a peace process as well.

But the real winner of the Uribe Agreement was the FARC. The agreement was the start of the guerrillas coming out party, and the little-known rebel group was about to become a massive celebrity. In the months following the agreement's signing, the peace talks would help the FARC get its revolutionary message to millions of Colombians. The UP would help the rebels rein in new followers. And all of this could be done under the canopy of a cease-fire.

Perhaps the only man more pleased than President Betancur with the Uribe Agreement was the FARC's longtime, enigmatic political commander, Jacobo Arenas. Arenas had spent most of his adult life preparing for this moment and would relish in its glory. During the next few years, Arenas would obtain unparalleled fame for a rebel commander. He would become the protagonist in the talks with the government and write a book about peace and war. He would also be the UP's leading advocate and its presidential candidate. He would make the FARC a determining factor in national politics and himself a national figure. For Arenas, the UP was a vehicle to the prominence that had eluded him for so long in the mountains. But more than fame, the Uribe Agreement gave Arenas something he had sought his whole life: control over the Communist Party and the leading role in the revolutionary war. Fulfilling this goal, however, had come at a great cost.

Long before he became a FARC commander, Jacobo Arenas was a brash young union leader named Luís Morantes. He joined the Communist Party in the 1940s after a brief stint with the Liberal Party and quickly distinguished himself as a top-notch orator and organizer. Throughout the trou-

bled times of *La Violencia,* Morantes stirred crowds from the Andean mountain cities to the villages dotting the Middle Magdalena Valley. But he also
found himself at odds with Communist Party leaders over who should run
the organization. It was a fight that would plague the party for years to come.

Morantes vied for more worker and peasant control of the Communist
Party. However, the party hierarchy wanted more "professional" leaders. The
division wasn't just political, it was also about geography. These "professional" leaders wanted to run the "revolution" from the cities, while the
workers would fight the battles on the streets and the peasants in the countryside. It was, and has been, the prevailing model for all Colombian political parties in their bloody battles for power. The top leaders of the
Conservative and Liberal Parties rarely shed any blood in the long-standing
civil wars that have ripped the country apart for over a century. They have
left the fighting up to their peasant supporters. Communist Party leaders do
the same. Morantes and his colleagues lost the debate. The party stayed city
based and was run by the Marxist intelligentsia. It was a blow the future
FARC leader wouldn't forget.

Despite this early ideological rift, Morantes remained loyal to the
Communist Party. Throughout the 1950s and early 1960s, he bided his time
by organizing unions and helping the Communists fend off army assaults
during *La Violencia.* He was a firm advocate of the Communist strategy of
combining legal and illegal forms of struggle to topple the government, popularly known as *la combinación de todas las formas de lucha.* In fact, Morantes
was fascinated by military affairs, which he would gladly mix with politics to
meet his own ends. He had spent his childhood in military academies studying strategy and later jumped at any opportunity to help the Communists'
"self-defense" groups in the countryside. Indeed, party leaders underestimated Morantes's enthusiasm for leading a war. In the early 1960s, they sent
him to the mountains of Tolima to help the beleaguered guerrilla commander
of the Communist self-defense groups, Manuel "Sureshot" Marulanda. To
their dismay, Luís Morantes never returned.

Soon after he arrived in Tolima, the government attacked the
Communists' "independent republics." The Communists lost the battle, but
the newly christened Jacobo Arenas had found his place. Almost immediately, Arenas nestled into his new role: He would be the FARC's political
adviser, the complement to Sureshot Marulanda. Born Pedro Marín,
Marulanda was himself a one-time Liberal Party supporter, and had been
fighting the government for fifteen years already. After escaping from dozens
of army assaults—and being pronounced dead on more than a few of those
occasions—he had the well-deserved respect of the troops. Arenas would

earn their respect as well but more because of his charisma than his battle savvy. Over the next few years, Sureshot Marulanda ran the army, while Arenas decided rebel political and long-term military strategy. The powerful twosome eventually became the face of the FARC. Whereas "Sureshot" saw the enemy through his viewfinder, Arenas envisioned it in its offices planning its counterattacks. They were a formidable team, but for the moment, they continued receiving orders from the Communist Party.

Meanwhile, the debate over strategy continued. While both the party and the FARC agreed that they would use *la combinación de todas las formas de lucha*, they disagreed over where to set the boundaries of the armed struggle. The Communist Party wanted to limit the FARC to the rural areas. But the rebels saw the city as an important political and military battleground. The debate was a rehash of the early "intelligentsia" versus "peasant" discussions in the 1940s. Only this time, the peasants had more guns.

In the early 1970s, the battle for "revolutionary" control over the cities came to a head. Rival guerrilla groups sought to establish militias for petty terrorist acts and recruiting. Urban rebels knocked off some banks, kidnapped a few wealthy Colombians, and set up a newsletter to publicize all guerrilla attacks in the countryside. At first, the Communist Party acquiesced to the rebels' push into the cities and allowed the FARC to send in a crack team of urban troops. But then, just as the militias' work was beginning, Communist Party leaders reversed their decision. Several urban guerrilla leaders revolted. When the Communist leadership sought to reprimand them, these leaders broke from the party to form a separate guerrilla group they called the M-19.

From its beginnings in 1974, the April 19 Movement, or M-19 for short, was the antithesis of the FARC. The group focused on the cities, not the countryside. These rebels also proclaimed they wanted to reform democracy in Colombia, not replace it. At first, the M-19 was small, but its flashy style made the other rebels seem flat-footed and outmoded. While the old guerrillas idled in remote rural areas, these new rebels stole milk, food, and medicine right in front of the police and handed them out to the poor in the city slums. The M-19 would score political and financial points by holding business executives captive until they gave their employees raises and paid the guerrillas handsome ransoms. Their bravado was especially appealing to college students who saw their bacchanal attitude as *chévere* or "cool." "The revolution is a party," the M-19 leaders would say, and they made it so. Masked M-19 members would appear in university assemblies to deliver rousing speeches and invite people to rallies. Then they would recruit students to be everything from soldiers to messengers.

It was during the M-19's early years that the Communist Party's double standard with regard to the FARC—revere it, but don't join it—finally began to unravel. If they couldn't join the FARC, these same revolutionary wanna-bes would join the M-19. The Communist Party watched helplessly as their younger members filtered into the M-19's urban platoons. Party leaders were furious but held to the principle of no urban guerrillas. It would compromise their "legality," they reasoned. Their rivals just laughed and called them "pussies."

In the countryside, FARC leaders like Jacobo Arenas clenched their teeth. The rebel group was still small, relatively insignificant; the Communist Party controlled it. But Arenas could see the tide turning. The M-19 was growing exponentially, and the popular movement was exploding. In the late 1970s, unions, student organizations, and peasant syndicates organized massive protests against the government, the biggest of which culminated in a national strike in 1977. For two weeks, the country was paralyzed. Clashes with the army followed, during which at least fifteen strikers were killed. Dozens of others were jailed.

The strike was a "revolutionary moment," Arenas would declare later, a time in which the only thing that was missing from a mass insurrection was guns. Arenas decided then that he could no longer accept orders from the Communist Party, and he began developing a master plan to prepare for the next revolutionary moment. The plan included building a larger army and replacing the Communist Party with a new, more dynamic one that represented his interests. He understood that to win the country, the FARC had to have a stronger political presence in the cities. And although he hated the M-19 for defecting from the FARC, Arenas knew the rival rebel group had proved this.

As the fight over the cities was coming to a head, Arenas began solidifying his control over the countryside. Unlike the other guerrilla groups in Colombia, who received assistance from third parties like the Cuban government, the FARC was dirt poor and got little or no help from its natural ideological ally, the Soviet Union. These were the lean years. For instance, the FARC got its weapons from the "neighborhood store" in Bogotá. Messengers would hear that a pistol or a small rifle was for sale and put in their bid. Sometimes a sale would fall through while the messengers were waiting for money from the rebel commanders. Other times, someone else would bid above the FARC and take the gun. In those days, the FARC relied heavily on a "war tax" in the countryside and the Communist Party's Solidarity Committee in the cities. To complete his master plan, Arenas knew he had to have more money and be financially independent from the Communist Party.

To this end, the FARC began kidnapping. Kidnapping has a long history in Colombia. Crime syndicates have kidnapped wealthy Colombians for years. In the 1970s, for instance, the future drug kingpin, Pablo Escobar, secured a $100,000 ransom for a Medellín executive. During *La Violencia*, guerrillas and later "bandits" kidnapped to put pressure on political foes and secure some financing in the process. In the early 1970s, a new wave of rebel groups started their own brand of kidnapping. The M-19 and the ELN took bankers and wealthy landowners captive and then collected healthy ransom payments. The boon made FARC leaders jealous. But at first the FARC, under strict orders from the Communist Party, could only kidnap for "political" reasons. One of the FARC's first kidnap victims was a diplomat. They called it a "retention" and eventually released the man.

With time, however, the FARC's definition of "political" evolved. Defying Communist Party leaders, the rebels began targeting wealthy landowners and big businessmen. In the guerrillas' eyes, these people were "war criminals" who needed to pay a price for their freedom. During the FARC's VI Conference, a national meeting in 1978 of all guerrilla commanders, the rebels formalized the practice of kidnapping for political reasons. At the time the guerrillas had a half-dozen columns or what they called Fronts. But depending on the money it made, each Front could spawn more Fronts. What's more, Fronts were encouraged to give birth, which was an indirect way of encouraging more kidnapping. In the four years that followed, the FARC doubled in size to reach close to one-thousand troops, which were spread out in eleven Fronts.

The money and the growth were impossible to ignore. By the early 1980s, the rebels' definition of "political" had evolved even further. What's more, kidnapping was easy. The government had little control over the countryside, and the FARC took advantage. The FARC "retained" shop owners from small towns, middle-class lawyers and doctors from midsize cities, peasant farmers from alongside highways, and street vendors from lonely markets. The supply seemed endless and the financial scheme risk-free. The short-term result was another boost in earnings and FARC Fronts, but the long-term effects of this strategy would be catastrophic for the rebels and their supporters.

In his quest to become financially independent, Arenas also added another source of funding: illegal drugs. As it was with kidnapping, other guerrilla groups like the M-19 were already raking in the profits by taxing drug traffickers. The FARC felt left behind again, especially since it had direct access to the drug traffickers who were beginning to operate in the rebels' domain.

The drug boom in Colombia had begun in the early 1970s with marijuana. Cannabis plantations sprang up in FARC strongholds throughout southern Colombia. At first, under orders from the Communist Party, the rebels denounced drug trafficking as against communist ideals. They burned some plantations and sent the owners running. But once again, the benefits were too big to ignore, and the guerrillas' logic shifted. Soon, what was against their ideals became "just another crop" that the rebels decided to tax.

When coca replaced marijuana, the profits rose, as did the stakes. Colombians quickly realized that coca was big business. Steadily larger, and more dangerous, drug traffickers filtered into FARC territory to set up cocaine-processing laboratories. The drug traffickers struck a deal with the guerrillas: lay off the business, and we'll pay the taxes. The rebels charged for everything. There was a tax on each cocaine shipment, another for protection of that shipment, and still another for use of the jungle to establish a lab and a secret runway. The costs rose over time, and some traffickers quickly grew weary of paying the guerrillas so much of their profits. It was an arrangement that couldn't last.

But in the beginning, it was bliss. The FARC used the protection money to buy weapons, new uniforms, and communications equipment. The rebels drew in more recruits and secured control over wider areas. The guerrillas also became a ready replacement for an absentee government. In regions where the coca boom was beginning to resemble the Wild West, the FARC established a police and judicial system. The guerrillas punished drunks, adulterers, and murderers. They also protected these villagers from aggressive drug traffickers and forbade the use of dangerously addictive coca derivatives. The FARC was becoming a virtual state, and Arenas was beginning to see his master plan take shape.

By the early 1980s, other pieces of the puzzle had come together. Nicaragua was Communist, a product of the armed revolt that overthrew the long-standing dictatorship of the Somoza family in 1979. El Salvador and Guatemala seemed to be next. The United States, under Ronald Reagan, was in a panic and sending aid to fight the "Reds" in Central America. And in Colombia, President Julio César Turbay had done Arenas and the FARC a huge favor by smashing the popular movement. Hundreds defected from the beleaguered unions and student organizations to join the guerrillas. With more money, more troops, and more control over the regions under FARC domain, Arenas was prepared to hatch his master plan.

In May 1982, Arenas and the other FARC commanders gathered in the cold, barren Sumapaz mountains for their VII Conference. The VII Conference was the most important national meeting the rebels had had to date, and Arenas was ready. Over the previous twenty years, he had emerged as the thinking guerrilla, the long-term strategist. He paid special attention to all the details: finances, weapons, recruiting. He was a slow, methodical worker. He was not, as one former colleague noted, an artist but more of an artisan. His work might take years to accomplish, but it would get done with care and precision. Since his arrival in the FARC in the early 1960s, he had become the man of big projects, and this would be his biggest.

The new income from kidnapping and illegal drugs allowed Arenas and the FARC leaders at the VII Conference to think long-term. And over the next few days, amid the cold mountain backdrop, they developed an eight-year plan to win the war. It wasn't complex. In fact, the main facet of the plan was simple: Build an army, then slowly surround the major cities. The plan called for 28,000 troops by 1990 and a multimillion dollar budget. "As soon as we have an army," Arenas would later tell a colleague during the peace talks with the Betancur administration, "We won't have to go anywhere. Everyone will come looking for us."

To emphasize this point, the leaders added the words *ejército del pueblo*, "army of the people," to their name. The FARC officially became the FARC-EP. Arenas called it "The New Way of Fighting." It meant that the rebels were finally on the offensive. The FARC will "strike blows of national importance," rebel leaders wrote in the conclusions of the conference. "We will no longer wait for the enemy."

Like the military tactician he had always wanted to be, Arenas broke down the country into regions. Starting with the easternmost mountain range, the FARC would split Colombia into pieces, making it even harder for the army to bring the country back together. Over time, the rebels would also slowly surround the major cities along these mountains: Bucaramanga, Cúcuta, Villavicencio, and most importantly, Bogotá. The cities, Arenas believed, was where the war would be won. And for that he didn't just need an army, he needed to get rid of the old political party and replace it with a new one that represented his interests.

Following the VII Conference in 1982, the rebels started to stake their independence from the Communist Party. Despite the party's opposition, the FARC continued to collect taxes from drug traffickers and drug producers. The guerrillas also sent urban assault teams into Bogotá to kidnap and collect lucrative ransoms from the victims and their families. When peace talks began with the Betancur government, the FARC kept most of the Communist Party in the dark. Only the five members of the party's Executive Committee knew of the negotiations. What the Executive Committee didn't know was that, through the talks, Arenas was positioning himself to head the entire organization, and his new political party, the UP, would be an integral part of this plan.

The Communist Party was also jockeying to maintain its position, but it was being outmaneuvered at every turn. At the VII Conference, the party squeezed the FARC into accepting two of its leaders—Guillermo León Saenz Vargas, a.k.a. Alfonso Cano, and Luís Edgar Devia, a.k.a. Raúl Reyes—into the rebels' board of directors, the Secretariat. In this way, the Communist Party thought it could control the rebel group from within. But once again the party underestimated Arenas's resolve and his charisma. It didn't take long for both Cano and Reyes to submit to Arenas's will, and soon the FARC leader had etched away the party's last hope to regain control over him and his budding guerrilla army.

Meanwhile, peace talks with Betancur moved quickly, and Arenas seized the opportunity to take over party affairs for good and, at the same time, upstage his rival rebel group, the M-19. President Betancur pushed through an amnesty for jailed guerrillas; in return, the FARC promised to slow the pace of kidnappings (which it did, even while increasing the pace of tax collection in the countryside). The rebels also began setting the stage for their final trump card, the creation of the *Unión Patriótica*. Arenas wrote up a draft of the UP's mandate and its demands and included them in the historic Uribe Agreement the FARC and the government readied for early 1984.

When the Uribe Agreement became public, Communist Party leaders were stunned. They had been fooled again. Only this time it was worse than they thought. By negotiating with the rebels apart from the Communist Party, the government had unwittingly handed a tremendous amount of political power to the FARC. The announcement of the creation of the UP was an even bigger shock for the Communist Party. It was almost as if the FARC was rejecting its founders. And in a way, the guerrillas were. With the UP, the FARC was saying that it was no longer going to take orders from the party, that the rebel group was the vanguard now.

A debate within the Communist Party ensued about whether it should support the FARC's new political project, but most of the party leaders knew the answer before they even started talking. They had been outmaneuvered again by the clever rebel leader, and now there was little the party could do to stall Arenas's project. Communist leaders had to accept his new rules: They were Arenas's servants. From now on, the party would form the rearguard, while the rebel group took the reins of the organization. And whether they wanted it to be or not, the Communist Party would form the backbone of Arenas's political project, the UP.

For the first time in years, the FARC had also stolen the stage from the M-19. The M-19 was very popular. One poll in 1985 found that if the elections had been held during that year, the M-19 would have garnered a remarkable 36.7 percent of the vote. But the cease-fire and the peace process with the government suddenly made the FARC the protagonists in the guerrilla war; the UP solidified the rebels' position on the political front as well. The M-19 was as hamstrung as the Communist Party by Arenas's connivance, and the guerrilla group began its steady decline, which would eventually lead to disaster.

This was Arenas's finest moment, something he'd been waiting for his whole life. In the months following the 1984 Uribe Agreement, FARC leaders were making headlines daily, and FARC commanders were reaching celebrity status. Arenas had a "red telephone" installed in FARC headquarters that he could use to call the president's office whenever he wanted. He launched a book about war and peace, which was published by Gabriel García Márquez's publisher, *Oveja Negra*. And other FARC leaders started appearing regularly on magazine covers and drawing huge crowds across the country. With the UP, Arenas had gotten his revenge against both the Communist Party and the M-19. Now he could turn his efforts toward building his army.

As peace talks between the government and the FARC began in earnest in 1984, the country watched closely. The two sides met officially for the first time in October in the rebels' headquarters, the *Casa Verde*. The Green House was located on the far edge of a barren hill, a three-day hike through the Sumapaz mountain range. By all appearances, it was nothing more than a wooden shack held up on stilts. What's more, it was cold. The delegates dressed in thick sweaters and wool hats. They smoked pipes, sipped whiskey, and drank buckets of hot chocolate. But they also talked peace. An ex–military general who had fought against Sureshot Marulanda was there, as were members of the country's most powerful business associations. Photos from the talks showed FARC commanders like Jacobo Arenas in his customary train conductor's cap, dark glasses, and Red Baron scarf embracing government reps. "All difficulties will be overcome," the government's chief envoy confidently told reporters.

Newspapers, radio, and television covered the talks with great fanfare. Journalists asked about the cease-fire and the peace agenda. They asked about the secret meetings between the FARC and the government, and the Uribe Agreement. Most of all, they swarmed the mysterious rebel leaders with questions about their past and their future. When will the UP campaign begin? one journalist asked Manuel "Sureshot" Marulanda. "We haven't decided that yet because we can't count on the government giving us the guarantees to be able to campaign," the FARC commander responded.

But for Sureshot Marulanda and his counterpart, Jacobo Arenas, the talks at *Casa Verde* were all part of a show. Behind the scenes the two were carrying on a long-standing Colombia tradition: Talking peace on one side, while waging bloody war on the other. Around the time peace talks were starting with the government, Arenas gathered with his FARC commanders to discuss the master plan they had made during the VII Conference a couple years earlier. The peace talks with the government, Arenas explained to them, were nothing more than a means to an end. It was an opportunity, he explained, to expand on the master plan of building an army. The Colombian military couldn't attack, and so the FARC could regroup and "sun their bellies," as the Communist Party stalwart Alberto Rojas Puyo had once playfully joked with them. The rebels could also train, recruit, and look for new weapons contacts. They could strategize and define political positions. They could reaffirm control over their units and try to establish a strong central command. A cease-fire meant time, the FARC had decided during the VII Conference, and time was working in its favor. Talk of peace, it seemed to Arenas and the other FARC leaders, was a perfect opportunity to get ready for war.

In this context, the UP was nothing more than a part of Arenas's master plan, a way for the FARC to develop its army in the countryside and bring its politics to the cities. The UP would do what the FARC couldn't do: take the rebels' message to a broad public. It would also introduce the FARC's leaders to Colombia and be the vehicle through which they could make a national impact. Nowhere did Arenas even mention to the commanders that they would hand over their guns. Indeed, he spent much his time assuring them this wouldn't happen. The eight-year plan developed at the VII Conference was intact; the UP would accelerate this plan. The party would be the FARC's lackey, an errand boy in the larger struggle for power that was just getting started.

Following the meeting with his commanders, Arenas was more confident than ever.

CHAPTER 4

GUERRILLA POLITICS

For a bold and adventurous rebel leader, Jacobo Arenas was notoriously paranoid. Some said it was related to his mother, who never ate food she didn't prepare herself. But others simply said it was part of being a guerrilla. Since he had joined the FARC in the 1960s, Arenas had obsessed over the various plots to assassinate him he was absolutely sure were afoot. The CIA was his biggest nemesis. The U.S. spy agency, he constantly reminded his fellow commanders, was hatching plans in its Langley, Virginia, headquarters to slip poison into his food or gun him down as he rode his horse through the woods. Arenas's list of attackers would later include drug traffickers and paramilitaries who, of course, were working closely with the CIA. When perestroika began in the Soviet Union, Mikhail Gorbachev became a suspect. Arenas had reason to be afraid. In the late 1980s, drug traffickers did hire British and South African mercenaries to lead a group of paramilitaries in an attack on the FARC headquarters, the *Casa Verde*. The assault, however, never happened, as support for it fizzled during the training for the operation.

Given Arenas's paranoia, it seemed fitting that the commander who he picked to lead the UP carried a pendulum in his pocket. Carlos Enrique Cardona, a.k.a. Braulio Herrera, used the pendulum to snuff out plots against him and his top commanders. He swung it over his own food to check for poison and over his injured soldiers to diagnose their ailments. And when he was in trouble, he swung the pendulum in front of himself and whispered to his gods. But Braulio was a reluctant showman. One time, the government helicopter flying him and Alberto Rojas Puyo, the Communist stalwart, through the treacherous mountain pass to *Casa Verde* began spinning out of control. "I told him to take out the pendulum to see if we were going to make it," Rojas Puyo told me many years later. "And we both started laughing. But

then the pilot got nervous and turned around and said, 'This isn't a game.'"
The two made it, and the peace talks continued.

Herrera was a longtime member of the Communist Party before becoming a FARC rebel. Since joining the guerrillas in the late 1970s, he had built a reputation as a good commander and gained the trust of his troops despite being another *comandante de media-carrera*, intellectual half-timer from the city. He had also forged a strong relationship with Jacobo Arenas, which paved the way for his rapid ascension in the organization. Now Arenas decided that Herrera was the man to carry his master plan ahead and move the FARC into the cities through the *Unión Patriótica*. But first Herrera had to find out who the UP was.

When the UP was created in 1984, Herrera was training in Vietnam. In fact, the first time he heard the words "*Unión Patriótica*" was when he stepped off the plane from Asia. "What's that?" he asked when a fellow guerrilla called Álvaro Salazar told him he was the new party's president. But Herrera caught on quickly. It helped that he was smart. It also helped that he was a charismatic and lovable-looking character—tall and a little round at the waist. With his thick beard and furry arms, he resembled a big teddy bear and quickly began to campaign like one too. But he never really got past his fears. Although he kept the pendulum hidden, he hired extra security and rode in cars with a pistol between his legs.

To help Herrera with the UP, FARC commander Jacobo Arenas assembled a small team. A towering and understated guerrilla leader named Luciano Marín Arango, a.k.a. Iván Márquez, was Herrera's first mate. Márquez was about 6'1", and his curly hair made him look even taller. But Márquez didn't intimidate; like Herrera, he gathered people around him with ease. He had a welcoming smile that caught most off guard. When people spoke to him, he looked at them through his large square-rimmed glasses and listened to what they had to say. His brazen sincerity sometimes scared even his closest friends.

Herrera and Márquez became the UP's public face. But behind them were several guerrillas who worked to keep the party under rebel control. Guillermo Banguero, a veteran of the FARC's urban militias, ran the finances. The hefty, dark-haired Banguero was a good operative, and he had slipped past the security apparatus on his way to becoming a highly respected rebel leader. Álvaro Salazar, the man who met Braulio Herrera at the airport, was the chief of propaganda. Of these men, it was Salazar who had the most experience with the UP, and it was Salazar who would play a decisive role in its future.

When I met him some years later, it was easy to see why Álvaro Salazar had escaped imprisonment and death all these years and why he was perfect for helping Herrera and Márquez organize the UP. He was indistinguishable from everyone else that teetered up and down the Bogotá streets. He had the look of a high school teacher: a round face with small eyes; short, straight hair with a part on the right side. He wore plaid button-downs, jeans, and hush puppies. He had shaven his mustache, but that was about the only thing he had changed since working with the UP. His smile, which he displayed often, always gripped his teeth just before he let out a big belly laugh.

Salazar was also observant and careful. Like Guillermo Banguero, Salazar was an urban militiaman before becoming part of the UP. For years he had been working out of Bogotá's back alleys, dark cafés, and student cafeterias. He had shuttled medicine, guns, and uniforms to the rebel troops. He had written reports, recruited new members, and passed coded messages between guerrillas. Those first few years were the most exciting. Salazar occasionally saw his old comrades in the Communist Party, who would acknowledge his revolutionary spirit with a nod and a dip of the eyebrow. But contact between him and his Communist colleagues was limited. "The party was very strict about this," Salazar insisted to me when I met with him in his apartment. He was happy in the guerrillas. He felt he was in the vanguard now; it didn't get any better for a budding revolutionary.

Later, Salazar graduated to running errands and issuing reports to the press about the rebel group. After a time, he'd created a niche for himself as the "information officer." The FARC had also begun using him as an intermediary for its first contacts with the government. Salazar shuttled messages between the FARC and President Belisario Betancur and served as the rebels' official representative in Bogotá as the two sides revved up peace talks.

Salazar's skills as an intermediary were also put to use with the Communist Party. When the cease-fire and the creation of the UP were announced, Salazar had the difficult job of mitigating the effects it might have on the relationship between the Communist Party and the FARC. The day after the announcement, he met with a prominent member of the Communist Party for breakfast who had learned of the Uribe Agreement via the news. There, Salazar gently explained to him what the FARC was doing with the peace process and the new political party, the UP. Of course, Salazar didn't tell him everything. Arenas's master plan was kept secret from most of the Communist Party. Only a select few would ever get the real story that the FARC was using the peace process and the UP to build its army. The rest simply believed what they wanted to believe. They may have even thought the FARC was really seeking peace.

But for Salazar, Herrera, Márquez, Banguero, and the rest of the FARC guerrillas working for the UP, there was little doubt as to what their orders were. "The UP was nothing more than a political instrument that would allow the FARC to grow even more," Salazar explained to me. "The different Fronts were to implement this new policy. The FARC was to sell the idea that it was a political movement. Each Front would have someone designated to control the political project. They were to create *Juntas Patrióticas*. It wasn't directly recruiting people, but indirectly it had the same effect."

These *Juntas Patrióticas* were a crucial part of Arenas's master plan. During the 1982 VII Conference, the FARC talked of "solidarity cells," small groups of fervent followers who would organize unions, student groups, and peasant leagues. Originally, these were to be clandestine cells. But with the UP, they could work in the open. The advantages were immeasurable. They could sell the FARC's ideas, organize political rallies for rebel leaders, and recruit new members in public.

To set this plan in motion, Salazar set up a small office for the UP in Bogotá. It had just a few desks and chairs and was located in the red-light district, but it was a place to launch the party. From there, Herrera and Márquez began to organize "the masses." The two were good emissaries. Both bought little notebooks and set to work. "They [Herrera and Márquez] listened to the problems of the people day and night," one former UP member told me. "And they'd asked questions: 'What are your streets like? Are there potholes? Do you have running water? Drinking water? What about electricity?' They were very committed. They went into the *barrios*. And then they put everyone to work. Sure, Herrera took out his pendulum once in a while. But it was very rare; it was almost like a myth. He had a warmth to him. They both did. They'd been gone so long that when they arrived, they handed themselves over to the people."

The two met with community leaders and politicians, schoolteachers and Communist militants. They held rallies in markets and public squares. The reaction was immediate. *Juntas Patrióticas* started appearing in Communist-dominated neighborhoods and the green and yellow UP colors in people's doorways, on telephone polls, and in store windows.

It was an exciting time in Colombia. The presence of these high-level FARC leaders campaigning in Bogotá gave many the impression that the FARC was serious about the peace process and the new party. It wasn't long before the UP office was flooded with volunteers. The possibility that the UP was just a pawn in a larger game didn't seem to occur to many of the militants, new and old. They believed their new party was going to alter the face of Colombian politics forever, and some of them were willing to sacrifice their lives in order to achieve this goal. Others simply didn't know their lives were on the line.

"We were totally committed to the UP project," one ex–party member told me. "To push the UP forward wasn't helping the guerrillas but rather contributing to peace and a policy that would end the guerrillas, or at least demobilize the guerrillas." The quickness with which the organizing campaign was going only galvanized these members. "'This could work,' we told ourselves."

And it did. The combination of peace, politics, and guerrillas had people rushing to sign up for service. "I had a stack of résumés next to me," a former UP secretary told me. "Everyone wanted to work for the UP."

What did it feel like? I asked her.

"It was almost like *I* was a commander," she replied.

Jacobo Arenas had his military Fronts do similar work in the countryside. The commanders started in the smallest villages, then steadily made their way to the cities. Each Front had a *"político,"* a politician, to guide the troops through the process. One of these *políticos* was a bespectacled university dropout who called himself Sebastián González. Sebastián met with me a number of years later and told me how the FARC mobilized support in the rural areas.

Sebastián was a wiry character with straight hair and thick glasses, the type you might mistake for an extra in *Revenge of the Nerds*. But his frail-looking body belied his strength. As a high school student, he was a tough soccer player, and when I met with him, he still had a little competitive fire in his eye. He was so excited to reminisce about the FARC, he could barely contain his emotions. He sometimes talked himself into a frenzy emitting words and saliva at an equally bewildering rate. "A lot of people say, 'My best years were in school,'" he told me. "But the best five years of my life were in the FARC. I gave military service to the people. It was an experience, a commitment. It was like I'd gotten a graduate degree in defending the people who were getting fucked by the establishment."

He grabbed another beer and opened it. We had been drinking steadily for most of the day. There were about ten empty bottles in front of me, and he was starting to get sentimental. "It was like I entered the real world, you know," he continued. "Like they say, 'You're a lawyer, go and practice law,' or, 'You're a doctor, go practice medicine.' It was like that." The FARC would get bigger, but it would never regain the romantic appeal it had when Sebastián entered its ranks in the early 1980s. At the time, the rebels were unknown. Kidnapping was still limited. Drug trafficking was a new phenomenon. The war was just getting started, the FARC were still heroes to many, and Sebastián was in the prime of his life. Like UP propaganda chief Álvaro

Salazar in Bogotá, Sebastián was on top of the revolutionary world. And he took advantage of the opportunity.

Sebastián was part of the FARC's IX Front, which operated in the lush, green coffee belt that spread over three provinces in western Colombia. He had arrived with great expectations, he told me. But the majority of his comrades weren't like him. They had never shared dreams of revolutionary struggle during marches at the universities or over a coffee at the cafeteria like he had. They were peasant farmers with little knowledge of the outside world. Still, they were far more prepared than he was. Not only could they shoot a rifle better, but they could walk for days on end. It was a tough fit for Sebastián at first, but his induction was made easier because one of his childhood friends was a commander in the IX Front. Once, after he dropped one of the Front's extra large cooking pots into a steep valley, his friend relieved him of carrying any more heavy items.

Sebastián also benefited from the FARC's years of experience. Gone were the days when every soldier had to do every task. Over time, the rebels had learned to use people's strengths. Sebastián was a teacher, his commanders quickly decided, the "*político*." They soon got him a small chalkboard, which he carried around with him wherever he went. When they stopped to rest, Sebastián would take the board out to give the peasant soldiers mini-lessons in math, science, English, and anything else he could remember from college. He also organized soldiers to perform plays and write poetry.

Sebastián was a natural leader. From an early age, he had been involved in drama clubs and had played on all the sports teams. After he was kicked out of college, he had been the head of a bottlers' union. He loved anything that had to do with academics and politics, and his enthusiasm was contagious. Sebastián also knew his trade well. With his soldiers, he always kept things simple and light. He taught many of the peasant troops geometry by playing billiards with them and explained physics by kicking around a soccer ball. In return, the FARC kept him from the front lines. After the Uribe Agreement, the rebels' foresight would start to pay off, and things would get even better for Sebastián.

In October 1984, a few months after the FARC and the government signed the Uribe Agreement, Sebastián got the order to start creating what they called the *Juntas Patrióticas*, the "patriotic cells" of support for the FARC's party, the UP. Shortly thereafter, Sebastián gathered forty of the IX's most able soldiers, established a little classroom in a small tent in the hills, and began training them in guerrilla politics. "Take one," he would say to his students as he spread pieces of scrap paper in front of them. "Now talk about whatever it says on the paper for three minutes." The subjects ranged from sports to current affairs to philosophy. The peasant soldiers struggled. "I can't do this," they would constantly complain. But Sebastián pushed them. They stumbled again, but Sebastián persisted—and his perseverance began to pay dividends.

After three months of this political training, Sebastián's IX Front started touring villages. He and his troops would break up into small groups. Half were dressed in civilian clothes, the other half in fatigues. Each group visited several houses in the morning to notify the villagers that they were holding a meeting in the afternoon about the guerrillas' new political party, the UP. The visits, however, didn't always go as planned. Even though many people had seen the guerrillas passing through their pastures, some locals were too frightened to speak to the rebels. At one house, Sebastián had to chase down an entire family that had scampered out the back door. At another small farm, Sebastián had to slowly approach a scared peasant farmer and offer him a smoke. The elderly man's hand shook as he reached for the cigarette. "Don't worry," Sebastián tried to calm him. "We're not here to collect a fee; we're not here to take your kids away."

Others were much more hospitable. They offered the guerrillas breakfast, and the rebels rarely refused. Sebastián would sometimes eat four or five breakfasts in a single day. The rebels were heroes to many of them. The locals often sought to get a glimpse of the FARC soldiers when they walked by, and if they were close enough, the children would reach out and touch them before running away laughing. Some of the more aggressive rebel admirers grabbed the guerrillas by the hands and arms to tell them their problems or their fears. Sebastián was once asked to resolve a dispute between two village families whose children were fighting over a pet bird.

The FARC's fans were not limited to families. The women swooned, and Sebastián had to keep his boys from the local girls. He started including sex education in his lectures and handing out condoms to the soldiers. It didn't always work. For instance, one of Sebastián's soldiers convinced a local peasant girl that nothing would happen if she simply ate a dry, uncooked lentil. Not surprisingly, the girl got pregnant.

Sebastián had to keep his soldiers from getting too involved in the towns' habits as well, the most dangerous of which was drinking. This was difficult for Sebastián since he enjoyed alcohol so much himself. On one occasion, the commanders sent Sebastián to pull a drunk *compañero* from a cantina and discipline him. He found the FARC soldier slumping over his seat talking to himself. "You're going to get your ass shot off," Sebastián yelled at him.

Sebastián had barely gotten the soldier out of the cantina when the drunk one convinced him to purchase a bottle of *aguardiente*, Colombia's local anis-laced hooch. With the liquor in hand, the two soldiers headed into the woods, where they drank until morning. "What are we going to tell the *jefe*?" they laughed as they stumbled back to camp. The commander disciplined the Sebastián's colleague, but Sebastián convinced the *jefe* to buy some whiskey so the two of them could get drunk.

Whatever the side effects, the rebel visits to the towns were starting to work. Guerrilla troops would arrive in the mornings, and entire villages would show up for the afternoon meetings. By the next week, they would have a new *Junta Patriótica* and a new green and yellow UP flag swinging from a handmade wooden pole at the entrance to the village. War and politics were coming together to make way for hope. The FARC inspired this confidence, and it presented itself as a ready replacement for an absentee government.

Soon Sebastián and other commanders started visiting bigger towns and villages, and the UP began to creep into the national political scene. By election time two years later, the FARC had organized four thousand *Juntas Patrióticas*. Arenas's master plan was proceeding perfectly.

CHAPTER 5

BLACK VLADIMIR

Every genocide must have what you might call its "doctor," its cruel and merciless master of death, its unwavering murderer. These men put the ideologies to work. They systematically dispose of the enemy, surgically remove it. But few of them are political idealists. They are more mercenary than philosophical, more calculating than soulful. Before the UP came along, Colombia had had its share of "doctors." During *La Violencia*, a paramilitary known as "Blackblood" once drank several liters of his dead adversary's blood to illustrate his resolve; another known as "The Butcher" hung his victims in a tree before cutting off their faces. During the period of the UP, there was a "doctor" called Black Vladimir whose specialty was chopping his victims to pieces before disposing of them in a river.

Vladimir's real name was Alonso de Jesús Baquero. And to all who encountered him as a youngster, he seemed a willing and able student. In the strange world that is Colombia, Baquero's first teachers were members of the FARC, long before they had created the UP. The UP, in the end, would become one of Baquero's favorite targets. But in the beginning, Baquero was a model rebel soldier, the type his guerrilla commanders would use as an example of revolutionary spirit and camaraderie. It was the 1970s when Baquero joined the rebels, and the FARC was starting to extend its reach. Willing boys like Baquero were filtering into the guerrillas' ranks on a massive scale. But few could match Baquero's gumption. He was simply fearless.

The FARC taught Baquero at their *centro de pioneros*, its "Pioneer School" in the eastern foothills of Antioquia, where he had grown up with his peasant family. The area was part of the Middle Magdalena Valley, where Baquero would later kill countless UP militants. After they trained him, the guerrillas made him a messenger and a spy. The rebels gave the eleven-year-old Baquero ammunition and sometimes rifles to carry into heavily militarized areas. The army didn't stop boys back then, and Baquero passed through practically unnoticed. He also watched the army soldiers carefully and noted their movements for the rebels, who planned their ambushes using his information.

At age thirteen, Baquero joined the Communist Youth, JUCO, as a cover for his real work in the guerrillas' urban militias. There he learned how to move clandestinely in the cities, a lesson he would value later when he started hunting the UP. The FARC also taught him how to manage weapons, set up booby traps, prepare ambushes, and kidnap the wealthy. He mastered these skills with ease. Baquero was a prodigy and rapidly rose through the rebels' ranks. Although not very tall, he intimidated all who encountered him. He had powerful forearms, a thick chest, and a neck as wide as his head. He was courageous and took on a brazen ideological air with his new nickname, *El Negro Vladimir* or "Black Vladimir."

But as the years passed, Vladimir the prodigy became Vladimir the ruthless commander. What may have been a fun game for the young kid became a job for the teenager and a bore for the young adult. Vladimir's rebel prowess was eventually matched only by his coldhearted nature. Somewhere something had cracked, and Vladimir had stopped feeling for anyone other than himself. "They take you when you're young, and they make you aggressive," he tried to explain to me about the FARC when I met him inside a jail some years later. "They made me aggressive. But now I'm different." He smiled, and his round baby face stretched to meet my approval.

Vladimir was serving out a thirty-year sentence in a high-security prison near the city of Cali when I saw him. He was in his late thirties but looked like an oversized teenager in his Bermudas and T-shirt. He had confessed to more than eight hundred murders, he told me, many of whom were members of the UP. But repent, I found, wasn't in Vladimir's vocabulary for his was rarely an ideological war. He was a doctor of death, a mercenary.

Still—before the UP, before the paramilitaries—his FARC teachers thought of him as nothing less than the premier soldier in his class, the new type of guerrilla the FARC needed to make itself into an army. Vladimir had his own squadron before he was eighteen, and with more battle experience than most of his comrades, the FARC decided to make him a war instructor. He was just over twenty when a new student caught his attention. Celia Acero, or "Berta" as she was known in the FARC, fell for the physically imposing light-skinned "black" guerrilla leader as quickly as he did for her. Six months later, the two got permission to form a "union." Shortly thereafter, Berta bore a baby girl; their lives would never be the same.

In the FARC, children of soldiers are usually sent to live with relatives. But under the cover of their tent, after several late-night discussions, the couple decided they wanted to keep the baby and made a pact to desert. With Vladimir's help, Berta and a fellow guerrilla, who had also just had a child, fled into the jungle. The two women walked with their children for three days before coming to the town of Puerto Boyacá. It was the beginning of a new life for Berta and her daughter. They had stumbled into the center of Colombia's anti-guerrilla movement. It wasn't long before they brought Vladimir down the same path.

Vladimir was part of the FARC's IV Front. During his first few years as a rebel, the guerrillas moved with relative ease in the Middle Magdalena Valley. The IV divided the area with the XI, and the two Fronts held a virtual monopoly on power. The Communist Party held sway over much of the region, making the FARC's job even simpler. The XI Front was particularly infamous for its kidnapping. The rebels would take as many as twenty people a month. Cattle ranchers and businessmen were the first targets, but soon the list grew to include small shop owners and middle-class farmers. It got so bad that these people would receive notice that the guerrillas wanted to speak to them and they would pack their bags for a month's stay in the jungle.

Kidnapping led to anger, which led to organization, which led to war. The first formal paramilitary meetings in Puerto Boyacá took place in 1982. Military personnel, police, local politicians, businessmen, and cattle ranchers came together to form "self-defense" groups, or *autodefensas*, to protect themselves from the FARC. These groups took on names like "Death to Kidnappers," "Embryo," "Small Fry," and "Black Faces," and they attacked without mercy. By the time Berta and her friend made their break for freedom with Vladimir's little girl in 1983, hundreds of "Communists" were dead. Hundreds of others had fled. Human rights groups called out for justice, but it was too late. The *autodefensa* model had shown its worth, and its promoters didn't waste time in solidifying it. The epicenter would be the city of Puerto Boyacá.

Berta arrived in the city in tatters with a child to feed and a story to tell. She immediately went to the mayor's office, where she thought she might get a sympathetic ear. It came by the name of Luis Rubio. Rubio was a small, unobtrusive man who wore square-rimmed glasses and the short-sleeved golf shirts favored by the locals. He was also the town mayor. He listened to the deserter's story with consternation and compassion. He could help, he told her. But there would be a cost: Berta would have to be a paramilitary informant; in the months to come, she would participate in the slaughter of her former comrades, the "Communists."

In the Middle Magdalena Valley, deserters like Berta were the cornerstone of the paramilitary strategy. Dozens of them helped the right-wing groups identify and, in some cases, kill rebel collaborators. The military did its part as well. It provided intelligence and protected paramilitary soldiers in the field. In this way, the death squads had the means to find their victims and dispose of them without fearing the enemy would compromise the mission.

Over time, the paramilitaries complemented their military strategy with a political one. In 1983, Mayor Luis Rubio, along with several of his Liberal Party colleagues created an organization they called ACDEGAM, which stood for Association of Middle Magdalena Ranchers and Farmers. ACDEGAM's programs dovetailed perfectly with the ideas of military officers like General Fernando Landazábal. For years, the pointy-nosed, outspoken Landazábal had advocated the union between peasants, businesses, and the government. ACDEGAM made it happen. The association set up more than thirty schools in different parts of the Middle Magdalena Valley. These schools created what ACDEGAM called a "patriotic and anti-Communist" educational environment. The association also established health clinics and cooperatives where local farmers could get technical and financial assistance. ACDEGAM built roads and bridges. Financing for these projects came from all types of businesses, including Texas Petroleum Company, a Texaco subsidiary.

Yet behind the nonprofit facade, ACDEGAM was the *autodefensas'* center of operations. Recruiting, weapons storage, communications, propaganda, and medical services were all run from ACDEGAM headquarters. The association had a printing press that put out anti-guerrilla pamphlets, and it had a clothing store that furnished uniforms for paramilitary soldiers. It had "Medical Brigades," who spent most of their time curing injured paramilitary soldiers. And, of course, there were politicians. Mayor Luis Rubio was the local *autodefensa* political voice. Pablo Guarín was the national one.

Guarín was the most outspoken of many imposing political figures in the paramilitaries. He was an exceptionally tall, dark-haired man and the son of an old party boss in the area. His dominating physical presence was as strong as his party connections, and he was elected to congress several times over because of his firm pro-Boyacá stance. Although a staunch member of the Liberal Party, Guarín had a long history of power sharing with the Communist Party. He had broken this alliance, however, when the FARC's appetite for kidnapping grew insatiable. Then he had led the first efforts to form the *autodefensas.* Soon afterward, he became their national political representative. Even his language mirrored that of the most practiced counterinsurgency strategists. "The war will be won by the one who wins the hearts of the peasants," Guarín told the local Puerto Boyacá paper, aptly called *Puerto Rojo* or *Red Port*, of which he was one of the founders.

Guarín sought—and often got—political support from nationally prominent politicians as well. For years, he had a working relationship with President Belisario Betancur's interior minister, Jaime Castro. And eventually, as President Betancur became more skeptical of the guerrillas' intentions, Guarín's work in the region would be recognized by the president himself. On a visit to the region in 1985, Betancur called on Colombians to "come to the Middle Magdalena and see the show in Puerto Boyacá. . . . I can see it on the people's faces, which before were stricken with fear and terror because of the war. . . . Now, everyone in the Middle Magdalena has risen and made himself a defender of the peace next to our army and next to our police. . . . We've received the lesson of peace in this region."

Vladimir had risked his life to get Berta out of the FARC, and now he would risk his own to find her. Whatever remorseless nature he carried in his job, Vladimir was in love with his girlfriend and his child. After facing down a rebel tribunal for Berta's escape, he planned his own getaway. Two years after Berta left, in 1985, he got his chance. The burly rebel leader convinced his commanders in the FARC to allow to him to seek medical treatment because he said he was deathly ill. Still wary of Vladimir's intentions, the commanders sent one of their sentries to chaperon the ailing guerrilla.

The two men made their way to a small village hospital, where they persuaded the attending nurse that Vladimir was a poor peasant farmer. In the middle of the night, he snuck past his guard and onto a bus headed for the town of La Dorada. There he spent weeks looking for news of his wife and child. With no money he begged for food, until he finally got a lead that his family was in the neighboring village of Puerto Boyacá.

When Vladimir arrived, he went straight to Mayor Luis Rubio. Rubio had taken in Berta and Vladimir's daughter and put Berta to work, but he greeted the ex-FARC's story with skepticism. The *autodefensas* were growing now, but they had had problems with infiltrators. Ex-guerrillas who joined would get a thorough interrogation, which sometimes included torture. Entry was not assured, and if a former rebel was not accepted, he usually met his end. In addition to the interrogation, each candidate had to take a questionnaire that asked, among other things: if he had been a victim of the guerrillas; the names and addresses of his family; if he was capable of killing a family member who was a guerrilla. Once accepted, the paramilitaries would inject a little of the U.S. government's National Security Doctrine into the new soldier by telling him: "You're entering a war that has no end. . . . The only enemy is communism."

After Mayor Rubio interrogated Vladimir for several days, he relented and brought him to his wife. Soon after, the *autodefensas* integrated the former FARC into the fold as well. Reunited with his family, Vladimir's new life was cushy compared with his old one. He had a house, a little land, and some livestock. His family was well protected. He could walk on the streets again, go to the park with his daughter, and have a picnic with his wife. He had new friends and was making money for the first time since he could remember. Although it was just a few hundred dollars a month, he could buy clothes and music. It was almost a completely normal existence except for one thing: He was a paramilitary.

As Vladimir found out, the job of a paramilitary in the mid-1980s was similar to working in a slaughterhouse. The men gathered their prey, brought them to designated areas, and massacred them. They then frequently dismembered their victims—first the hands, then the feet, and finally the head—and removed the intestines in a process they called a *picalesco* or "gutting." In this way, the corpses would sink to the bottom of the rivers, where no one would find them. Without the body as evidence, investigators had a difficult time prosecuting anyone.

Each paramilitary had a job: patrol, guard, driver; there was even a torture coordinator. Vladimir wasn't the torture coordinator, but he liked to help when he got the chance. He played good cop and bad cop all at once. First, he would untie his victims' hands from the two ropes hanging from the wall, get them some water, and start an informal chat. The giant man with a childlike smile would then gently warn the prisoners of the consequences if they refused to cooperate. If the accused still didn't answer his questions to his liking, Vladimir would start applying electric shocks and proceed steadily to worse forms of torture involving the testicles, the bones, and the face. Within a few hours, the men were usually dead, and Vladimir would have the information he needed to look for more victims. Then came his favorite part: the *picalesco*. With a smile on his face, Vladimir would chop up his victims and dump them in the nearest river.

"When you're in the paramilitaries, you kill a lot of people," Vladimir told me when I met with him outside his prison cell. "Every day, they brought in 5, 10, 20 people to the school [his name for the detention center]. Some of these guys were tortured so bad they couldn't even think. They'd go crazy. Some had half an arm, their knees shattered." He paused, then looked right at me. "I did them a favor by killing them."

Vladimir worked in the paramilitary slaughterhouses near Puerto Boyacá not far where he and his colleagues would round up their victims. Sometimes, the people would be killed within a few hours of being corralled. Other times, it would take days while they tortured them and squeezed every bit of information they could from the mangled humans in captivity.

The *autodefensas* in the Middle Magdalena Valley didn't confine themselves to killing just suspected guerrilla collaborators. They also murdered
street vendors, bank managers, store owners, political opponents, judges,
policemen, vagabonds, prostitutes, leftist politicians, trade unionists, community leaders, local criminals, and anyone else they believed might disturb their
project. They often killed one another as well. They were prone to disputes
over territory, guns, and, eventually, illegal drugs.

Since the mid-1970s, illegal drugs have become the gasoline that fuels
Colombia's war. And just as they spurred the FARC's growth leading up to the
famous VII Conference, they would spur the paramilitaries' growth leading to
the slaughter of the rebels' political party, the UP. Drug traffickers weren't often
wedded to ideas as much as they were wedded to money. Their alliances shifted
when they saw opportunity or, conversely, when their money was in peril.

At the time Vladimir joined the *autodefensas*, the illegal drug trade was
the biggest business on the planet, and few did it better than the Colombians.
In 1988, *Fortune* magazine declared, "The illicit drug trade is probably the
fastest-growing industry in the world and is unquestionably the most prof-
itable." The magazine estimated that Colombian cocaine exports alone were
worth $4 billion per year, more than Colombia's coffee and oil exports com-
bined. The biggest problem drug traffickers had was handling the crates and
crates of money. "Since the trade is conducted entirely in cash," the magazine
noted, "narcotics leaves a trail of $20 bills." The trails are legendary, and
Colombians are still scouring for the traffickers' hidden stashes.

Leading the narcotics business in the 1980s was the Medellín cartel. The
cartel was a loosely knit network of smugglers who imported semiprocessed
coca "paste" from Peru and Bolivia, processed it into powdered cocaine in
Colombia, and then transported it to the United States. *Fortune* marveled at
the Medellín cartel's business and organizational savvy. The cartel had teams
of police, customs officials, businessmen, cattle ranchers, bankers, military
personnel, and politicians on its staff. It established multiple routes that frequently involved third parties and included foreign government officials. It
had the most sophisticated radar equipment in the world on its airplanes,
and, in the United States, the cartel had its own distributors. It had a financial division responsible for collecting revenues, making investments, and
laundering money, *Fortune* noted. "An 'enforcement' division took charge of
bribes, guards, and hit men," the magazine said. The return on the invest-
ment was stunning: $18,000 a kilogram wholesale in the United States.

Tops at the Medellín cartel was the infamous Pablo Escobar. The beefy
and forlorn Escobar was a man of multiple personalities: robber baron and

socially conscious citizen; ruthless killer and amiable host; pedophile and
upright family man; entrepreneurial genius and incessant dope smoker. The
son of a poor farmer and domestic servant, Escobar started his criminal
career by robbing gravestones and refurbishing them for resale. After gradu-
ating to car theft and contraband, Escobar got a break: Someone asked him
to move coca paste, the gooey, semiprocessed leaf that is turned into cocaine.
His own coca-shipping business wasn't far behind. Eventually, he had killed
his way to an empire and earned a reputation that made even Italian Mafia
bosses shudder. When his friends betrayed him, he might shoot them in the
head. To payback his enemies, he would rape their wives and kill their children before ending their lives. One of his favorite ways of murdering was to
hang his victims upside down before he lit them on fire. In his path Escobar
buried judges, policemen, and rivals.

Still, Escobar thought of himself as Robin Hood, a crusader in a crooked
nation. He built housing for the poor, constructed soccer fields in slums, and
hosted bullfights. His enemies were the "oligarchy," and the Colombian and
U.S. governments who unjustly tried to incarcerate him. While spreading his
wealth, he vilified these enemies, raising his stature with the poor even more.
"It was a song for which he could always find an appreciative audience south
of the border," the *London Times* wrote of the drug kingpin's social and political crusade, "and Escobar had financed his share of gullible or corruptible
Colombian journalists to sing it for him." At one point, Escobar offered to
pay off the country's $13 billion debt. He even won a seat in congress as a
Liberal Party substitute in the early 1980s. "Pablo equals food," the Medellín
poor scrawled along the walls of their slums.

But his popularity was eventually matched by his infamy. He was *Don*
Pablo on the streets, but *pablito* in congress. Inevitably, Escobar's world began
to crumble. "The average law-abiding Colombian is not an admirer of
Escobar," one Colombian told the *Orlando Sentinel*. "He has never been
accepted by the country's high society." Indeed, not long after he won his
congressional post, the wealthy shut him out of their elite country clubs. His
Liberal Party colleagues tried to revoke his membership in the party. Law
enforcement issued warrants for his arrest. Escobar went on the run. And
when on the run, Escobar found few places better than the Middle
Magdalena Valley.

By the mid-1980s, the Middle Magdalena Valley had become a drug
traffickers' safe haven. All over the region, drug traffickers were buying up
land in startling quantities. To the south of Puerto Boyacá, Pablo Escobar's
strongman and business partner in the Medellín cartel, José Gonzalo "*El
Mejicano*" Rodríguez Gacha, owned large swaths of property. Victor

Carranza, the emerald czar and sometime drug trafficker, was buying land to the north. A smattering of smaller traffickers were picking up other plots with or without the permission of the locals.

Just north of Puerto Boyacá, in a dusty cattle village called Puerto Triunfo, Escobar himself established a fifteen-thousand-acre ranchhouse, the *Hacienda Napoles*. In *Napoles*, Escobar felt safe. He easily bought himself favor in the town by giving away Christmas presents, which included televisions and washing machines. He also imported exotic animals and opened up his ranch like a zoo. For less than a penny, locals could see rhinos, deer, zebras, giraffes, gazelles, buffalo, and antelope roaming the light green pastures. They could watch pelicans, herons, and hippopotamuses splash around in the *hacienda*'s sixteen artificial lakes. Visitors were also constantly reminded who the *patrón* was: The airplane that carried Escobar's first drug shipment was mounted at the entrance, and various cars said to belong to Al Capone were littered throughout the zoo. *Napoles* had other advantages as well. The Middle Magdalena Valley was in the heart of the country, so Escobar, the world renowned drug trafficker, had access to six different provinces and multiple smuggling routes; and Escobar, the overweight fugitive, had escape routes through mountains, rivers, and tunnels.

The narco-landgrab in the Middle Magdalena Valley was originally a way to launder money and gain the social status that had eluded many of the ones who, like Escobar, came from poor families. Drug traffickers bought cattle and carved out huge spaces for their opulent mansions. It was a trend that would continue throughout the 1980s and eventually change the face of the Colombian conflict forever. The drug traffickers were purchasing their way into the landed gentry, and as such, they would need increasing protection from their new neighbors, the guerrillas. The *autodefensas* were perfect for the job. It was only a matter of time before the two joined forces.

The drug traffickers and paramilitaries already had some shared history in Colombia before Escobar and others bought land in the Middle Magdalena Valley. In fact, Colombia's first modern-day paramilitary group was formed by drug traffickers. In 1981, the M-19 guerrillas kidnapped Martha Nieves Ochoa, the daughter of the powerful drug lord *Don* Fabio Ochoa, Sr. It was one of a series of M-19 kidnappings of drug traffickers and their relatives. It was also a serious miscalculation. Shortly after the kidnapping, the Ochoa family organized a meeting in the southwestern city of Cali with local businessmen, fellow drug traffickers, and military personnel. Pablo Escobar was one of those in attendance, since Ochoa was a business associate of his. The result was a death squad they baptized as *Muerte a Secuestradores* or MAS, which literally means "Death to Kidnappers." MAS announced its presence by dropping pamphlets on Cali, then killed their enemies in the M-19 until the rebel group submitted to their will. After a few dozen M-19 and their family members had been gunned down, the guerrillas made a pact with the traffickers vowing never to kidnap any of them or their relatives again.

The original MAS fizzled shortly after it had forced the M-19 to stand down, but many say the cooperation between drug traffickers spawned the Medellín cartel. More importantly, the MAS idea spawned an entire generation of paramilitary groups in the Middle Magdalena Valley. The new generation also worked under the MAS banner. But unlike the original MAS, this second wave of paramilitaries in the valley was both anti-guerrilla and anti-drug, and their military leader, Henry Pérez, didn't accept drug traffickers in the areas he controlled.

Pérez was a short, dark-skinned son of a cattle rancher who thought of himself as a hard worker and of his groups as ideologically superior to the drug-financed death squads operating in other parts of the country. Pérez even had strict penalties for the *autodefensas* who were caught using or trafficking drugs. Still, Pérez understood that traffickers were willing to help organizations like his even if he wasn't yet willing to accept that help. Pérez envied their resources, and with the *autodefensas* expanding, he needed their money.

As the story goes, the first contact between Pérez's *autodefensas* of the Middle Magdalena Valley and the drug traffickers came in 1985. About the time that Black Vladimir was entering the paramilitaries, one of Pérez's patrols intercepted a four-by-four as it sped along the maze of dirt tracks that cut through the jungles in the area. The car was filled with processed cocaine. The owners of the drugs were close associates of Pablo Escobar. The confiscation of the jeep gave Pérez an opportunity. Although he could have stolen the goods or turned the traffickers in, Pérez decided to give back the car and the drugs to their owners. To return the favor, the traffickers sent Pérez a new Toyota four-by-four. Direct contact followed, and an alliance between the most powerful drug cartel and the most formidable group of *autodefensas* was forged.

The drug trafficking money was the huge windfall Pérez's *autodefensas* needed to complete the "cleanup" of the region's communists. Soon Pérez's soldiers were using the traffickers' airplanes and jeeps. They also had a seemingly endless supply of sophisticated weaponry and communications equipment, and they could finance more recruits. Paramilitary sentries patrolled with new walkie-talkies. The commanders had satellite communication. Smaller communications centers were established throughout the region.

These centers had a direct line to each other and the local military bases. Pérez could also monitor all incoming and outgoing telephone calls through his contacts at the local telecom. Even Pérez, once a staunch anti-narco, made the most of his new partnership. His new white Toyota pickup had a telephone and a radio. He also rode with three bodyguards, two machine guns, an R-15 rifle, grenades, and four pistols just in case he ran into trouble. And he quickly became a partner in the drug business. He stashed guns, cash, ammunition, and processed cocaine at his home. If anyone tried to search his house, the guards had orders to shoot to kill.

Over time, Pérez sought to bring all the pieces together. He began channeling the new money for the project through Congressman Pablo Guarín's and Mayor Luis Rubio's politico-military organization, ACDEGAM. Two local banks handled the paramilitaries' salaries and gave Henry Pérez a $10 million credit line. From the oil industry to the cattle ranchers, everyone contributed a little bit of gas or food. Medical donations for ACDEGAM came from nightclub owners in Bogotá, radio equipment from drug traffickers in the nearby town of Puerto Berrío. Other drug dealers from around the country joined the *autodefensas* as well. Together they formed a loose national paramilitary network whose unifying factor was their hatred for the guerrillas, in particular the FARC. With the lure of money, they had also begun recruiting the likes of Vladimir. As he had with the rebels, Black Vladimir quickly impressed his superiors. Before long, Henry Pérez made him one of his top commanders. With drug money, the project had consolidated its forces and was becoming increasingly hard for the enemy to penetrate.

But the partnership with the drug traffickers came with costs as well. The new *autodefensas* were split into two groups: some protected the drug dealers' laboratories, transport, land, and even the capos themselves; others patrolled for guerrillas or hunted suspected rebel collaborators. At first, the extra work seemed worth it. In addition to more equipment, salaries increased and paramilitaries' families got perks like food and supplies while the man of the house was on patrol. Drug money also helped fix the local soccer stadium and finance local teams. The *autodefensas* sponsored beauty contests and huge parties. But over time, loyalties were stretched, and the war seemed to take a backseat to the needs of the new bosses. Being anti-guerrilla didn't mean as much as being pro-narco. Money was king, and the word *autodefensa* meant less everyday.

What's more, the FARC was proving to be a difficult target. The guerrillas still had superior numbers and decades of experience. The *autodefensas* could not confront the rebels head-on, so they opted for a different tactic. The year was 1985, and the guerrillas had launched their new political party, the UP. To the astonishment of some and the consternation of others, the UP was establishing an open, legal presence in rural areas across the country. For the paramilitaries, party members weren't just political representatives of the rebels—they were the FARC. And if they couldn't get at FARC soldiers, the paramilitaries would get the next best thing: the UP's politicians and supporters. Who better to do this job than former FARC commanders like the doctor of death, Black Vladimir?

CHAPTER 6

TOO MUCH TIC

By 1985, the FARC was running on all cylinders. Its top commanders were talking peace with the government of President Belisario Betancur. Its Fronts were organizing the UP in small villages and midsize towns, and guerrilla leaders were starting to make headway in the big cities. It had taken a long time, but the FARC was finally working in Bogotá, and rebel commander Jacobo Arenas was plotting his return to the capital, or so everyone believed. Arenas was to be the UP's presidential candidate, and the mere possibility that he would be campaigning in Bogotá was enough to prove, even to the skeptics, that the new party was a path to peace.

Getting to Bogotá had been a critical battle that Arenas had waged on all fronts. First he had taken on the Communist Party, then the M-19 guerrillas, and finally the traditional political powers. After almost ten years, his master plan of enveloping the country with his army was starting to come together. The guerrillas had already created several new Fronts since peace talks had begun. They had also organized hundreds of *Juntas Patrióticas*, the small cells of UP supporters, in towns across Colombia. If the national protests happened again, as they did in 1977, the FARC was going to be ready. Arenas had made sure of this.

Yet to most, Arenas remained an enigma. His book, which was published shortly after the FARC began forming the UP, was more political jargon than personal experience and gave little insight into Arenas's life. Still, it was a best-seller. His popularity confused people, not least because of the way he looked. Pictures appeared in the papers of the FARC commander wearing dark sunglasses, silly European-looking scarves, colorful shirts, and a train conductor's cap. It wasn't the image of a guerrilla commander, much less a presidential hopeful. It also wasn't altogether clear that he would risk his life to be the UP's candidate. In fact, the only certain thing was that he was afraid. Arenas constantly spoke of elaborate CIA plans to assassinate him. He developed a code that the rebels could use to communicate, but it was so complicated no one understood it. Most of all, he stayed close to his bodyguards.

To be sure, 1985 was a confusing and dangerous time for everyone in the UP. No one was really sure what the FARC was doing. The rebels talked peace but didn't relinquish their weapons. They created a political party but at the same time increased the size of their army. Politicians were getting suspicious. Some said the guerrillas were using their guns to coerce potential voters into supporting the fledgling party. Meanwhile, paramilitaries were beginning to harass and threaten the UP for its connections to the FARC. Amid it all, the UP kept growing.

Youngsters like Josué Giraldo—the frightened and courageous human rights worker I would meet in Bogotá many years later—were pouring into the new party's ranks. These were the core of the UP, the future martyrs. Most of them were from the Communist Party or its splinter groups: the Trotskyites, Maoists, or Castroites. They implicitly understood that there were dangers lurking in the shadows; they had dealt with these dangers during their university days. Of one fellow student who was found dead during those dark years of struggle on the campuses, Josué blithely noted in his diary, "They castrated him. They cut off his tongue. They ripped out his eyes. They mutilated his fingers, and they threw acid on different parts of his body."

These new members weren't afraid. In the cities, they volunteered to organize marches, make placards, and set up rallies. In the countryside, they worked closely with FARC Fronts already establishing *Juntas Patrióticas*; they handed out pamphlets, played revolutionary music, and shouted anti-government slogans. Perhaps they underestimated their enemies' growing resolve or were blinded by a dedication to an inspiring cause. The UP was their chance to change the system. Giving up meant losing, and losing was unacceptable. Josué typified this attitude.

When Josué returned to his hometown in the coffee belt after getting a law degree in 1985, he arrived with an infectious enthusiasm for the UP. To pull in supporters, he and some of his old classmates created a cultural group that organized plays, poetry readings, and art expositions. To many, they must have seemed like the harmless school kids they were. But to others, they represented the worst kind of nightmare: godless communist guerrillas posing as artists to lure in their prey.

Josué's group attracted intellectuals, professors, and students. It was a small contingent, but it was enough to challenge the Conservative Party's hegemony in the town. Of course, Josué's Conservative Party father didn't like what his son was doing. Josué's father had been a city council member for thirty years. But over time, even he accepted his son's political affiliations. "My father changed and ended up being more tolerant," Josué wrote later. "Yes, we had discussions. But the interesting thing is that he listened to me." However, most of Josué's father's Conservative Party colleagues didn't go through the same transformation. Their solution to the UP would be that of their forefathers during *La Violencia*: extermination.

But for every opponent, the UP had a proponent. Throughout the country, the party drew on a newfound legitimacy that came with the combination of peace talks, Arenas's candidacy, and guerrilla leaders campaigning in Bogotá. FARC commanders like the teddy bear–looking Braulio Herrera and the towering Iván Márquez were setting up *Juntas Patrióticas* in the city, and the two decided to run for congress as "substitutes," or stand-ins, when the primary candidate wasn't available. Their public appearances drew huge crowds, and the guerrillas took advantage of the opportunity. Herrera and Márquez constantly surprised people with their intellect and energy. Curious onlookers were drawn into the new party's fold with the excitement of working for the "smart" rebels.

The new party also broadened its scope to include towns traditionally controlled by the Liberal and Conservative Parties. In some areas, the UP even made alliances with the traditional parties. The Communist Party and the FARC often scoffed at these alliances, but they were an effective PR tool. "The UP is perhaps the only positive thing to come from [Betancur's] Democratic Opening," wrote the influential columnist D'Artagnán in the country's leading daily, *El Tiempo*. The political rallies attracted a wide cross section of people that had never before worked together. Academics, lawyers, housewives, small farmers, blue-collar laborers, and students joined to listen and applaud the new party. Together they chanted, "UP, UP, UP, with the people all the way to victory," and "You can feel it, you can feel it, the UP is in the house."

"The UP caught on in a way that surprised everyone," UP propaganda chief Álvaro Salazar told me later, "including us."

Over time, the campaign picked up steam. Even old Communist stalwarts like Alberto Rojas Puyo joined the senate race with a renewed enthusiasm for politics. He had never been a public politician. And in typical Rojas Puyo form, he had made an alliance with a Liberal Party leader in the province of Huila. For Rojas Puyo, it was always more about reconciliation than winning, and his presence on the ballot brought the UP even more credibility. He was a living symbol of the possibility of peace, a solid emissary for the FARC's message that it was serious about signing an accord and eventually handing over its guns. Nevertheless, Rojas Puyo campaigned fiercely.

And as he and his Liberal Party candidate running mate went ahead in the polls, Rojas Puyo laughed again at his ever-changing fortunes.

The UP also recaptured some of the Communist Party hard-liners. The Communist Party had reconciled itself to the idea that the FARC was launching the new party. With momentum building, Communists embraced the UP and eventually even tried to subsume it to the party's interests. For the moment, though, the Communists were content to have their members as leading UP candidates. The green and yellow UP banner replaced the hammer and sickle. New recruits filtered in and party candidates surged. The Communist party was rejuvenated, and the UP was the main reason. Not even the Stalinists could dispute that.

But by mid-1985, the year before the UP's first general elections, trouble was already brewing. Despite the cease-fire agreement, army and police officers began harassing UP militants, who they saw as nothing more than rebels in civilian clothes. In the mountainous province of Tolima, just south of Bogotá, the military detained propaganda chief Álvaro Salazar as he made his rounds. It held him for several hours before releasing him. Others were jailed as well, and the death threats were starting to flow in.

Then the dam broke. On September 28, suspected paramilitaries dragged UP militant Hernán Dionisio Calderón from his house and shot him dead in front of his family. Calderón had been protesting military abuses in his hometown of Yumbo in the southwestern part of the country. Fifteen thousand people attended his funeral and shouted at the military to stop targeting them. But it didn't do any good. In the following months, UP activists were murdered in four different provinces across the country. Bombs went off in front of the UP offices in two major cities, killing another militant. In October, police raided the offices of the Communist Party newspaper, *Voz*. Belligerent graffiti like "UP assassins" and "Communist Party criminals" greeted the new party's candidates everywhere on the campaign trail. And it was only the beginning.

Despite the assassinations and threats, preparations for the UP's national convention, scheduled for November 1985, continued. It was a surreal environment. With killings and bombings going on in the countryside, *Voz* announced that UP presidential candidate and FARC commander Jacobo Arenas would be speaking in Bogotá's central *Plaza de Bolívar*. Militants put up posters on city streets with pictures of Arenas, Manuel "Sureshot" Marulanda, and UP president Braulio Herrera, announcing a benefit for Arenas's candidacy and giving directions to the scheduled events. For his part, Herrera continued his stand-up job as Arenas's emissary. With Herrera touring the country to packed houses, momentum continued to build, but so did the tensions.

Critics began to wonder aloud what the FARC was doing with the new party. At UP rallies, green and yellow party banners waved side by side with flags that displayed images of Ernesto "Che" Guevara. To its foes, the rallies looked like the television images they were seeing coming from Communist Cuba and Sandinista-run Nicaragua. FARC leaders aggravated the situation with revealing comments to the press. After being asked how he evaluated the months since the UP was formed, Adán Izquierdo, a commander along the northern coast, told *Voz*, "I would say we're progressing quicker than we thought. . . . In the peaceful and civil village of Santa Clara, 10 boys joined our forces."

Comments like these startled people and fueled the fire. Opposition politicians and analysts began to question the FARC's attitude and the UP's role in fostering peace. In September 1985, just a couple months before the party's national convention, the debate hit the front pages. Some senators said the FARC was "armed campaigning," scaring the people into supporting them. Congress then passed a new law that forbade parties from "creating, maintaining, assisting or financing" armed groups "who, even without guns, intimidate or hinder the participants in the electoral processes." The law also threatened to cancel the votes of any party found guilty of violating the new legislation.

The government recognized the UP as a legally constituted party and, per the Uribe Agreement, afforded it all of the protections under the law. But the accusations of armed campaigning were quickly eroding the party's credibility. The criticisms also had another more sinister consequence: To many people, UP members were becoming "legitimate" military targets, and their opposition was beginning to take advantage of the political climate. Now retired, General Fernando Landazábal told anyone who would listen that the party was part of a FARC scam. "If the next government doesn't take the necessary means to apply its authority and continues to cede political power to the subversives, the country is going to enter a more generalized conflict," the former defense minister told a leading radio station. Landazábal threatened to create a right-wing party of his own, and the mere presence of his paramilitary cohorts in the countryside warned of the coming calamity. Landazábal's ranting worked. Suspicions remained high. As one banana worker in Urabá said to the *Washington Post* at the time, "In meeting with us, the FARC presents itself cordially, discusses things, is willing to compromise. But I believe they are dangerous."

Some UP members were worried. Since his meetings with FARC leaders in the wooden shack on the side of a cold Sumapaz mountain,

Communist stalwart Alberto Rojas Puyo had been warning party members what could happen if their intentions were misinterpreted. "If we didn't embrace democracy and peace in a way that was perfectly open," he told me when I met with him in his home much later, "but rather continued playing on both levels with the UP and the party in the legal sphere and the FARC in the war, we were headed for a holocaust. I said this to the party, and I said this to the leadership of the FARC."

Specifically, Rojas Puyo told rebel leader Jacobo Arenas. Since the cognac-laden meeting in the small rebel ranchhouse in Sumapaz, the UP leader had maintained a strong relationship with the FARC commander. The two exchanged letters for years, which were later published in an illuminating book about the development of the peace process and the political party. The debate again centered on the old Communist Party strategy of combining legal and illegal forms of struggle to topple the government, *la combinación de todas las formas de lucha*. On a number of occasions, Rojas Puyo told Arenas that he needed to be careful about how he presented the FARC's positions. "You can't leave the slightest impression that this may be a trick," he wrote to Arenas in 1983. "That a minority is trying to impose reform using bullets. As I told you in another letter, the tendency is to think that for you a cease-fire means breathing space so you can reinforce your military."

Over time, Rojas Puyo's worries grew. He wasn't mystical like the pendulum-carrying UP leader Herrera or paranoid like FARC commander Arenas. He was simply practical, almost to a point where it interfered with his revolutionary fervor. Since his first murmurs of dissent in the early 1980s, he had come to represent the moderate wing of the party, the "social democrats." It wouldn't be long before the social democrats clashed with the more radical party militants, the "orthodox." Already the battle lines within the UP were being drawn. In 1985, Rojas Puyo wrote to Arenas, "What the government and virtually everyone else thinks, including me, is that you can't campaign with guns in your hands, and, if you're going to accept peace, the guns should disappear, even if you don't hand them in."

But to his dismay and extreme disappointment, Rojas Puyo found that Arenas was less amenable to change than the Communist Party. Even as the pressure on the UP leaders increased and the deaths began to mount, Arenas insisted to Rojas Puyo that it was the rest of Colombia that was confused, not the FARC. For the rebel leader, handing in guns and creating a political party were completely unrelated. "People misunderstand the subject of demobilization," Arenas wrote to Rojas Puyo. "The Uribe Agreement had two proposals that people tend to combine into one."

Other FARC commanders and some UP leaders became just as defensive. In one UP rally, the teddy bear–like Braulio Herrera called on the crowd to "celebrate twenty-one years of the strongest guerrilla movement this century." Party leaders also defied calls to lay down their weapons. "Let's suppose hypothetically that tomorrow we accept [the proposal] to disarm and demobilize," Herrera attempted to explain to one reporter at the time. "What happens in the middle of the violence, in the middle of the terror, in the middle of the restrictive democracy, in the middle of the hunger and the broken pieces of our people? Will other Colombians take up arms to fight the ignominy, the violence, and the terror?"

His answer, of course, was that only the FARC would defend the people. But while snubbing their noses at the establishment was romantic, the reality carried with it grave consequences. The political race had become a game of chicken, and for the UP who weren't members of the guerrillas, it was increasingly a no-win situation. If the party denounced the FARC for refusing to lay down its weapons, then it would lose credibility with many of its followers and its rebel sponsors. If it didn't denounce the guerrilla group, the opposition would vilify it. All the pieces were falling into place for a "political genocide."

In the middle of the controversy sat FARC leader Jacobo Arenas. He was exactly where he had always wanted to be: in the eye of his own hurricane. His popularity was perhaps at an all-time high. Despite its convoluted message, his book on war and peace was selling well. He even had notions of writing another one or perhaps producing a play, which he eventually pitched to his publishers. His name was plastered all over the city, and he was quoted as often as any politician in Colombia. His political capital could not have risen any higher except maybe during a bid for the presidency or, conversely, a renewed attempt to topple the government. "If the truce is broken," Arenas warned, "we will resume warfare with the support of a considerable part of the Colombian people."

But while the notion of increasing his notoriety appealed to him, Arenas's decision about running for the country's highest office also carried with it tremendous responsibility. The FARC leader held the keys to UP legitimacy—and perhaps the party's safety. Arenas's name on the presidential ticket was the FARC's best argument that it took the new party seriously, that the UP was a possible avenue to peace, and that the rebel group considered demobilizing its forces. Arenas would run or risk putting all of those who followed him and his political experiment in grave danger.

But there remained real doubts about what Arenas's intentions were with regard to the party. Was the UP just a means by which the FARC could grow? Were the rebels seriously considering handing in their guns? Would the FARC become a legal political party at the end of the peace process? All of these questions might have been answered if Arenas had decided to run for president. But then something happened that changed the face of the war and, in a strange way, made Arenas's life easier.

Just two weeks before the UP's national convention, forty rebels from the M-19 stormed the Palace of Justice in central Bogotá. The guerrillas said they were putting President Belisario Betancur on trial for breaking a cease-fire the M-19 had signed with the government a year earlier. The takeover was a blow for President Betancur's peace efforts. He had put all his energy into forging these cease-fires, and it had blown up in his face. Now it appeared that he had had enough of the guerrillas. From the beginning of the crisis in the palace, he refused to even negotiate with the rebels. Instead, he abdicated to the military. He had simply given up.

Army tanks rushed the palace and began firing indiscriminately. Dozens of rebels and perhaps over a hundred hostages were left dead, including eleven of the 12 chief magistrates being held captive. The holocaust at the palace turned the country on its head. President Betancur took full responsibility. "Our pain is like no one's pain," Betancur told Colombians in a national address. "We have been victims both of terrorist delirium and the blind force of nature." But it was clear Betancur had lost his political edge and his ability to control his military. Analysts called the army's counterattack on the palace the "26-hour coup." The president would not make any more peace overtures to the other guerrilla groups, and for a moment, the peace process with the FARC was in doubt as well. The army's position of ending the peace talks had won, and the palace was the first major sign of things to come.

UP leaders had already been assassinated and were getting harassed throughout the country, but the Palace of Justice was the first time party leaders began to openly question how wise their strategy was. "It created a strange political environment," Álvaro Salazar told me. "Suddenly, people were more pessimistic about the UP's future." The army had pursued some members of the M-19 all the way to the hospital to kill them. Innocent Palace of Justice employees also simply "disappeared." The UP could be next, party leaders and militants began to say.

Under these circumstances, FARC leader Jacobo Arenas couldn't run for president. More importantly, we may never know if he was really going to run. The tragedy at the Palace of Justice gave him the perfect excuse to opt out; he could not have designed a better escape hatch himself. History will have a hard time judging the FARC leader for something he just couldn't do.

As UP delegates and supporters gathered for the national convention in late November, word had already spread: Arenas had withdrawn his name from consideration. To compensate for the seemingly abrupt change, the FARC sent a video of Arenas and the rebels' military commander, Manuel "Sureshot" Marulanda, which the UP put on a big screen at the convention hall. The two leaders—Arenas wearing his signature sunglasses, scarf, shiny shirt, and train conductor's cap, and Marulanda with his weather-beaten face and curly hair waving in the wind—apologized to their followers and urged them to continue the struggle. Meanwhile, they would continue "the struggle" from the safety of the mountains.

Following the disaster at the Palace of Justice, the UP needed a savior. A dark cloud hung over Colombia. The country split between those who blamed the government for the debacle and those who blamed the guerrillas. But the military had already begun covering up its tracks, and the M-19 had refused to accept any responsibility for what had happened. Peace suddenly seemed like a distant dream.

The UP was in the middle—a representation of what could be, or could have been. With the withdrawal of Arenas's name from the ballot, the party was reeling. No FARC leader could conceivably be the presidential candidate. And Communist Party leaders had little credibility. Many communists were still bitter about the FARC's move to create the UP, and some had boycotted the national convention.

On their own, UP leaders had to act quickly. They surveyed the choices. Herrera would have been the logical choice but was excluded for the same reasons that his commander, Arenas, had opted out. A top union official was also disqualified because of his overbearing communist past. Arenas's replacement, they decided, had to be an outsider, someone who wasn't a politician. After some debate, the group settled on Jaime Pardo Leal, a Communist Party lawyer. Arenas could not have picked a better candidate himself.

On the surface, Pardo was not the savior type. Although well educated and married with kids, the veteran judge cared little about his appearance. He seemed to take pride in his old, out-of-style suits and his five-o'clock shadow. Sometimes his ties were as wide as they were long and barely reached the middle of his shirt. The look went well with his short, stocky figure and his slight tic that sometimes startled those who didn't know him. His belly pushed over his pants, and his pudgy round face almost always bore a mischievous smile.

Pardo was a base, even crude, character. Former colleagues told me he would eye female party members up and down and say things like, "You're lookin' sooo good." Some would blush, but others would get angry at his *machismo*. Nearly everyone in the office would chuckle. Pardo was equally cruel to those he didn't find attractive. The UP leader told one particularly homely woman working in the party's office that he had dreamt about her. After she brightened with pride, he added, "The dreams were so scary, I couldn't get a hard-on for a week."

Despite his sometimes gross nature, people loved Pardo. He was a real person, not a politician. Although a member of the Communist Party, Pardo was not part of any party committees and often joked that he was way behind on his dues. His passion was the judicial workers' union he had helped form. There, his colleagues nicknamed him, "*Paro Ilegal*," a play on his full name, Pardo Leal, meaning "illegal strike." "That's what I never ask," he explained to a reporter once, "if the strike is legal or not—only whether it's just."

Pardo was not a typical Communist either. Communists had a reputation for being stale, lifeless, and dogmatic. Pardo was the opposite. He didn't take life or himself too seriously. "We used to have a meeting before the meetings just to tell jokes and trade stories," Álvaro Salazar told me. At one of these "meetings before the meeting," Pardo told Salazar and the rest of the UP leadership a story about a campaign stop. While the other candidates were talking, Pardo got down from the platform and started walking toward a bar with a bathroom. "He tried to be discrete," Salazar explained, "but everyone started to follow him, so he turned and told the crowd, 'Don't follow me, you idiots! Haven't you ever seen a presidential candidate take a shit?' Then he found a toilet. But the bathroom had run out of toilet paper, and, so Jaime says to us, 'The only thing I could find to wipe my ass were flyers with a picture of me on them. So I had to wipe my ass with my own face.' Then he laughed."

This unpretentious demeanor was perhaps Pardo's most endearing quality. It was obvious he wasn't seeking fame or money from his candidacy. He just liked to be with people. On a typical day, he would stroll down to the corner store near the UP office, where some construction workers or house painters would be talking about the latest tabloid headline or soccer match. Pardo would sit on a sack of potatoes beneath the pay phone and join in the conversation. Nothing could drag him away. "Jaime, RCN Radio is at the office," his UP colleagues would run to tell him. "Just tell them to fuck off," he would respond with a big smile on his face. The whole store would burst out laughing.

But as a presidential candidate, Pardo wasn't a clown. He was a riveting and passionate public speaker. He mixed his humor with his emotional politics and riled up the crowd with his biting sarcasm. He poked fun at his own inexperience but chastised his opposition for their machine politics. On the road, he connected to people by clasping their hands and flashing a big smile. He spoke to them about their problems and their dreams. And he was a master at spinning the bad into good. He made people forget the massacre at the Palace of Justice without forgetting why it had happened. More importantly, he made people remember why the UP was their hope for the future.

Pardo could also bridge the widening gap between the "social democrats," represented by the Communist stalwart Rojas Puyo, and the "orthodox," represented by people like Jacobo Arenas. The social democrats sought to discard the armed revolution and embraced the democratic process as the principal means of changing the system. The orthodox sought to win the war through *la combinación de todas las formas de lucha*. They drew young and virulent recruits to the cause like Josué Giraldo, who didn't mind having the guerrillas as the vanguard. For the moment, these two tendencies coexisted. It was easy back then. The peace process between the FARC and the government was still progressing, albeit slowly. And repression hadn't yet begun in earnest.

For his part, Pardo delicately balanced his rhetoric to appease both sides. In the months preceding the presidential elections, Pardo voiced his support for the FARC, as "the ones trying to act within the constitution, protecting life, honor, and the well-being of Colombians." But Pardo also rallied the social democrats. "As we advance and as we rise in the polls, the more they'll fear us and the more victories and happiness we'll obtain," he screamed at one convention. "Compatriots, *compañeros*, friends, and comrades: We have begun the long walk toward taking power and there's no doubt that with your help no one will stop this march toward victory, not even the traffickers of death."

Pardo was the final pillar the UP needed to make its leap into prominence. While guerrilla leaders like Braulio Herrera and Iván Márquez brought a romantic appeal to the UP, Pardo gave their ideas meaning. While Alberto Rojas Puyo paved the political path to legitimacy, Pardo kept the new party unified. While young, energetic Communists like Josué Giraldo were the core, Pardo was the spirit; while they did the dirty work, he made them believe it was worth it.

On election day in 1986, the emotion was palpable and fear temporarily put aside. Thousands of new followers wearing yellow and green UP T-shirts, baseball hats, and visors swarmed the polls. They screamed for the party, for peace, and even for the FARC. They had been reinvigorated by the UP. They had invested time, money, and energy organizing support for a fledgling project they believed represented an alternative. They had a wide variety of can-

didates and some support from the traditional parties. Perhaps most importantly, they had active guerrillas running for congressional positions, making
the possibility of peace seem even more tangible. Peace, as an idea, wasn't yet
destroyed, they decided. The new party would save it.

The UP had raised the aspirations of many Colombians that the rotten
regime running the country could eventually be overturned. The new followers were convinced they were seeing a revolution and voiced their support for
it any way they pleased. On election day, some of the young UP sympathizers shouted, "Long live the FARC! Long live Pardo Leal! Long live
[Sureshot] Marulanda Vélez!" Pardo then cast his vote alongside Braulio
Herrera and screamed, "*Viva la UP!*" The crowd responded in kind.

As the results trickled in on election night, Pardo yelled them out to the
crowd. He would then turn for a drink and usually crack a joke. "How was
that interview?" he asked one confused journalist. "Too much tic for ya?" A
howling belly laugh followed. The results weren't in, but Pardo knew that the
party, without actually winning the elections, had scored an historic victory.
In less than two years, the UP had become a major player. The UP wouldn't
run the country, but the FARC had shown its political strength. The people
would party in the streets that night, while the ruling classes trembled in their
homes.

PART TWO

CHAPTER 7

THE "DISPOSABLE ONES"

On May 25, 1986, Jaime Pardo Leal had a reason to celebrate. He had just made history. In the presidential elections, the boisterous and charismatic UP presidential candidate had garnered 328,752 votes. It was a tiny percentage compared with the winner, Liberal Party candidate Virgilio Barco, who received 4,212,510 votes. But it was the most that any leftist candidate had ever gotten in Colombia. And it was four times as many votes as the Communist Party candidate had gotten in 1982. It was considerably higher than anyone, including the UP, expected. It was so stunning that Pardo himself couldn't control his excitement.

On the night of the election, he ran around the headquarters screaming at his people about the need to organize more UP "cells" of support. "If we could have visited 1,100 municipalities instead of 80, we would have gotten a much higher percentage," he spit out with an enthusiasm that startled his guests and riled up his followers. "This just forces us to work harder and create many more *Juntas Patrióticas*, thousands of *Juntas Patrióticas*. . . . We can't rest. We have to combine our organizing with future mayoral campaigns. How beautiful would it be to elect one hundred revolutionary mayors?"

Newly elected Colombian president Barco wasn't as excited about the UP as Pardo. Barco was the opposite of Pardo in every way. He was a tall, light-skinned man with thick, square-rimmed glasses and graying hair. In his dark suits and bright red ties he looked a lot like what he was: a Liberal technocrat from the old-school wing of his party. He had won the presidency on the back of this machine. But like so many others, he also hoped the UP would fare well so that its founders and progenitors, the FARC rebels, would end the war with the government. It had been over thirty years since the guerrillas had launched their fight, but only now was the country beginning to take them and their new political party seriously.

As a measure of goodwill, President Barco gave the UP control over fourteen mayoralties. He also continued talking peace with the FARC in its jungle lair, the *Casa Verde*. Barco spoke of "direct dialogue" and promised more results. "I'm not going to savor victory," the president, whose aides liked to describe as Calvinist, told reporters. "Instead, I'm going to rebuild Colombia." To prove he was serious, the new president sent his top peace adviser to speak to FARC leader Jacobo Arenas. The talks gave the UP an added measure of security—as long as peace was on the horizon, the new party had a chance; it was a thin layer at best. Still, President Barco's blessing, the continuing peace talks, and the euphoria surrounding the party's accomplishments smothered the sense that anything could go wrong with the UP. Besides, everything else that mattered seemed to be going so well.

In the congressional and local elections in March 1986, some two months before Jaime Pardo's triumphant day, the UP had elected twenty-four provincial deputies and 275 municipal council representatives. The party had also elected four senators and four congressional representatives. The experiment was proving a success, maybe too much so.

Among the new congressmen were the lovable and intriguing FARC leaders Braulio Herrera and Iván Márquez. Both were elected as congressional substitutes, or stand-ins. They were the first and only congressional representatives the FARC has ever had, and they took advantage of every moment. They spoke to magazines, newspapers, radio programs, and television stations, getting more airtime in their short stints in congress than most official representatives do in their entire tenures. To the swarming reporters, they gave glints of their warm and engaging personalities. To their congressional colleagues, they gave a piece of their mind. They spoke of war, peace, and violence in ways that gave new meaning to old words. "What's characterized this conflict," Braulio Herrera reminded a packed congress just a few months after his election, "is that no one has been able to defeat anyone."

Herrera's speech wasn't a revelation, but congressmen began to nod their heads in agreement. With rebels as politicians, it felt like a new era. And for a few weeks, no other congressmen could match the two rebels' apparent sincerity and earnestness. The FARC's credibility and confidence soared. But the two leaders' newfound fame also gave them a false sense of security to say things that simply weren't true. "The results of the elections were very important," the teddy bear–like Herrera told congress during the same session, "and a true reversal to militarism. It was [also] a profound 'yes' to peace and the politics of a democratic opening."

Others shared Herrera's hope. "We didn't think about [the possible consequences] of our success," the UP propaganda chief, Álvaro Salazar, said to me later. "There was a lot of optimism. The UP was very well received by the press and the public. The press, in particular, gave it a lot of support. Braulio Herrera was a virtual hero. There were rallies all over the country. There was a real hope for peace. In general, people received us with a certain amount of romanticism."

But the celebrations were tempered by the bloody events that slowly began to encircle the UP. The deaths were starting to pile up just as the fledgling project was surging. For a political party with little more than a year on the books, twenty-four members elected to provincial assemblies was a startling accomplishment matched only by the number of dead it had already put in the morgue. Herrera told congress in September 1986 that more than three hundred UP members had already been assassinated, and the party hadn't even had its first anniversary.

One typical victim in those early months was Nelly Flórez Uribe, a former FARC soldier who'd recently laid down her gun to join the UP. Nelly and her brother Edgar Flórez were shot and killed in the small village of La Putana in central Colombia. Her father and four others were injured in the attack. Other victims were longtime Communists and popular movement leaders like Leonardo Posada. Posada had been elected a UP congressman in March 1986, but he was shot eight times in the back while leaving his office in the oil town of Barrancabermeja to grab a beer with some friends. Leonardo was a romantic revolutionary to the end. While his legs went numb and his breath fell short, Leonardo requested that "no hymns be played at my funeral, only a series of *boleros*."

As the deaths mounted, UP leaders like Jaime Pardo tried to keep the party's followers focused on the future. "Where's Leonardo?" Pardo asked a crowd of ten thousand at Posada's funeral in the grotty cemetery of downtown Bogotá. "Leonardo, where are you?" he repeated, to which the people responded, "Leonardo is in the streets of Barranca, fighting for peace."

What's amazing is that the majority of UP militants, including Jaime Pardo himself, seemed to accept these initial fatalities as part of the business of doing politics in Colombia. Colombians had had nearly two centuries of practice. The Liberal and Conservative Parties had lost thousands to assassination. Hundreds of Communist Party members had also been murdered, many of them in the years prior to the creation of the UP. This legacy seemed to dull the UP's senses to the mayhem around it. Dozens of UP militants were killed in the first six months following the presidential and congressional elections, including one senator. Thousands went to their funerals, clamored for justice, then dared the enemies to strike again.

"The coward paramilitary assassins can take the lives of one or two of our *compañeros*, but they can't assassinate all our leaders," FARC congressman Herrera stridently told a reporter from the Communist newspaper, *Voz*. "And what's more," he added, "the people will accompany us and respond to the assassins with more political vigor using *la combinación de todas las formas de lucha*."

And for a while, the people did continue to join the new movement. These people were hopeful, naive, and "revolutionary" all at once. They didn't question the direction of the UP or the nefarious strategy they may have suspected was being implemented behind the scenes. They didn't think the repression would get worse. They believed the movement could outlast its killers, even if they themselves died. They were the martyrs, and they seemed blind to the fact that they might be getting used.

"We achieved the highest number of votes ever for a leftist party," Álvaro Salazar explained to me. "We got more congressional reps than ever before. In less than a year, the UP got two leaders who had a national profile: Braulio Herrera and Jaime Pardo Leal. Who was going to question this? Who was going to say that behind this was a devious strategy? Only the ones who were behind the scenes and involved in that strategy. But the others were very excited with the UP project and the cease-fire and the possibility of leftist political gains. But simultaneously the FARC took advantage of this phase to grow, to recruit a lot of people, to increase the size of its army, its Fronts, to continue the process of forming its military."

For FARC leader Jacobo Arenas—sitting in his mountaintop hideout, wrapped in his scarf, surrounded by hundreds of rebel guards—things were moving as smoothly as they possibly could. Arenas was troubled, of course, by the loss of life but continued to insist on having his strategy work both ways: In Arenas's estimation, the FARC could grow militarily even while developing a legal political party. And they did. Between 1984 and 1988—the peak of UP popularity across the country; the time when leaders and militants were working tirelessly to form what they hoped was an avenue to peace—the FARC added fourteen Fronts, more than doubling in size. If that wasn't suspicious enough, many of these Fronts emerged in areas where the UP had done well at the polls and where UP mayors took power. Some even suspected municipal funds were channeled directly into rebel coffers for the creation of these Fronts.

The strategy became even more dubious as time passed. Salazar told me that some UP militants secretly recruited for the FARC in the party's office in Bogotá. And others said the same occurred in the party's offices in the countryside. With the UP, Salazar said, "The FARC got space to spread its gospel and draw many young idealists who were feeding off the [revolutionary] news coming from Central America. People also went to the headquarters of the UP to join, so the party processed these requests, and many of these people ended up in the FARC."

But while the rebels' duplicity helped them grow militarily, it also gave its enemies the leverage they needed to attack the party. *La combinación de todas las formas de lucha*, the longtime Communist Party strategy of combining legal and illegal struggles to topple the government, may have been a secret to many UP followers, but to the military and their proxy allies, the paramilitaries, it was simply an open book. "From the Uribe Agreement [for a cease-fire in 1984], I saw the danger," the old Communist Party stalwart Alberto Rojas Puyo told me when I met with him years later. "They were going to assassinate all of us. Maybe the army wasn't able to finish off the guerrillas, but it was capable of finishing off the membership of the *Unión Patriótica* and the Communist Party. . . . They [the Communist Party] persisted with *la combinación de todas las formas de lucha* and made the UP an easy target for the assassins."

Like many others during those first euphoric moments following the 1986 elections, Alberto Rojas Puyo held on to the hope that the party was real, a means toward peace. During those early years, he convinced himself that the misunderstandings between him and FARC leader Jacobo Arenas over the use of the party were natural in such a complicated process—that disagreements were part of growing, becoming more mature as a movement. But years later, he wouldn't have a problem deciphering just what Arenas was doing with the UP. "From the beginning," Rojas Puyo told me, "the FARC and the [Communist] Party considered the UP to be a political instrument of *la combinación de todas las formas de lucha*, one more political instrument for their project of insurrection."

Even more disheartening was the fact that the result would be lasting and equally useful to the FARC and Jacobo Arenas. A dead UP would prove that the only way to change Colombia was through military insurrection, a position Arenas had been subtly advocating for years. It was the final and most disturbing element of Arenas's master plan that had culminated in 1982 with the creation of the FARC's "army of the people." "Jacobo never wanted the party to be anything more than something that could open up political space for the military movement," Álvaro Salazar said. "This was part of their war plan. We were the sacrificial battalion so they could justify their war. Every war needs some sacrificial lambs. Jacobo knew this. We knew this. . . . We were the disposable ones."

One of the most important "disposable ones" was Jaime Pardo Leal. And almost from the beginning, he was ready to take on his role. The FARC's decision to use the party as a sacrificial battalion was being made behind closed doors, and the excitable UP presidential candidate wasn't always invited. But Pardo didn't mind. From the moment he took the job as president of the UP, he knew there was a good chance he would die. He wasn't so much a martyr as a fatalist. It was only natural. Death surrounded him. He spent a good deal of his time going to funerals and wakes, and he was constantly reminded that he was a target as well. There was a neverending barrage of threatening phone calls and letters to his home and office.

Up to a point, Pardo took these threats seriously. He had several full-time bodyguards and wore a bulletproof vest. But in typical Pardo style, he also made jokes about his own predicament. "They can't shoot me in the chest," he would say tapping on his bulletproof vest. "If they shoot at my head, they'll miss because of my tic. And if they shoot at my balls, that's not a problem either, because I'm so scared that my balls are in my throat."

Like many of his UP colleagues, Pardo hated having bodyguards. He would slip out the back door of the office when they weren't paying attention, then phone them from a bar where he was having a drink with some friends and ask for "*Doctor* Pardo Leal, *por favor*." The guards would frantically search the office before Pardo would say, "It's me, you fuckin' idiots."

Pardo's wife, however, pushed him to take care of himself. And when he didn't, there were consequences. One colleague recalled to me that he dropped Pardo off at his house after a late night of drinking, and his wife had locked him out. Pardo crossed the street and called her from a pay phone. "He's not here," she replied to Pardo's standard query about himself. "He's not there because you won't let him in!" he screamed back.

Still, Pardo never resigned himself to the fact that what he did might be futile. He believed in the Communist Party and the UP, and he refused to condemn the FARC. He wasn't part of the rebel cadre and never would be. But for a long time, his romanticism made it difficult for him to see the larger project at hand. "I'm a revolutionary," he liked to say.

During the presidential campaign, Pardo had to face down his enemies who bombarded him with questions about his revolutionary fervor. One television interview with a prominent Colombian journalist, Yamid Amat, was particularly awkward.

YA: The guerrillas kill. Is it OK to kill?
JPL: No, it isn't OK to kill. But the ones who suffer the most are the
      guerrillas. It's an enormous sacrifice for the country, for them. No
      one wants to die and much less use violence. What happens is the
      army kills and other forces also kill without shame. And we have to
      avoid all this. We have to love peace and believe in peace.

YA: Would you be a guerrilla?

JPL: Yes, when in our country the oligarchy makes it impossible to talk about solving our problems; when a new regime imposes its indiscriminate terror on the country, there wouldn't be any alternative. And I'm sure, Yamid, you'd be a guerrilla too.

YA: Would you shoot a soldier in our army?

JPL: If my life was in danger, yes. But I don't want to be put in that situation.

Like his FARC colleagues, Pardo didn't back down from the verbal challenges. The rebels frequently sent him letters, one of which he read aloud to his followers. "[The guerrillas] asked me what do I want them to do for me," a chuffed Pardo told an audience in the mountainous city of Bucaramanga. "To which I respond: Do what you've always done. Come together and work for the people and together, you, the 'army of the people,' workers, and peasants will construct a huge Front so that this democratic opening is possible."

But as pressures increased after the 1986 elections, Pardo became sad and despondent. He had won a major victory by garnering over 300,000 votes, but he felt powerless to stop the murders. What's more, it was increasingly obvious to him that the Communist Party's and the FARC's strategy of using *la combinación de todas las formas de lucha* wasn't working. Still, it was hard for him to envision a strategy that didn't include the guerrillas. "He was very radical," one colleague told me, "and very loyal."

Yet there was something churning inside Pardo, and some of his former colleagues said it might have been the beginning of a political transformation that would have led him to abandon the *combinación* strategy forever. "He [Pardo] had this internal conflict," one of his close friends told me. "If they'd let him live, this would have made him more pro-UP, and he would have left the Communist Party. It's very risky for me to say this, but everything pointed this way. He was in the UP groove, and he understood it. And he had a way of campaigning that was very generous, very open, very democratic."

It wasn't just Pardo who felt the need for change. Within the UP, there was growing tension. The *combinación* strategy was taking its toll, not on the FARC but on the new party. Tensions were building between the orthodox, who adhered to the *combinación* strategy at all costs, and the social democrats, who were pulling away. Pardo maintained his public position, but the ground beneath his feet was shifting, and so was he. "If they'd let him live," his colleague said to me, his voice trailing off. The problem was, of course, they didn't.

The UP's enemies were many and growing. They were members of the traditional political parties who saw the new guerrilla party as an emerging electoral challenge, especially in rural areas. They were officers in the military establishment who saw the FARC's and the Communist Party's nefarious plan to use the UP as part of the revolutionary strategy of the *combinación*. Most importantly, they were drug traffickers who saw the UP as threatening their newly achieved status as landowners and cattle ranchers and saw the UP's progenitor, the FARC, as threatening their old business interests in illegal drugs.

The peace process and the cease-fire between the FARC and the government had given the UP the space it needed to proliferate. In the first few years after the UP emerged, many drug-producing areas became party bastions and would serve to strengthen the rebel army in the years to come. But the FARC's expansion in these areas ran head-on with a similarly ambitious project. Drug traffickers and their private armies saw any stateless territory as their domain as well. For reasons similar to the rebels, they sought more and more remote areas to establish their fiefdoms and process their drugs. These drug traffickers included some of the most powerful capos in Colombia and the world: *Don* Fabio Ochoa Sr., Pablo Escobar, Fidel Castaño, Gilberto Molina, Victor Carranza, and José Gonzalo "*El Mejicano*" Rodríguez Gacha. All of them had a gripe to pick with the FARC, which they would happily take out on the UP. But none of them made the battle as bloody as *El Mejicano* Rodríguez Gacha.

For such an enormous personality, Rodríguez Gacha was an elusive character. In 1988, *Forbes* magazine put the drug capo on its cover with the title, "Inside the Global Drug Trade." The picture was the most famous of the powerful drug trafficker—his square jaw, large nose, and half-closed eyes seemingly ducking the camera, and a Panama-jack hat covering his head. The magazine estimated that Rodríguez Gacha was worth close to $1.3 billion at the time. He ran the largest drug-processing laboratories in the country, including several in FARC-controlled territory. One, "*Tranquilandia*," had the capacity to produce five thousand kilos of refined cocaine per week. In 1984, the U.S. Drug Enforcement Administration (DEA), with Colombian police, raided the lab and found 13.8 tons of cocaine, with a street value of $1.2 billion; the biggest bust "by far," one DEA agent remarked. The profits from the trade were nearly as big as Rodríguez Gacha's ego. "We produce a lot more for this country than [the government oil company] Ecopetrol," he was often heard saying.

El Mejicano got his nickname because he loved ranchera, the Mexican country music, and Mexican culture. In his hometown of Pacho, just north of Bogotá, he built several mission-style *haciendas*, which he named after Mexican towns like Cuernavaca and Mazatlán. One of these ranches had a disco that resembled a Mexican restaurant. Rodríguez Gacha also tried to pose as a populist. He and several other drug traffickers had come from poverty. They were famous for their handouts—appliances, cash, soccer stadiums—and believed this qualified them as social visionaries. "We're defending the people and fighting for the people," Rodríguez Gacha once told the Colombian weekly magazine *Semana*. "If it wasn't for drug trafficking, we would have had a civil war here five years ago. You know that the politicians here only worry about what they can steal." Rodríguez Gacha surely knew. Colombian officials said he had half of Pacho on his payroll. "He has the sympathy of the majority of the town," an official said matter-of-factly.

Still, it was clear that the drug capo had little ideology aside from his worship of money and penchant for violence. Rodríguez Gacha killed anyone in his path. And unlike Pablo Escobar, who stayed away from cocaine, Rodríguez Gacha was said to have a habit that resembled Tony Montana's, the fictitious kingpin from the movie *Scarface* who liked to plop his head in the powder and snort like a pig. At the height of his pathology and drug-induced rage, Rodríguez Gacha organized the slaughter of his former boss and mentor, causing one U.S. official to remark that he was "the most dangerous of all the heads of the cartels."

But for a while, Rodríguez Gacha's power and wealth made him almost untouchable. He had a smattering of other coca laboratories throughout the country and land as far as the eye could see. He owned territory in a half dozen provinces, some of which were in FARC strongholds. Only his closest drug-trafficking colleagues could match his lust for land. They bought with gumption and arrogance anywhere they could. At the time, it was a buyer's market. Many cattle ranchers were fleeing the business and leaving their land due to guerrilla encroachment. Prices were low, demand limited to a few unsavory and insistent clients. Virtually overnight, drug traffickers became some of the most powerful cattle ranchers in the country. Fellow drug trafficker and cattle rancher Fidel Castaño once bragged to a visitor that he was the only one in the country who could sell 450,000 calves at the annual Medellín cattle auction. But some of his colleagues, like *Don* Fabio Ochoa Sr. and *El Mejicano* Rodríguez Gacha, probably could have come close.

In land, the drug clans had discovered a way to launder money and gain prestige all at once. One political scientist calculated in 1996 that the narcos had purchased over 660 million acres of land in the previous twenty years, or one-third of the most fertile grazing land in the entire country. The magazine *Semana* reported in 1988 that drug traffickers had bought more land in the previous five years than the government's own agrarian institute designed to parcel out plots to landless peasants. It was a revolution in reverse, analysts argued, and the result was *La Violencia* all over again. Only this time, the big landowners were drug traffickers, whose methods were even more unscrupulous than their predecessors and whose cash flow was endless. The birth of the paramilitaries stemmed from a combination of this cash flow and the drug traffickers' new needs as landowners and old needs as drug traffickers. The shifting landscape had direct implications for the FARC and the UP.

The death of Jaime Pardo and so many other UP leaders and militants came from a confluence of factors, which included both ideology and personality clashes. While the "political genocide" was set into motion with the development of the paramilitary death squads in the early 1980s, some of the carnage might have been avoided if there had been a rational response to the growing dangers facing the party. There were some within the UP who could see the enemy gathering its forces. There were others who were in the privileged position of knowing how the FARC was using the UP to grow militarily. But there were few who could see both of these factors converging and who had a chance to do something about the coming calamity before it happened. One of these people was UP propaganda chief Álvaro Salazar.

Salazar was the appointed peacemaker, the man with the unenviable task of being the party's unofficial mediator in all things related to the UP. He had played this role even before the UP was created. In the early 1980s, Salazar had run the awkward messages to the government to start the peace process. When there were problems with the negotiations, Salazar was the messenger and sometimes the interpreter. A little later, he had deflected the criticism that came from the Communist Party after the FARC suddenly announced the creation of the UP in 1984. But his toughest task was still to come: He would be the emissary the UP sent to the paramilitary camp to arrange for a cease-fire.

It was a huge weight to carry, not least because Salazar was beginning to question his own beliefs and actions. He had shared in the hope that came with the rise of new leaders like Jaime Pardo and Braulio Herrera. He had even found himself caught up in the excitement of the new political party and had begun to extricate himself from the FARC's grip. Indeed, he would be one of several FARC members who would eventually leave the guerrillas because of his disgust with the rebels' strategy. But in the meantime, Salazar was a guerrilla-lackey, and the UP was still under FARC control. Although he saw the dangers mounting, he couldn't say anything to his civilian colleagues about the FARC's nefarious strategy. Instead, he could only watch as the FARC's battles became the UP's battles. And one of the FARC's biggest battles was with Rodríguez Gacha.

In late 1986, the fight between the FARC and Rodríguez Gacha had come to a head, and the drug capo contacted the UP for a meeting. The party sent Salazar. He flew to Colombia's notorious drug-trafficking epicenter, Medellín, where Rodríguez Gacha had set up the meeting. The UP propaganda chief was terrified. The drug empire was as big as it had ever been. Pablo Escobar and Rodríguez Gacha had the capability of paying off the country's foreign debt, and Escobar even offered to do it. When that didn't work the drug traffickers began holding the government hostage: buying off or killing most of their enemies. Rodríguez Gacha had also made his intentions clear with regard to the UP. He was angry with the FARC but would happily take out his anger on the rebels' political party. Even if he hadn't yet attacked the UP directly, the growth of his private army was an unmistakable sign that he would not tolerate interference in his affairs.

In downtown Medellín, Salazar met Rodríguez Gacha's lawyer, who took him to a plush hotel room. There, Rodríguez Gacha was waiting. The two greeted one another and Salazar relaxed a little bit. "He seemed like a normal guy," Salazar told me later. Then the drug capo told him his side of a curious story that to Salazar rang true: The FARC, Rodríguez Gacha said to Salazar, had recently occupied three of his ranches where he processed cocaine, each worth about $3 or $4 million; the rebels had ransacked a few of his laboratories and stolen some of his "merchandise"; the FARC had intercepted some of his middlemen who were going toward the jungles of the southern province of Guaviare to buy some coca paste and stolen an estimated $10,000 as well. Rodríguez Gacha told Salazar he had spoken to some of the local FARC commanders. But these commanders didn't have the power to give national orders, the drug capo complained to his UP guest. "He [Rodríguez Gacha] said he just wanted to have an agreement with the [FARC's leaders in the] Secretariat," Salazar told me, "so they'd let him work."

To emphasize that he was serious, Rodríguez Gacha did the math for Salazar. He told the UP leader that he exported 2,000 kilos of cocaine a week, which he sold for $16,000 per kilo. "This was $32 million per week, or more than $100 million per month," Salazar explained to me. "He said he had the capacity to arm a militia of one thousand men. And if the FARC wanted war, he would give it war." By the time of their meeting, Rodríguez Gacha was already in the process of creating an army. Within a year, government investigators estimated that Rodríguez Gacha, and his cohorts Henry Pérez, Fidel Castaño, and Victor Carranza, had close to five thousand men at their disposal. Many of these paramilitary soldiers were under Rodríguez Gacha's command.

After the meeting, Salazar went to the FARC's leadership council, the Secretariat, with the drug capo's proposal to "let him work." It was a critical moment in the UP's history, a time when the young party could have weathered a small onslaught and still made a dent in Colombian politics. New supporters expected some deaths; they didn't expect the bludgeoning that would follow when Rodríguez Gacha unleashed his men on them. But Álvaro Salazar didn't get very far with the FARC leaders—his was a weak position that would only get weaker with time as he broke from the guerrillas' clutches. FARC commander Jacobo Arenas flat out rejected Rodríguez Gacha's proposal to "let him work." "Jacobo said he wouldn't negotiate with this guy, this criminal," Salazar told me. "The only one who said this was a dangerous attitude was [FARC leader] Alfonso Cano," Salazar continued. "He told me, 'We're pushing *El Mejicano* [Rodríguez Gacha] to ally with the army, and this could be a problem.' But Jacobo Arenas was for the war against *El Mejicano*."

The two camps—the FARC in its mountainside hideout and the UP in its city offices—were losing touch with one another. It appeared that rebel leaders had stopped listening to reason, especially ideas that came from the cities via discredited FARC members like Salazar, who had already begun to lose the rebels' trust. As the murder rate of the UP rose, guerrilla leaders became more intransigent and UP leaders increasingly desperate. Each sought refuge in their own ideas, in a belief that something positive would eventually emerge from the chaos. But nothing ever did. In fact, the FARC went a long way toward making it worse. "We will not be provoked," Arenas said at one point, before adding curiously, "We will not just lay down and die."

Over the next few months, the rebels' position became more belligerent toward everyone. Guerrilla leaders became particularly suspicious of the recently elected president, Virgilio Barco. Somewhere in their discussions, the peace process lost currency, and both sides turned aggressive. Light skirmishes evolved into full-scale battles. In June 1987, the rebels ambushed a squadron of marching soldiers in the southern jungles, killing twenty-seven soldiers and wounding forty others. The government followed the attack with an ultimatum. "If the FARC do not disarm and dissolve, the only option left for the government is to wipe them out militarily," Barco's interior minister told congress, "no matter how much that might cost." In his usual way, Arenas remained steadfast. "Of course, these kind of incidents are natural in a truce of this sort," Arenas said about the FARC's ambush of government troops. "The important thing is that we are not turning our backs on dialogue." Nor was the FARC turning in its guns. Peace talks were over.

The end of the peace process had an immediate impact on the UP. For its part, the FARC withdrew its leaders from the new party. Iván Márquez abandoned his congressional post and went north to the banana-growing region of Urabá to continue the fight. Braulio Herrera left congress and returned south to a chilly Sumapaz.

But what about the UP? The party had been created as a messenger for peace. But now the negotiations were over. UP leaders tried to calm the coming storm with words. In a press conference, they claimed they were independent from the FARC. The truth, however, was something of a mystery, even to some of them. Things were suddenly spinning out of control. And Arenas's comments to the press weren't helping matters. "If the government tries to annihilate us, they will have to annihilate the rest of the country, too," he declared.

El Mejicano Rodríguez Gacha fulfilled the promise he had made to Álvaro Salazar almost immediately. One of his first victims was Pedro Nel Jiménez, the youngest of the three newly elected UP senators. Jiménez was shot just two months after taking office as he was picking his daughter up from school. News reports attributed the assassination to a tit-for-tat that had begun between Rodríguez Gacha and the FARC over drug proceeds. Other victims followed. In all, the tally of UP dead reached five hundred in the first two years of the party's existence. The majority of these murders were attributed to Rodríguez Gacha, but *El Mejicano* had help. As FARC leader Alfonso Cano feared, the drug capo had firmed up his alliances with the military. Rodríguez Gacha met regularly with members of the XIII and XIV Brigades. Officials from the Calvary School spent time on his ranch in the mountains just outside Bogotá. Many police were on his payroll as well.

"The government gives them medals," Rodríguez Gacha once told the Colombian weekly *Semana*, referring to the military. "I give them money." The relationship was mutually beneficial: The army supplied him with information; he supplied it with dead Communists. Witnesses said Pedro Nel Jiménez's killers drove into the local military battalion following the shooting. Dozens of similar accounts followed UP assassinations across the country. Rodríguez Gacha's murderous network stretched throughout Colombia. He used police, intelligence officials, army soldiers, and hired killers to do his work. His terror, and that of his fabled boss, Pablo Escobar, was settling on the country like a blanket. Anyone who openly opposed them was destroyed, most notably the UP. "It's a shame," Rodríguez Gacha told *Semana* magazine, referring to the rebels' theft of his properties, "that they [the FARC] took that route, that they attacked us like they did some seven, eight years ago. If they hadn't attacked us, then the war would be over. But they tricked us. They wanted to finish us off."

The worst was yet to come. On a weekend in early October 1987, Jaime Pardo took his family to their cottage in La Mesa, a small village in the mountains west of Bogotá. He had given most of his bodyguards a few days off. His wife later said that Pardo wanted his guards to enjoy the weekend as much as he did. In the countryside, the UP leader was his usual jovial self. His friend and colleague, UP propaganda chief Álvaro Salazar, was getting married that Sunday. The morning of the wedding, the family gathered their things and started back to Bogotá. Pardo wore a cowboy hat. His wife later remembered that he looked silly, and his children poked fun at him. He turned the hat backward, then sideways. They all laughed. It was a good way to die.

Pardo drove his jeep while some Communist Party bodyguards rode behind him. About fifteen minutes after they had left the ranch, a car passed them. The Communist Party chauffeur later said that a person in the other passing car insulted them before adding, "You have no idea what's in store for you." The Communist chauffeur thought the man was angry that they were driving too slow. Then another car appeared. The two squeezed the caravan and pumped a dozen rounds into the UP president. He died on the spot.

CHAPTER 8

A MORAL VICTORY

By the time Josué Giraldo arrived in the Eastern Plains in late 1987, his party had been decimated and he had lost his confidence. Once a young and brash political leader, he had been reduced to looking over his shoulder at every corner. He never stood in one place for too long and sometimes even refused to answer the telephone. Jaime Pardo Leal had been shot as he drove to a wedding with his family a couple of months earlier. The prominent Eastern Plains' senator, Pedro Nel Jiménez, was killed as he picked up his daughter from school. Others were hiding or fleeing the onslaught. The assassins seemed to be everywhere, and Josué was still wounded from the recent attempt on his own life some months before. "When I arrived," he wrote of the time, "the rosary for the UP who'd died was an everyday thing."

The man who had given the first order to kill Josué was one of his childhood friends. The two had gone to school together, been playmates, and "shared dreams," Josué wrote later. It was May 1987, a full year after Jaime Pardo and his UP colleagues had shocked the country with their electoral showing, and several months before Josué would arrive in the Eastern Plains. Despite their hard work setting up plays and passing out pamphlets, Josué's UP cadre in his hometown in the coffee-growing region hadn't won any political posts. But they had scared the local power brokers who'd given the order to gun down the UP leader. Josué said that his childhood friend was part of a group of paramilitaries who were financed by the local drug trafficker in the area. He wasn't José Gonzalo "*El Mejicano*" Rodríguez Gacha, but this trafficker was powerful enough to rid himself of his enemies. Josué and his UP colleagues were at the top of that list.

The FARC had also paved the way for the first attempt on Josué's life. As peace talks with President Virgilio Barco of the Liberal Party unraveled, the guerrillas had begun showing their teeth again. They had grown since the cease-fire that came with the Uribe Agreement three years prior, and they didn't mind showing it. In Josué's area, the FARC targeted paramilitaries and their suspected supporters. Just a short time before assassins went for Josué, the rebels ambushed a small column of paramilitaries and "nearly wiped them out," Josué recounted later. The paramilitaries, it was said at the time, had connected Josué's political work with the attack. And who could blame them? For weeks following the break in the peace talks between the FARC and the government, the guerillas and the UP were still officially part of the same organization. The party's public declaration of independence a little later hadn't convinced anyone it had really separated from the rebels. "Everyone still treated us like spokespeople for the FARC," UP propaganda chief Álvaro Salazar told me.

For his part, Josué remained defiant. He said he had nothing to hide. "We never uttered a single word of conspiracy," he would write later. "We bet with our hearts on democracy so that we could overcome war." Of course, it was never that simple. Josué had regular contact with the guerrillas, but he kept much of his life secret. In fact, few knew of the FARC's continuing support of the UP. Even within the UP, there was little understanding of what the arrangement really was. Meanwhile, the UP's enemies were taking advantage of the ambiguity, and Josué became one of their many targets.

Even before some of his old schoolmates had told him he was on a hit list, Josué could feel an attack coming. The army "militarized" the town. The police began to tail him. There were rumors that the military was going to search his home and office. Josué complained to the local authorities. He told them of the plan to kill him, of the police following him, of the possible search and seizure at his office. Sensing the enemy was closing in, Josué changed his routines. In the weeks leading up to the attack, he had left for work later and returned earlier. He had exercised more in case he had to run. "Psychologically, I prepared myself for the worst," he wrote, "so that the fear wouldn't paralyze me." His preparation might have saved his life.

On the day he was shot, Josué noticed that the police followed him. He went to a youth sports clinic where he did some part-time work and then to the town's central plaza, where he grabbed a coffee. At the café, Josué spied the would-be leader of the assassins—his childhood friend who had given the order to kill him—at another table. Sitting with his childhood friend were the police chief and two strange men. Josué assumed the two strangers were the gunmen. When Josué got up to leave, the two men followed him, so Josué ducked into a church to hide. From a distance, Josué saw the two men enter a hotel. Then he went to another café to wait out the assassins. There he stayed for a few hours before heading home.

Josué never saw the first shot. It hit him in his collarbone and knocked him to the ground. "I felt as if someone had opened a huge hole in me and I'd fallen on a pile of trees, rock, and black dirt, a lot of black dirt," he wrote of the incident. Josué rapidly got to his feet, covered his head with his poncho, and began running wildly down the street. The assassin gave chase and fired a shot at Josué's head. The bullet went through the poncho and tore off a piece of Josué's ear. The assassin kept shooting. Josué jumped, and a bullet hit a girl just behind him in the leg. Others along the street scrambled for cover. Undeterred by the screams, the assassin fired again, piercing Josué's clothing. The fifth shot missed, but the sixth got Josué in the stomach. Having emptied his revolver, the assassin fled from the scene.

Josué stumbled into a café and fell to the floor, clutching his stomach. A friend recognized him and got him to the hospital, where Josué lost consciousness. But Josué was not out of danger yet. As dawn broke the next day, Josué's schoolboy paramilitary friend tried to enter the hospital with his two accomplices to finish the job. Luckily, Josué's brother and some of his friends were there. They fired their guns in the air, sending the assassins into the morning light.

With danger still lurking in the area, the UP ferried Josué to Bogotá, where party leaders like Jaime Pardo lifted his spirits by visiting him in the hospital. Then the party sent Josué to Moscow, where the medical treatment from the Communist Party was better and the dangers mitigated. To his surprise, Josué ran into two other UP members in Moscow who were also recovering from attempts on their lives. Many more wounded would follow. In the hospital, the three of them praised their luck, then cursed their country when they found out that Jaime Pardo had been killed. After three months in Moscow, Josué returned to Colombia. Then he decided to go to the Eastern Plains.

When he arrived, he was a different person from the one who had gone to his hometown to work for the UP. He had seen the guns now and had felt the terror rip through his body. He could also picture the assassins, and they looked like his best friends from grade school. Invincibility had turned into vulnerability. "I always went home right after work," Josué wrote later of his first few months in the Eastern Plains. "I didn't take offers to go out, not even to drink a coffee. This may have saved my life because the majority of *compañeros* were shot having a soda or a beer in any old place."

Josué had also lost his confidence and his spirit. He was particularly intimidated by the *Llaneros* or plainsmen. These were the closest thing Colombia had to cowboys—meat eaters, drinkers, and fighters. As opposed to the peasant farmers who scurried up and down the sidewalks unnoticed, the

Llaneros immediately came into focus: ten-gallon hats and jeans; a swagger of undisturbed conviction. Their bravado reminded Josué of what he used to be.

It would take more death and violence for Josué to recoup his conviction. After moving to the Eastern Plains, the young lawyer got a job as the district attorney of Villavicencio, the capital city of the province of Meta. But he spent much of his time in the countryside. There was a certain calm to the Eastern Plains. It was a land of endless green pastures, cebú cattle, and long wooden fences. It was deathly hot, but the locals were friendly and inviting. Josué felt at home.

Slowly, the UP leader recovered his revolutionary spirit. A modern-day rehash of *La Violencia* had begun in the region; what had started out as a refuge for these people in the 1950s had turned into a full-fledged war zone by the mid-1980s. The army and its proxy allies, the paramilitaries, were attacking the villages where the UP had power. Hundreds of victims, including dozens from the UP, were looking for help. As the district attorney with connections to the UP, Josué had an advantage: The Eastern Plains were a FARC and Communist Party stronghold, so it didn't take him long to gain the refugees' trust. They sought him out in Villavicencio. The young lawyer also traveled to their towns and villages collecting testimony and learning about the region's history, geography, and economics. Soon he was enamored with the region and its spirit.

The courage Josué saw in these people eventually rubbed off on him. Some of the victims were running for the second or third time in their lives. One man fled from a village he had helped create after leaving home during *La Violencia*. Another returned to the village she had left during *La Violencia*. These were Colombia's migrants or "colonists." They were mostly families who moved about the country like the Joad family in a violent Colombian version of *The Grapes of Wrath*. Some of them had traveled hundreds of miles with their kids, grandparents, and all of their belongings strapped to their backs in the 1950s. Millions of them had pushed the country's frontier toward the jungles along the Brazilian, Peruvian, and Ecuadorian borders in the decades that followed. Like their North American brethren, they carved a life out of the woods. Yet even when they found a piece of land and a little serenity, it never seemed to last.

One couple Josué met along the way had been there from the beginning. Julio Cañón and his wife, María Carmen, already had one child and María was expecting another when they had set off to the Macarena, a vast jungle in the heart of the Eastern Plains. Even under the best of circumstances, conquering the Macarena when the Cañóns moved there in the 1960s was a formidable task. The jungle was littered with wild, man-eating animals, and the region features a mountain that seems to suddenly jut up from the middle of the tabletop terrain. Broke and with very little water and food, the couple had walked for two days to an unpopulated area. There, they staked a plot of land and strung a few palm leaves onto some wooden stilts to build a roof. María Carmen tore out the high grass so snakes wouldn't cross through their new living room. Julio got his shotgun, and the two of them took turns playing sentry against the tigers.

By the time Josué arrived and the UP was launched some twenty years later, the area now known as Vista Hermosa "Beautiful View" was an officially recognized municipality, and the Cañóns had established a sizable ranch that had four hundred cebú cattle, some yucca, maize, and plantains. The Communist Party and the FARC were in control of the area. Julio was a prominent Communist Party leader, head of the local community association, and a member of the powerful peasant farmers' syndicate. He was also rapidly moving through the ranks of the UP, the rebels' nascent political project.

It hadn't been easy, though. From almost the beginning, the army had harassed Julio and his family. Julio was first arrested and held for several days in the local army battalion in 1974 "for carrying Marxist literature," María Carmen testified in her complaint to the authorities at the time. They'd arrested and beat him on several occasions thereafter. Julio was a tall, wiry figure with curly hair and a thick beard, hardly strong enough to handle a long torture session. One time, the army dropped by the house posing as guerrillas looking for "informants." But María Carmen had the kids surround their father. He cried out of shame and fear, while his children held his hands tightly and the army made veiled threats.

The family's scant and antagonistic relations with the government made living with the FARC the easy option. The rebels were the law in the area. The FARC settled domestic and interfamilial disputes and ensured the land remained in the hands of the "colonists." Government neglect of the area put an exclamation point on FARC control. There wasn't a health clinic in Vista Hermosa, so when someone was ill or injured, their neighbors had to carry them in a hammock to the closest hospital. There were but a few dirt roads to and from the "*casco urbano*" or main village, which, as in the rest of Colombia, took on the name of the municipality, Vista Hermosa. And the only road to the principal market in the region was not paved and in constant disrepair.

Not surprisingly, the UP surged in Vista Hermosa. When I asked María Carmen some years later why she had joined the new party, she smiled. "We read the platform," she told me. "And we could see it covered all the bases, all our concerns. Everyone liked it, even the priests."

When I met with her, María Carmen was a short, fair-skinned woman
in her mid-forties. She had dirty blond hair that was getting a gray tint to it.
She dressed simply, like a peasant farmer, without any clear color coordination or style. Her purple sweater clashed sharply with her light gray skirt, but
she didn't care. She was well beyond that stage of life. "It didn't say Liberal
or Conservative," she continued telling me about the UP's platform. "It did-
n't matter what religion you were, Adventist or Catholic. Anyone who didn't
like the way things were going could join, so it kind of caught our attention.
We said to ourselves, 'Yeah! This thing lets us fight for our rights, for our *real*
rights, for what belongs to us poor people.' Then the guerrillas came and they
formed the *Juntas Patrióticas*. And that's when it all started coming together.
That's when we started to get some momentum, just before the elections."

In 1986, a little over a year before Josué arrived in the Eastern Plains, the
UP elected six city councilmen in Vista Hermosa. María Carmen told me the
celebrations lasted for days, and the party began to think big. If they were
lucky, they said to one another in the meetings that followed, maybe they
could set up a health clinic, fix the schools, even pave the road to the central
marketplace in the neighboring town of San Juan de Arama.

More than anywhere else in the country, the province of Meta became the
UP's. In the 1986 elections, the party won fifteen municipal council seats.
The UP also elected one congressman and Senator Pedro Nel Jiménez, who
was assassinated just a few months after he took office. The new party's electoral victories presented the political status quo and elite business interests
with a difficult problem. Meta was the gateway to the Eastern Plains, an area
of increasing value to cattle ranchers, oil producers, and, of course, drug traffickers. The UP, they determined, could disrupt the flow of business.

This conflict wasn't limited to Meta. The UP challenged for power in
some 280 of the country's 1,098 municipalities. The municipalities represented a small portion of the population, but more than half of the country's
surface area, producing almost all of Colombia's oil, gold, bananas, and coca,
the raw material used to make cocaine.

What's more, the UP's rise in power coincided with an important legislative change. In 1985, congress passed a law that paved the way for the
people to elect their own mayors. Prior to the so-called *ley 34*, the mayors
were appointed by the leading vote getter in the province. The legislation also
called for municipalities to have greater autonomy over their budgets.
Decentralizing the government, the proponents argued, was an important
step in galvanizing democracy in Colombia. And in a way it was. Small
municipalities like Vista Hermosa could, for the first time, set their own pri-

orities instead of waiting for the province's traditional political power to determine its budget.

But proponents of the plan probably didn't expect the UP's sudden rise in the polls. In Meta in 1988, during the country's first popular mayoral campaign, the UP elected four mayors outright and another in coalition. Across the country, the UP elected 16 mayors and 256 municipal councilmen, including 47 in Meta. The UP's surprising showing had many advocates of the new plan rethinking their positions. In places like Meta, the new party threatened to overturn the traditional parties' dominance and completely alter the political agenda to include things like agrarian reform and new roads. What's more, the UP would finally have the money to do it.

To complicate matters further, Meta was the home of the FARC. The rebels' headquarters was located at the base of the mountains just about seventy-five miles northwest of Vista Hermosa. And with the UP victories, critics wondered whether the guerrillas would get their hands on the municipal funds under UP control. The rebel group was mute about the subject but seemed poised to turn the region into FARC-*landia*. The traditional parties were already shaking with fear.

Power brokers, new and old, immediately mobilized against this sudden shift in regional politics. The mighty drug lord José Gonzalo "*El Mejicano*" Rodríguez Gacha gathered his men on one side of Meta. The emerald czar, drug dealer, and cattle rancher Victor Carranza gathered his men on the other side. Paramilitary groups emerged in a half-dozen municipalities. Their assassins took on names similar to those of their forefathers in *La Violencia*— "big balls," "large mustache," "three tongues," "big shirt," "doll," "death," and "scar"—then began to blaze their now familiar trail of death.

The paramilitary groups worked closely with political and military leaders in the region. In Meta there was a sophisticated police and government intelligence network led by officers who also took on nicknames with a twinge of the past, such as "surgery," "the killer," and "little lieutenant." The paramilitaries carried the officers' telephone numbers at all times. The rightwing groups also had direct contact with national politicians, city councilmen, provincial deputies, mayors, and their assistants. The big landowners, in particular the ranchers, were there to help as well with safe houses and money. The groups traded weapons, shared cars, and at the end of the day, had a few beers. They also ran "errands," meaning "hits," with the army's VII Brigade in Villavicencio acting as headquarters.

Senator Pedro Nel Jiménez was one of the first to die, gunned down in front of his screaming daughter as he picked her up for school in Villavicencio. Dozens more followed. Soon selective assassinations turned into massacres. Whereas in 1986, 32 UP militants were assassinated in Meta, in 1988, the first year mayors were popularly elected, at least 142 party members were murdered and 11 more "disappeared."

When Josué visited Vista Hermosa in 1987, he was stunned by what he saw. "The town was divided by the Guejar River," he noted some years later. "On one side was the political and social opposition: the peasant unions, civic leaders, 'colonists,' and members of the *Unión Patriótica* who created 'self-defense' groups and asked for the guerrillas' help; on the other side of the river, the paramilitaries, the army, and the police set up camp. No one went from one side to the other. It was the front line. . . . They set up a type of Berlin wall that you couldn't see, but everyone felt."

Julio and María Carmen felt it the most. Their eldest son, Gerardo, was shot just a few months after the 1986 elections by a man María Carmen said regularly ferried people across the Guejar River. She said the neighbors chased the assassin down the river until he fled into the local army battalion. A few dozen UP deaths later, the army caught up to her second oldest son, Nelson, as he headed toward a wake for the UP mayoral candidate.

"He ran down the river banks," María Carmen recounted to me. He had a hard time keeping his feet along the uneven ground, she explained. He stumbled, then got up, then stumbled again. "That's when they [the army] yelled, 'This guerrilla is very agile,'" she said. Some soldiers closed in on Nelson upriver. The rest followed from downriver. Nelson was trapped. The army surrounded him, then gunned him down in plain view of two of María Carmen's children. "They [the army] said he was a guerrilla, shot in combat," she told me. "My kids went to the other side of the river. There the [army] commander said, 'Who's going to cry for this son-of-a-bitch?' My kids didn't budge; they didn't cry, but their hearts were broken in little pieces."

The mayoral candidate had been shot just a few days earlier, paving the way for María Carmen's husband, Julio, to become the new candidate. In the 1988 elections, Julio won in a landslide, then immediately sent his family to live in Bogotá. He couldn't afford to lose anybody else to the violence, he told his wife. "I was crying when I left Vista Hermosa," María Carmen told me later. "We heard the roosters crowing, the cows mooing, but we had to leave everything behind. . . . Julio came with us. He said, 'I've got to take care of my family. If they kill me, well then so be it, but they're not going to kill my whole family.' That's when he brought me to Bogotá and got me an apartment. Then he turns to me and says, 'I'm going back.'"

I asked her why Julio didn't just stay in Bogotá. "I guess because he wanted a better future for the community, for the municipality," she replied.

"He wanted to pave the road from [the neighboring village of] San Juan [de Arama] to Vista Hermosa. He said, 'We're with the UP. We can tell them to pave the road. This road's going to give us a way to connect and do business.' This is what he fought for; so they'd give us that. . . . I pleaded with him but he said, 'No, we've got to stay and fight. Because if we all go, who's left to fight? And besides, we have the farm there that we have to take care of. Listen, to get what you want, you have to fight. . . . They killed my two boys; they forced my family to run for their lives. And now, on top of that, I have to run too. No! I'm staying.'"

Like so many others in the UP, Julio never quarreled with fate; he seemed to accept his role as a martyr. The dangers were always evident, but the path to avoid those dangers never seemed so simple. Stop being politically active was the easiest answer. But nothing was ever that easy. Julio was a fighter, and he would rather die battling for his party than live in fear. He believed in myths. He believed that David could still defeat Goliath.

But the challenges Julio faced were daunting. The paramilitaries had made it clear from the beginning that all UP mayors were targets. A few months after the elections, paramilitaries stopped a truck carrying eighteen people, most of them UP militants from Vista Hermosa's neighboring municipality of El Castillo. The gunman wove their way through the crowd looking for the UP mayor. When they didn't find him, they shot and killed seventeen of the people on the truck, including a ten-year-old girl and a five-year-old boy.

The paramilitaries sent Julio his first notice through the mail. "Those votes have given you three months to govern," it said. The paramilitaries kept their word. Men shot at the startled mayor from a moving vehicle in his town just days before the El Castillo massacre. Julio's bodyguards repelled the attack. Four days after the assault, the army went to his home, and an army captain stood outside yelling for the mayor. "Come out! My finger is itching to pull the trigger on you, you son-of-a-bitch!" When Julio didn't appear, the soldiers walked away and in an act of frustration shot their guns into the air.

Throughout this time, Josué met with Julio on several occasions and marveled at his courage. "Julio had to create his own team of bodyguards," Josué wrote later. "He'd often go to Villavicencio and Bogotá to complain to the local and national government about the daily assassinations, the forced 'disappearances' committed by the army against the civilian population."

Back in Vista Hermosa, Julio faced his own mortality every day. Graffiti near his office read, "We don't want a guerrilla mayor" and "Go away UP-FARC." The press also constantly harassed him and even tried to frame him. Just a few weeks after paramilitaries shot at him, a bomb exploded at a small store in town. Radio reports in the capital city of Villavicencio blamed the

Communist Party and Julio for the attack. The owner of the store wrote a letter to the radio station denying its version of events.

But the attacks didn't stop Julio. He was determined to get his municipality a health clinic and improve the decrepit road that stretched to the next
town, San Juan de Arama, even if it cost him his life. "The situation is troubling," he said to the Communist weekly newspaper, *Voz*. "But we're still
optimistic; we're going to continue to push our projects forward."

A couple months after being shot at, Julio took the road to Villavicencio. He
wanted to talk to the governor about getting funds to pave this road. He also
wanted to see his family. It was September 7, the anniversary of his son
Nelson's tragic death. María Carmen would be mourning, he thought. The
kids would be consoling her, but it wouldn't be enough. He had to be there
as well, despite the dangers.

On the bus to Villavicencio, Julio noticed that two men were eyeing him
suspiciously. It was hard to tell who was who anymore. As it was for Josué,
Julio's life had taken a paranoid turn since the paramilitaries tried to gun him
down: Everyone had become a potential assassin; Julio didn't take any
chances and now assumed the worst in every situation. In Villavicencio, Julio
decided to dodge the two men by switching buses when they weren't looking.
He didn't really know if they were after him, but he'd arrived in Bogotá frazzled nonetheless. "What do you think of this?" he told his startled family as
they stared up at him. "They're going to kill me."

While in their small Bogotá apartment, the family said a prayer for
Nelson. María Carmen made a meal, and then they sat around and told corny
jokes. After dinner, María Carmen and Julio took a walk. She was depressed.
She didn't want him to quit his job, but she also wanted him alive. She needed
him, she explained. Finances were already tight. Julio had arrived with barely
enough money to cover the rent. And the owner of the apartment in Bogotá
told María Carmen he would evict the family if her husband was killed. As bad
as that sounds, the Cañóns were lucky. In other places, owners wouldn't even
rent to UP families because of the high possibility of losing the wage earner to
sudden death.

After the meal, Julio started to prepare for his trip back to Villavicencio.
He was as worried as his wife. He knew he was a marked man, and he knew
that the paramilitaries might be waiting for him as he traveled back to his
town. Before he left, he arranged for two government bodyguards to accompany him along the deadly road to his town, Vista Hermosa. He also asked
the governor for a car, but one wasn't available. Fine, he thought, two bodyguards and the bus should get me to Vista Hermosa.

He gathered the family and told them point-blank, "I think they're really going to assassinate me this time. But it's not important. I know they'll kill me for speaking the truth. But I'm in so much pain. There have been so many innocent people who've died, and they killed my sons." Everyone was crying now, and they started to hug one another and tell Julio, "Don't go!" But he replied, "Tomorrow, I'm going." The next day, Julio left.

On his way, Julio stopped by the UP offices in Villavicencio, where he met with Josué again. The two talked about the threats and Julio's inability to get a car and extra bodyguards from the governor. "We said goodbye to each other," Josué recalled later. "I wished him luck, although luck doesn't matter much when you're in the eye of the hurricane."

Julio died in a poetic sort of way: He was bouncing up and down the unpaved road that he dreamt of fixing. Paramilitaries caught up to him a mere ten minutes before arriving in Vista Hermosa. They got on the bus and asked for him by name. He stood up, it was said later, to avoid causing a massacre like the one that had happened to the neighboring UP supporters from El Castillo. The gunman took him off the bus and shot him twenty-seven times while the passengers watched helplessly. The paramilitaries also killed one of his bodyguards. The other was spared.

In Bogotá, his children got the news from the radio. "*Atención! Atención! Acaban de matar al alcalde de Vista Hermosa, Meta!*" María Carmen had gone for a walk. When she returned, she only had to hear the wailing coming from her apartment to know what had happened. She entered into an emotional coma and was still trying to wake up when I met with her more than ten years later. "Every death is tough because it's your blood," she told me crying. "But this one was harder. It's not like it's easier to lose a son. But losing your husband is very difficult. I wouldn't wish it on my worst enemy because it's like losing your best friend, the person who looks out for you. You'll never see that person again, not even to get mad at him."

For the funeral, the family organized three cars to Villavicencio. There the attorney general's office assigned two more cars and some bodyguards to the caravan, and they set off for Vista Hermosa. Like Julio, they bounced along the unpaved road for a few hours before arriving at the town. "It was a huge funeral," María Carmen remembered. "All the villages, community associations, neighborhoods, leaders, politicians—even the church—went to his funeral. There were so many people that we couldn't even fit everyone in the church."

In between the rabble-rousing speeches of Julio's colleagues, his fourteen-year-old son, Chesman, spoke. Chesman was as fearless as his father and perhaps as naive as his two slain brothers. He took to the podium with the humble charisma his father had once displayed. "They killed my dad," he told the packed hall. "They think that by killing the leaders of the UP, they're going to shut us up. They're wrong, because every day we're getting stronger."

Sitting in the audience, Josué felt the same way. He was frustrated and angry. His return trip to Vista Hermosa just a few months after Julio was killed only infuriated him further. "I saw only desolation," he wrote later. "Starving dogs and emaciated donkeys. In virtually all the houses there were 'For Sale,' 'For Rent,' and 'Will Swap' signs; they were empty and the doors were boarded up. This was a ghost town. There were only two bars open with a couple of old guys playing billiards. There wasn't a single teenager. Not a single woman. Not a single kid. There was no future."

The constant death that surrounded him in the Eastern Plains made Josué feel as if he were at war as well, and he began to take on a soldier mentality that he confused with becoming more in tune with the local spirit. Like Julio, he became defiant of death and afraid of being considered afraid. Josué was heavily threatened, but the thought of leaving his bloodied UP comrades behind disgusted him. He, too, believed in myths.

"It would be like abandoning their memories, the struggle for which they had given their lives," he later wrote, undoubtedly thinking of people like Julio Cañón. "If I survived, it was like I was a coward; I would never forgive myself. What's more, there's a tradition of the plainsman: he's a man of his word, a man who never backs down in front of the obstacles but rises to the challenge. This is very important there and worked on my mind. Leaving the Eastern Plains would be like reducing my manliness. Just thinking about leaving was an act of cowardice in front of these people who—knowing they were going to die—never gave up their struggle. On the contrary, they stepped up the pressure so that when death was upon them they had already won a moral victory over their assassins."

(*Vox*)

Jacobo Arenas surveys the scene near his headquarters in the cold, barren Sumapaz Mountains just south of Bogotá. Arenas was the architect of FARC strategy for twenty-five years before dying of natural causes in 1990. He devised the plan to develop the FARC into a massive army and created the rebels' political party, the *Unión Patriótica* (UP). Arenas's popularity surged as the FARC launched the UP. He wrote a book and was even the UP's presidential candidate until just before the party's first national convention in 1985. But Arenas also used the UP for his own devious ends.

(Voz)

Jacob Arenas (right) and Manuel "Sureshot" Marulanda contemplate their next move at the peace talks held in FARC headquarters in Sumapaz in 1984. From the rebels' beginning in 1964, these two men led the FARC. Arenas was the political strategist, Marulanda was the military strategist. The two men steered the FARC toward a ceasefire agreement with the government, which led to peace talks. As talks progressed they built up the FARC's army and arsenal.

(Voz)

Jacob Arenas addresses government and rebel delegates at the peace talks. The peace process lasted three years during which time the FARC created the UP. When talks fell apart in 1987, the FARC called back its members who had participated in the UP. The UP, meanwhile, continued to vie for political posts. The strategy of combining both guerrilla and political movements to win power—known as *la combinación de todas las formas de lucha*—was the cornerstone of the FARC's strategy in Colombia.

(*Voz*)

UP leaders Jaime Pardo (second from left) and Braulio Herrera (third from left) speak with
Colombian president Belisario Betancur (far right). With the UP, Pardo and Herrera became
national political figures virtually overnight. They met on several occasions with much-maligned
President Betancur. Betancur struggled to keep the UP safe, the peace talks going, and the increasingly aggressive Colombian military at bay.

(*Voz*)

Government, civilian, and rebel delegates line up for a photo at the peace talks held in FARC
headquarters in the Sumapaz Mountains. Shown in the photo are Sureshot Marulanda (far left),
Alfonso Cano (back row, first on the left), Alberto Rojas Puyo (back row, second from the left),
Jaime Pardo Leal (far right, standing), and Jacobo Arenas (far right, kneeling). By all accounts, the
meetings were cordial. But the peace talks suffered as both sides constantly accused the other of
violating the cease-fire.

After being a circuit court judge for many years and heading up its union, Jaime Pardo Leal became the president of the UP in 1985. He was known as much for his charisma and revolutionary beliefs as his sense of humor. In the presidential elections of 1986, Pardo garnered 328,752 votes, the most to date of any leftist candidate in the history of Colombia.

(*Voz*)

Bernardo Jaramillo addresses UP supporters at a campaign rally. Jaramillo took over the UP in 1987 following the assassination of Jaime Pardo Leal. A hard-line Communist Party and FARC supporter when he began, Jaramillo softened his revolutionary rhetoric as he saw more and more UP members murdered.

(*Voz*)

A UP rally draws thousands in downtown Bogotá. The UP brought together disparate members of the student, labor, and peasant movements. In its first elections, the party elected twenty-four provincial deputies and 275 municipal council representatives. The party also elected three senators and four congressional representatives.

UP supporters get riled up on the streets on the day of the presidential elections 1986. Party militants expressed their love for the party by chanting revolutionary slogans, wearing Che Guevara-like berets, and shouting, "Long Live the FARC!" Opponents of the party said it was the political wing of the rebel group.

Iván Márquez smiles during a UP political rally. Márquez ran as a substitute, or stand-in, for congress and won. Along with Braulio Herrera, he would be the only FARC member to ever hold political office. When peace talks between the FARC and the government broke down in 1987, he returned to the mountains. Today he is part of the rebels' top command.

(Voz)

(Voz)

UP supporters surround their leader, Braulio Herrera (above, top center) during the 1986 presidential elections. The teddy bear–looking Herrera (also pictured left, addressing congress) was chosen by the FARC to be the head of the UP in 1984. He was a mystical character who carried a pendulum so he could decipher illnesses, test his food for poison, and get himself out of dangerous situations. He won a congressional post as a substitute in 1986. When peace talks between the FARC and the government ended in 1987, he returned to fighting in the Middle Magdalena Valley. But soon afterwards, he snapped and killed close to one hundred of his own soldiers for treason. Eventually he fled the country.

Alberto Rojas Puyo sits in his tenth story apartment in downtown Bogotá. Rojas Puyo was part of President Belisario Betancur's peace team in the early 1980s. He also was part of the early FARC discussions about how to form what would become the UP. Over time, Rojas Puyo became disillusioned with the FARC and the Communist Party's strategy of combining the political movement with the guerrilla war and worked to make the UP an independent political force.

Josué Giraldo addresses a workshop near his long-time home in the Eastern Plains. Josue joined the Communist Party while he was studying law in the early 1980s, then organized the *Juntas Patrióticas*, small cells of supporters, for the UP when the party emerged in 1985. He was a hard-liner who maintained contact with the FARC even after the rebel group and the political party officially announced they had parted ways. But he was also a tireless human rights advocate. He was murdered in front of his family in 1996.

(Voz)

Throughout the period of the UP, Manuel Cepeda was one of the Communist Party's most important leaders. He directed the weekly *Voz* before winning a congressional and then a senate position for the UP. He was also known as a staunch hard-liner who supported the FARC. In 1994, he was assassinated by two members of a military intelligence unit.

(Marcelo Salinas)

Álvaro Salazar, shown here in a recent photo, was a member of the FARC's urban militias in the late 1970s. He graduated to the role of guerrilla messenger in the early 1980s and eventually became the UP's propaganda chief. Like some of his colleagues, Salazar grew frustrated with the strategy of combining the political movement with the guerrilla war against the government. In the late 1980s, he and others sought to separate the UP from the FARC. His efforts to break from the rebels' grip nearly cost him his life.

Julio Cañón talks to *Voz* just a few weeks before his assassination in 1988. Cañón was the mayor of the town of Vista Hermosa in the Eastern Plains. Two of his sons were killed shortly after the UP was formed. After he was assassinated, one other son was murdered. The rest of the family fled to Ecuador, then Canada, except for his widow who remained in Colombia. Paramilitaries eventually caught up to her and threatened her with death unless she became an informant for them.

(*Voz*)

(*Voz*)

Wilson Borja speaks to *Voz* reporters not long after he was shot several times at the end of 2000. Borja is a former UP militant as well as a longtime union leader and Communist Party member. Despite his scant political power, he is one of the most threatened men in Colombia. He has ten bodyguards that he selects himself. In 2002, he campaigned with them by his side and won a congressional seat.

José Gonzalo "El Mejicano" Rodriguez Gacha (left) was one of the most notorious Colombian drug traffickers of the 1980s. He was Pablo Escobar's right-hand man and ran the biggest laboratories in the country in the some of the most remote places. But he and his jungle neighbors, the FARC, fought over this territory and this illegal crop. The fight would eventually include the FARC's political party, the UP. Rodríguez Gacha is thought to be responsible for the murder of hundreds of UP militants, including UP president Jaime Pardo Leal. Pardo's funeral (below) drew thousands of mourners to Bogotá's central plaza.

(Semana)

(El Tiempo)

Wanted posters of Fidel (left) and Carlos Castaño. Fidel was a powerful landowner, drug trafficker, and paramilitary. After Fidel's father, Jesús, died at the hands of the FARC in 1980, Fidel, Carlos and several of his brothers and cousins began attacking suspected FARC supporters. Eventually their targets became the UP. Pablo Escobar dubbed Fidel "2000," for the number of UP Fidel had allegedly killed.

(Semana)

General Fernando Landazábal was the Godfather of Colombian counterinsurgency and the UP's most dangerous enemy. Schooled in the U.S. and a veteran of the Korean War, Landazábal wrote countless articles and books on how to defeat communism. When he saw his message ignored, he pushed for a more dubious plan: creating paramilitary groups in the countryside. In 1997, he was assassinated by unknown assailants.

(Semana)

(Marcelo Salinas)

Carlos Castaño reviews his paramilitary troops. Carlos admits to killing "thirty or forty guerrillas outside of combat who were hidden in the UP." But he refuses to take responsibility for the murder of UP presidential candidate, Bernardo Jaramillo, despite being tried and convicted for the crime in absentia. After his older brother, Fidel, disappeared in 1993, Carlos became the unabashed leader of the paramilitary groups. He created a national paramilitary alliance that grew to include close to ten thousand soldiers. In 2004, he was ambushed by some of his paramilitary rivals and 'disappeared.'

Alonso de Jesús Baquero, better known as Black Vladimir, was the most ruthless of paramilitaries in the 1980s. After spending years as a member of the FARC, Black Vladimir defected to the paramilitaries where he became one of their preeminent commanders. He organized the attack on the UP stronghold, Segovia, in 1988 that left forty-three dead. Following his capture in 1989, he admitted to over eight hundred slayings, many of them UP supporters. "When you're in the paramilitaries you kill a lot of people," he said.

(Marcelo Salinas, Steven Dudley)

The FARC grew from having 980 troops in 1982, to 18,000 in 2002. The rebels used increasingly young soldiers to fill their ranks. They also obtained more sophisticated weaponry and better uniforms. The results, shown at bottom, did not always favor them. But over time, the FARC won some critical military victories, which led to the death and capture of hundreds of government troops. They also caught the attention of the U.S. government, which has sent billions of dollars to Colombia since 1999, to help the Colombian government fight the rebels.

(Voz)

FARC leader Alfonso Cano became part of the FARC's leadership council in 1982 and was there when the UP began in 1984. The former Communist Party militant has had a hard time garnering the full support of the troops given his "intellectual" background. Cano is shown here in 2000, after he officially launched the FARC's new political party, known as the Bolivarian Movement.

(Steven Dudley)

After winning major military victories in the late 1990s, the FARC pushed the government to cede a huge swath of territory to the rebels in order to make way for peace talks with the government. The area known as the "Demilitarized Zone" or DMZ was the size of Switzerland. As this picture of a rebel roadblock illustrates, the DMZ functioned as a virtual FARC state, which journalists began referring to as FARC-*landia* or "FARC-land."

Commander Omar of the FARC's 51st Front—also known as the "Jaime Pardo Leal" for the slain UP leader—surveys a village from afar. Omar and many other FARC members joined the rebels around the time the UP was being slaughtered. Because of what happened to the UP, Omar said, "The only way to struggle and reach political power in Colombia is with guns."

The author (right) discusses politics with a FARC commander in a rebel camp in the southern jungles of Colombia.

(Voz)

Manuel "Sureshot" Marulanda has been fighting the government for over fifty years without losing a limb or his revolutionary edge. Under his guide, the FARC has grown into the largest guerrilla organization in the western hemisphere. Like him, the rebel group shows few signs of age.

CHAPTER 9
THE RETURN OF BLACK VLADIMIR

The paramilitaries' effectiveness against the Communist Party could be measured by a statue. It was a bronze bust of paramilitary ideologue Pablo Guarín that stood ten feet high in a plaza in Puerto Boyacá. The bust was made after Guarín was shot under mysterious circumstances in 1987. The FARC said it killed Guarín, but some believe that Mafia boss José Gonzalo *"El Mejicano"* Rodríguez Gacha did it because Guarín opposed his drug business. For people in Puerto Boyacá, it didn't matter. Under Guarín's watchful eye and his omnipresent politico-military organization, ACDEGAM, the paramilitaries had "cleaned" the area of the Communists. The FARC's new political party, the *Unión Patriótica*, was never even an option. "If at the end of the road you find my body don't pick me up," it reads beneath the bust. "Let the vultures from the FARC devour me. Pick up my ideas, my flags, and continue ahead." Guarín said these words, and the people responded. At the entrance to the town, a sign read, "Welcome to Puerto Boyacá . . . the anti-subversive capital of Colombia."

But as effective as the paramilitaries were in some places, in others they continued to have trouble with the FARC and the UP. Selective assassination and even massacres didn't always work. The guerrillas held on, and the party would surge. These places warranted a different strategy than the methodical approach followed in Puerto Boyacá, something that would make a lasting impact. Almost like an atomic bomb, this strategy would be applied to one place, but it would have widespread implications. It would be a stamp that would kill the new party's will to continue and serve as a lesson for future would-be UP strongholds. It wouldn't simply be a massacre, it would be a holocaust.

The closest, most qualified pilot the paramilitaries had to drop an A-bomb was a hulking ex-FARC soldier named Alonso de Jesús Baquero, better known as Black Vladimir. For several years now Vladimir had done his job as few others could. As a guerrilla he had learned his lessons well, and he applied them to perfection in the paramilitaries. He knew where his enemies hid. He knew how to flush them out. He knew how to break them down— how to torture the weak for information and convert the strong to his side. Hundreds died at his hands as the baby-faced killer tore through the Middle Magdalena Valley with a generous grin on his face. The death toll was frightening to all but Vladimir himself.

By late 1988, the paramilitaries had set their sights on Segovia to drop their bomb. Segovia was a dank mining village of about 20,000 people in the picturesque mountains of eastern Antioquia. The battle lines in this city had been drawn thirty-five years before anyone even contemplated creating something like the UP. During *La Violencia* a harsh wing of the traditional Liberal Party, who called themselves the "Codfish," controlled Segovia with an iron fist; a multinational mining company exploited the local workforce. A radical peasant syndicate and miners' union mixed with the Communist Party—which had established itself in the 1930s—and later the rebels. The two sides clashed frequently, until the guerrillas eventually won out.

For years, Segovia remained the National Liberation Army (ELN) rebels' headquarters and one of its safe havens. They were joined later by the FARC, both of whom enjoyed a sense of invulnerability in the area, not least because of government ineptitude. In the early 1970s, the Colombian military launched an offensive in the region that drove the ELN to near extinction. Surrounded, the guerrillas said they were ready to talk peace. The government withdrew its troops. The ELN then retreated deeper into the mountains and regrouped. There were no peace talks, and the rebels simply trickled back later to retake control. The head of the military resigned over the debacle, while other officers fumed over the government's naïveté. Eventually these officers sought extrajudicial ways to exterminate their lifelong enemies.

In Segovia, the military found ready allies for this fight. In the early 1980s, the army teamed up with a group of young, rabid anti-guerrilla civilians from the same bloodline. The Castaño family—led by the eldest brother, Fidel—had moved to Segovia a few years earlier. They had been wronged by the FARC, who they said had killed their father after kidnapping him. The alliance paid immediate dividends. For a few weeks in 1983, Fidel's crew killed people in eights and tens—some of them women and children—using crude weapons like machetes. The military not only let them do their dirty work, they protected them forever afterward.

The Castaño family killing spree provided the spark for what would become the national paramilitary alliance. Dozens of the paramilitaries' first recruits came from the Segovia region. And according to his own account, Fidel's teenage brother Carlos shot his first victim there—one of the people allegedly involved in the kidnapping of his beloved father—thereby taking perhaps his biggest step toward becoming the head of this paramilitary alliance when it took shape some ten years later. "I was so angry," Carlos described the transcendental experience, "I kept firing the gun with my eyes closed even though there weren't any bullets left. And all I could hear was tic, tic, tic."

However, this first wave of repression didn't end guerrilla dominance in the area. Segovia's popular and rebel movements slowly recouped, and the guerrillas rebuilt their strong support network. When the UP emerged in the mid-1980s, the new party quickly usurped political power from the "Codfish" Liberals. Support for the UP came from the remnants of the exploited mining workers and the impoverished peasants who had teamed up with the guerrillas. It was a near-perfect illustration of *la combinación de todas las formas de lucha*, the Communist Party strategy of combining political and insurgent forces. Following the startling 1986 elections, both Segovia and the neighboring municipality of Remedios were in UP hands, and their enemies were scrambling their troops to counterattack.

Around this time, a death squad called *Muerte a Revolucionarios del Nordeste* (MRN) or "Death to Northeast [Antioquian] Revolutionaries" announced they were going to clean up the region. "We would like to remind everyone," one early pamphlet read, "just as our colleagues from [the paramilitary group] MAS ["Death to Kidnappers"], cleaned the communist filth from Puerto Berrío [in the Middle Magdalena Valley], we will exterminate the pro-Castro ELN, and we will liquidate the subversive *Unión Patriótica*, and we will end the cease-fire with the FARC. . . . We have the support of the police, the Colombian army, MAS, and the prominent sons and daughters of the region that occupy high government posts." The pamphlet also included a salute to the anti-communist godfathers in the U.S. government. "We recognize and value the effort that our allies in the United States are making under the guidance of their President Ronald Reagan to fight international communism. We cannot disgrace them given that they've put millions of dollars into our country." U.S. aid to Colombia was minimal compared with that to Central America, but Reagan's anti-communist ideology remained central.

Following Reagan's lead in places like El Salvador, Guatemala, and Nicaragua, the Colombian paramilitaries stepped up the pressure against the "communists." After assassinating several leftist political leaders, they distributed more menacing pamphlets. The army also increased its presence in the streets and began openly harassing UP politicians. But this seemed to have little impact. The UP continued to mobilize support, and after the 1988 elections, the party controlled both the mayoralties and city councils of Segovia and Remedios. For a while, Segovia seemed almost too difficult to handle. In fact, it was only when a mammoth ex-FARC soldier posing as a cattle rancher rolled into town that the paramilitaries could finally drop their A-bomb and send a message to the rest of the country that resistance was futile.

For Black Vladimir, going back to Segovia was a homecoming of sorts. He had grown up near the village and had shuttled guns for the rebels past army checkpoints in the area. He had also learned to be an urban militant and had taught recruits how to do the same in these foothills. Now, he had gone full circle. He had been sent by his boss, the son of a cattle rancher turned drug trafficker and paramilitary chieftain, Henry Pérez, to flush the area of his former instructors and students in the FARC. Vladimir had tortured and knocked off dozens of UP and FARC supporters on the other side of the Magdalena River, but he would make sure that Segovia would be his greatest triumph yet.

In Segovia, Vladimir had plenty of support. He worked with local military commanders as well as officers at the XIV Brigade—the Puerto Berrío–based army battalion that the infamous and angry General Fernando Landazábal had created so many years before to regain control of the region. Vladimir also had well-trained men at his disposal and, most importantly, political backing from the area strongman. At the time, a congressman named César Pérez headed up the "Codfish" cadre of the Liberal Party. Pérez was positioning himself to lead the national legislative body and could ill afford to have his constituency turn on him. But when his candidates lost the mayoral races in Segovia and Remedios, and his party was virtually eliminated from both municipal councils, he saw little choice other than to liquidate his enemies. César Pérez's fight was also personal. Just months before the 1988 elections, ELN rebels had tried to kill the "Codfish" Liberal Party leader. He had barely escaped but wouldn't take any more chances.

In testimony, Vladimir stated that César Pérez called Fidel Castaño, the would-be paramilitary leader in the region. But Castaño had since moved his operations farther north, and so César Pérez contacted Henry Pérez, the nominal paramilitary leader in the Middle Magdalena Valley. The phone calls set the Liberal Party's version of *la combinación de todas las formas de lucha* into motion. It wasn't that much different from the Communist Party's strategy except for one thing: The Liberals contracted the paramilitaries rather than integrating them into the party. After Henry Pérez talked to Fidel

Castaño, he met with Vladimir, who met with the military officials, who then began planning the operation to drop the paramilitary A-bomb. It was the beginning of the end for Segovia.

By 1988, the paramilitaries had evolved into a sophisticated national network. Henry Pérez and the mighty drug trafficker José Gonzalo Rodríguez Gacha ran the Middle Magdalena Valley. Fidel Castaño controlled the coastal province of Córdoba and bits of the northern part of Antioquia. The Eastern Plains were split between Rodríguez Gacha and the emerald dealer and cattle rancher Victor Carranza, while the mighty drug lord Pablo Escobar and his crew floated wherever they wanted. On occasion the leaders made decisions together, but each one was responsible for financing his own army and running his own dirty war. Death squads split their time between caring for the "merchandise" of their bosses and killing their political and business enemies.

The business association created by the political wing of the paramilitaries, ACDEGAM, had also evolved. A sister organization known as *Tradición, Familia y Propiedad*, "Tradition, Family, and Property" (TFP), had been formed. TFP and ACDEGAM made up the core of a new political movement they called MORENA. At the time, the Colombian magazine *Semana* compared the new party to ARENA, Roberto D'Aubisson's neofascist political movement in El Salvador that had close ties to the death squads in that Central American nation and strong connections to the Reagan administration. MORENA's platform spoke of democracy, respecting life, a right to education, and political, social, and economic development, but it ended with a virtual death threat against the Communist Party, "the enemy of democracy, and its [military] facade, the UP." As one Colombian columnist said at the time, "The only program MORENA has is to make war with the UP."

Like the UP, the paramilitaries sought to use the new laws concerning direct elections of mayors and more control over municipal budgets to their advantage. For a while, the project served its purpose. In the 1988 elections, MORENA, in alliance with traditional parties in the region, won six mayoral campaigns in the Middle Magdalena Valley. The newly elected mayors proclaimed themselves the "National Front of Anti-Subversive Mayors." Among them was Luis Rubio, the mayor of the paramilitary epicenter, Puerto Boyacá, former treasurer of ACDEGAM, and protector of Vladimir and his family. A few months after his victory, authorities issued a warrant for Rubio's arrest on charges that he helped mastermind the massacre of more than forty people in two small villages in the banana-growing region of Urabá.

The paramilitaries had also tried to professionalize their army. They set up training schools where recruits "ate mud" in the jungle and learned new loyalties. "To defend our children, our home, our belongings, our land," the paramilitaries' pledge of allegiance read. "We used to be communists forced to fight for things that are against peace. . . . [Now] we are *autodefensa* groups, and we are fighting for the defense of honor and good of the Colombian citizens. We fight against the Communist Party, the FARC, and all the subversive groups of Colombia."

The best school was at *Las Galaxias*, one of Rodríguez Gacha's ranches in central Colombia. There commanders like Black Vladimir trained the top paramilitaries in arms, explosives, personal defense, secret identities, intelligence gathering, counterintelligence, first aid, and communications. Over time, the training schools also became the loci of operations. The "01" school, for example, was converted into a detention center. Other schools became communication centers. Vladimir would call the schools if he needed men or war materiel for a job. And by 1987, there was an increasing need for both. The FARC had stepped up its attacks on paramilitaries and their supporters since the massacres of UP members had begun, which sparked the paramilitaries to shift their strategy.

Vladimir testified that, in late 1987, General Farouk Yanine Díaz, a former XIV Brigade commander who had since become an instructor in a military school in Bogotá, visited the "01" school. General Yanine had maintained regular contact with Henry Pérez since the two had met in the early 1980s when the first *autodefensas* formed. Vladimir said that Yanine and Henry Pérez often decided what the *autodefensas'* priorities were. Vladimir also testified that the general turned a blind eye to the drug-processing laboratories throughout the region. This was the grand quid pro quo: Get rid of the guerrillas, and the army will look the other way on drug trafficking (not to mention benefit from the proceeds militarily and, in some cases, personally). At "01," Vladimir remembered, Yanine gave a rousing speech to the paramilitary troops. The general called for them to move from the "defensive to the offensive . . . to do the things that the army can't." Vladimir also claimed that Yanine said they needed training from highly experienced professionals to "teach them new tactics."

The drug traffickers took the general's advice. In late 1987, active and retired Colombian military officers, at the behest of the drug traffickers, contacted five Israeli mercenaries to give a military training course. Pablo Escobar, José Gonzalo *"El Mejicano"* Rodríguez Gacha, Henry Pérez, and Victor Carranza pooled their money together to pay for it. The course took place at camp "50" in the flatlands of the Middle Magdalena Valley near the border of the Boyacá and Santander provinces. Escobar and Carranza sent five men each to be trained as bodyguards. Rodríguez Gacha and Pérez sent twenty men each, including Black Vladimir, for training in counterinsurgency and terrorism. Others received instruction in the art of assassination.

Vladimir met a lot of big-name killers at the camp: "*Trampas*" and "*El Perro*" of Rodríguez Gacha's gang, "*Caliche*" of Escobar's crew, Victor Carranza's nephew, and Carlos Castaño, Fidel's younger and more rabid brother. As it turned out, "new tactics" meant learning how to approach and take over an enemy house, and gun down a target leaning out of a moving vehicle. Students also learned how to send letter bombs with C4 explosives. In total, fifty men entered the six-week course; only thirty-five passed. Vladimir was considered one of the ten best. The Israeli instructors were especially impressed by this physically imposing ex-guerrilla; Vladimir had quickly taken to both the mercenary tactics and the Israelis' philosophy: Cut the enemy down by its roots.

At the closing ceremonies of the training, Rodríguez Gacha and Henry Pérez awarded Vladimir a prize. His status was as high as it gets for field commanders, and he was perhaps the Middle Magdalena Valley's most trusted commander. He was now making $1,000 per month; occasionally, Pérez would just give him several thousand dollars as a bonus for some work he had done. Even better, he had more than five hundred men at his disposal. They were spread throughout the Middle Magdalena Valley doing hitman work. Only in the blue-collar city of Barrancabermeja and the mining city of Segovia did Vladimir hesitate to leave his soldiers.

The A-bomb the paramilitaries dropped on Segovia took weeks of planning and coordination. Vladimir said he first talked with local army battalion commanders; they drew up a preliminary list of victims. One of these victims, the UP mayor of the neighboring municipality of Remedios, was soon crossed out. He was paying his bill at a hotel in Medellín when the MRN paramilitary group caught up to him and riddled his body with bullets. The mayor, who was going to take office just a few days later, had gone to Medellín to complain to the provincial government that he had no bodyguards.

A few weeks before the Segovia attack, Vladimir began to scout the city's streets. Posing as a cattle rancher, he looked for contacts with the guerrillas. During this search, his training as a FARC militant came in handy. One night, a small group of men pulled up to a garage in a four-by-four to get their car serviced. Vladimir recognized they were urban guerrillas right away, and he began casing the garage. His death list grew as he perused other streets. A few areas were obviously the principal centers of UP support, so he jotted them down as well. Names of people were replaced by the names of city blocks. Soon Vladimir's map of death covered virtually the entire city.

Vladimir then went to the business leaders in the municipality and secured some financial and logistic support, which included the use of the printing press at Frontino Gold Mines, the largest gold mining company in the country, to print out scare pamphlets. "We back the big *caudillo* in this region, César Pérez García, and his attempts to become President of the House of Representatives," one read. "We will not accept Communist mayors or municipal councils made up of idiotic peasants or vulgar workers like those who make up the *Unión Patriótica*. They don't have the intelligence to handle these positions and manage these municipalities that have always been ours. Now we will get them back NO MATTER WHAT IT COSTS! . . . You wait. . . . We will hit you with a mortal blow!"

Other ominous signs followed. Around this time, the army and police staged a drill to "practice," they said, against a guerrilla attack on the town. The streets were emptied. When the population emerged from their homes, paramilitary graffiti covered the walls and anti-Communist pamphlets lay on people's doorsteps. One spray-painted message read, "God loves us so much that he sent us to save you!"

Vladimir got the go-ahead to attack in early November and gathered fifteen of his best men. He got another fifteen from his fellow commander, "Jairo," who would lead the operation. For his part, the politician César Pérez had already met with Henry Pérez in Medellín. There the head of the "Codfish" cadre of the Liberal Party had agreed to use some of his men for the job as well. Vladimir then organized the transportation and waited for the nod to begin the operation.

It was a typical Friday evening in Segovia when the three trucks carrying Vladimir's men rolled into town. The city was hopping. The miners were just settling into their weekend: playing billiards, eating greasy chicken legs, having sex with the prostitutes at the brothels. Children rode their bicycles up and down the street and kicked soccer balls in the park. Women stopped at the corner store to get the last ingredients for dinner. Some people had fled Segovia because of the threats, but the rest tried to continue their normal lives. As it was in much of Colombia, these civilians were seasoned war veterans, accustomed to living with their fears.

From Vladimir's intelligence work and subsequent map, the paramilitaries knew where to find their victims. The three trucks slid slowly through the streets. Some men wore camouflage; others dressed in civilian clothes. They were heavily armed with AK-47s, R-15s, 9mms, and grenades. Their slow pace reflected their confidence that neither the police nor the army would interrupt their work. This was a bomb, but they weren't going to be rushed into dropping it.

One of the first trucks stopped at a popular bar and grill. The Johny Kay was full that night. Its clients were mostly miners. Vladimir and his paramilitary cohorts had pegged the workers as guerrilla sympathizers and UP supporters, and the grim reaper had arrived. One of the paramilitaries rolled a grenade into the bar. The explosion sent glass, tables, and bodies flying. Then several paramilitaries hopped out with R-15s and began indiscriminately pumping rounds into the clients. Some of the miners hit the ground and played dead. Others were dead. "I had to stay still and try not to drown in the blood of my colleagues," one Johny Kay survivor told the newspaper *El Tiempo*. "I knew that if I moved I was dead."

Down the road, the other two cars headed for different targets. On the streets Vladimir qualified as "UP," they went door to door. A man, his wife, his two kids, and his niece were shot while watching *The Fall Guy*. Minutes later the man's brother and his brother's wife were shot dead on the street. One of the paramilitaries shouted, "We're from the P!" as he fired his machine gun into the air. Paramilitaries moved through the town's central plaza and busted down some doors before firing at more civilians fleeing the scene. They killed a seventy-seven-year-old man in a wheelchair, a ten-year-old girl riding her bicycle, and a twenty-year-old woman who had gone to get some garbage bags from the store.

"We heard the gunfight," one witness told the Communist weekly, *Voz*, afterward. "We closed the doors, and we screamed, 'Hit the floor! Hit the floor!' We all started to pray, 'My God. What's happening?' Then we heard them knocking on the door, 'Open up you sons-a-bitches, or we'll kill you.' And they busted open the door. First they killed my father. They plucked him out of bed, and they blew his head off. My oldest brother said to them, 'You already killed him. Don't kill anybody else.' But they killed him too. My other brother told me to save myself so I climbed up into the attic with my nieces. That's when they threw a grenade at my brother. It was a grenade because everything was destroyed.

"After they killed my father and my brothers, they kept going. In another house, they killed a couple that was watching TV. One guy who went outside to ask about his son was also killed. A little boy who was carrying some food to his dad got it as well. A couple of girls that were in the street were also murdered. Everyone they saw they killed."

By the time the paramilitaries sped away, forty-three people were dead, another thirty-eight injured. Bodies were strewn across the town. Some lay under tables in pools of their own blood. Others were pressed along the side-walks, their hats blown off from the impact of the bullets. One man lay crumpled at a corner of a building, while a dead woman huddled over her seat on the bus. Another man looked as if he was shot just before he got through a door to take cover.

In all, the paramilitaries spent nearly an hour in Segovia. Witnesses said the police did nothing during that entire time, even though the station is about 150 yards from the Johny Kay, where the massacre began. The army was noticeably absent as well. "There are a lot of doubts, a lot of questions," UP mayor Rita Ivonne Tobón told the newspaper *El Espectador* by telephone that night. "It's very strange that the army, who is always patrolling [the streets], wasn't today. My police bodyguards also didn't show up for work today, nor did they give a reason why."

Fifteen minutes after the paramilitaries left town, the police surveyed the damage. Then the army arrived. One army officer was overheard saying, "It's all done." For their part, the paramilitaries sped past army checkpoints on their way to Puerto Berrío, where a celebration awaited them. They had done their job. They had dropped the A-bomb on Segovia. Some Segovians were shot because they worked with the party; others were killed because they allowed the UP to run the municipality. Others died simply because they were in the way of the bullets or the grenades. Either way, the warning was the same: With the UP in power, the town will suffer.

"I don't know how long we can take it," a distraught Mayor Tobón told *El Espectador*. "I don't what we're going to do tomorrow or what measures we can take. I only know that I will have to have strength, courage, serenity, know-how, [and] resistance to confront this situation. For the moment, we will continue to keep a close eye on the situation. I know that I should face it, and I will."

CHAPTER 10

THE *PERESTROIKAS*

From the moment they first met, Bernardo Jaramillo and Mariella Barragán talked about death. As the two drove to the beach in her beat-up Honda Accord, he casually mentioned that he and all his colleagues were probably going to die. Maybe he was trying to impress this woman who he wanted to sleep with. But for Mariella, it was less about seduction than insecurity. Behind the couple were several cars full of bodyguards. There were fifteen armed men in all. They were assigned to protect Bernardo, the president of the UP and arguably the most threatened man in the country.

Once at the beach, the two strolled hand in hand chatting aimlessly under the stars. The bodyguards followed. The couple had been introduced just a few hours before, but Mariella felt she had known Bernardo her whole life. "We understood each other immediately," she told me later. "It doesn't happen all the time, so you know when it does." She had seen him on television, and then suddenly he had arrived for a conference in her hometown, the coastal city of Barranquilla. The UP organized a party afterward, where he grabbed her during a steamy salsa. "He was charismatic," she said. "He had a presence. He was a leader."

He was also a lady's man. Standing just over six feet tall, with curly hair and a thick mustache, the women called him "*bizcocho*" or "sweetie." He liked his role and played up his romantic side without shame. He wrote poems and recited them to his admirers. He listened to and sang Cuban *boleros* and Argentinean *tangos*. "He was *cursi* [corny]," one ex-lover told me. "But he was one of those guys who could get away with it." Bernardo had been married and had two children. But his trysts continued, and by the time he met Mariella, he was separated and living every moment as if it was going to be his last. So the two of them, bodyguards in tow, walked the beach and talked about life and death. It was the beginning of something special.

When Bernardo sought Mariella's attention, he was thirty-three, a baby by political standards. Yet he found himself in an unenviable position. Following the brutal murder of Jaime Pardo Leal in October 1987, the UP had designated him as its president. The young leader had high political aspirations, so the decision to become party president at such a young age was a difficult one. Almost from the beginning, he understood that if he accepted, his fate would be the same as Pardo's. How do you think you're going to die, one reporter asked Bernardo shortly after Pardo's funeral. "They're going to kill me," he responded without hesitation, "on any corner, at any moment. It could even be in my house. I know they're going to kill me."

At the same time, Bernardo didn't shy away from death. Like other would-be martyrs in the UP, he embraced the thought of becoming immortalized. Do you think that dying for your country is valiant, the same reporter asked. "Yes, definitely," he responded. "In this way, I'm profoundly *Bolivariano*. We have the example of the Liberator, who was condemned to death for serving the government. Bolívar died trying to avoid a worse situation. We also have the example of Pardo Leal, who died struggling for peace and democracy."

In the early nineteenth century, Simón Bolívar had led a massive territory, stretching from Peru to Venezuela, to independence from Spain. Bolívar died trying to keep that territory together. Schools across Latin America immortalized the leader. Streets, towns, and provinces bore his name. But beginning in the 1970s, leftists and guerrilla groups in Colombia and other parts of Latin America began co-opting his legacy and his message, "He who serves the revolution plows the sea." By Bernardo's time, Bolívar had become more than the Liberator, he had become the Colombian Communists' Jesus Christ. No one hesitated to evoke his name in a spiritual vain, especially when it concerned death and martyrdom. Not surprisingly, Bernardo mentioned him all the time.

Things might have been very different for Bernardo. He was a bohemian, a partyer from a middle-class family in Manizales, a city in the heart of the coffee belt in central Colombia. His father even entertained offers to work in the United States and asked Bernardo if he would like go to *gringo-landia* with him. "Had my *papi* gone to the States," he once confided in a friend, "I would have been pro-Yankee." The thought made him laugh.

Bernardo was "saved" by the Communist Youth organization, the JUCO, a friend explained to me later. He quickly became a radical student leader in the state university in Manizales, where he was studying law. After finishing school, some of his comrades went to the mountains and joined the FARC. Bernardo, however, went to Urabá, the banana-growing region in northern

Colombia, where he opened a law office. There Bernardo put his new Communist comrades to work and used his country boy charm to quickly gain the locals' trust.

Like former UP president Jaime Pardo, Bernardo was good at drawing people to the UP. He had a sense of humor and laughed a lot. An old friend described him as "one of the boys." He played cards, drank beer, and poked fun at everyone. He loved soccer, although he wasn't a very good player himself. And his charisma at the podium brought in hundreds of new party supporters. In Urabá, Bernardo was their undisputed leader. In 1986, he was elected to congress, and under his guiding hand, the banana-growing region turned into a powerful UP bastion. The party filled dozens of town council positions and, by 1988, had elected a mayor in the unofficial capital city of the area, Apartadó.

As it was with Meta and the Eastern Plains, the UP's surge in Urabá troubled the traditional political and economic elite. Urabá is Colombia's banana-growing capital. Dole and Chiquita as well as a smattering of midsize Colombian producers dominate the local economy. Their bright green plantations stretch for miles on both sides of Apartadó and up toward the northern coast. Urabá also has a strong contingent of cattle farmers who supply some of the country's most savory beef. Both the FARC and the Maoist-inspired Popular Liberation Army (EPL) guerrillas vied for control over these resources and the money that came from taxing them. Each rebel group set up a banana-growers' union to pressure the companies. When the UP emerged, it appeared that the FARC was gaining the upper hand in the political battle against its rebel rivals.

The militant attitude of UP leaders only made it worse. At the time, Bernardo was a serious and uncompromising Communist and openly pro-FARC. "I think the FARC's presence has given credibility to the electoral process," he told the *Washington Post* after the 1986 elections, "and made people feel secure about electing whom they want." Bernardo believed in the rebels' project and the Communists' strategy of *la combinación de todas las formas de lucha*—fighting for power through politics and guerrilla war at the same time.

Just three months after he took over the UP, he wrote an editorial in the Communist Party weekly, *Voz*, titled "Combining All Forms of Struggle." He remained defiant to the press as well. "They [the deaths] at least prove we're growing," he told the *New York Times* after Jaime Pardo's murder. "If we were weak, no one would bother with us." On the first anniversary of Pardo's death, Bernardo gave a rousing speech over his grave during which he applauded the "heroic fight of the guerrillas." His strong opinions put him at odds with others who believed the *combinación* strategy was a huge failure. They sought his ear, but it would take several more months for them to get through to him.

Bernardo was an uncompromising boss. He would yell at his colleagues and underlings if they didn't get it right. He was often heard saying things like, "Don't screw it up" and "Get the fuck out of here with that shit." He had a good memory and rarely accepted when others didn't. Bernardo pushed his colleagues to do things they might not have otherwise. They accepted him and his faults; then they followed him into battle. It was a pattern that would repeat itself, even when the enemy became the Communist Party and the FARC.

As UP president, Bernardo's greatest concern was the nascent party's survival. Following the slaying of Jaime Pardo, the killings of UP members had continued unabated. In 1987, 111 militants were reported murdered. In 1988, that number increased to 276, and in 1989, 138. And these were only the reported deaths. The real number was thought to be much higher. The target areas were the same: regions where the party had emerged triumphant. The UP's momentum had continued through 1988. In the country's first mayoral elections that year, the party elected sixteen mayors. The mayors, it had been determined, would manage their own finances. But the killers didn't wait to find out what their policies were. Three were killed in 1988. Security increased, but it was like putting a finger in a ruptured dike. The dead just kept squirting through the gaps.

One of the first things Bernardo did as UP president was to obtain more protection for his party. After Jaime Pardo was assassinated, the UP signed an agreement with the government so that the president's special police force, known as the *Departamento Administrativo de Seguridad* or DAS, would provide extra security and arm and train UP bodyguards. The DAS brought UP recruits to its shooting range and taught them the basics of surveillance and marksmanship. It was this type of arrangement that made Colombia unique—DAS agents had and would be implicated in crimes against the party. Now they were protecting and training the very people who were their targets. But the agreement got stranger still: The military, an even more aggressive UP enemy, provided the party's bodyguards with many of their weapons.

The newly trained UP bodyguards fanned out to the areas hit the hardest by the repression. The UP in Urabá had a new standing army virtually overnight, as did the UP in the Eastern Plains. For his part, the UP district attorney in the city of Villavicencio, Josué Giraldo, got two permanent bodyguards. Until his death nine years later, he would never know the feeling of being free from the "protection" the government had dutifully provided during those first tumultuous years.

"I hate having these guys with me all the time," Josué would remark later. "It's like I have no privacy left." The guards accompanied Josué on his first date with his future wife and through the birth of his two daughters. "They [the guards] are part of your family and circle of friends to a suffocating degree," he complained. "Although they don't say anything, they're a constant reminder that death is near."

But in a sense, Josué was lucky. He only had two bodyguards. Bernardo had ten to fifteen at all times. Others had five or six. Still others hated or distrusted them so much that they refused to have any at all. They were going to play the odds—and why not? Despite the new and improved protection, UP members kept falling at a horrific rate. One of them, José Antequera, died in the presence of a plethora of state security agents. Antequera was shot in the airport as he stood talking to another heavily armed Liberal Party member, Ernesto Samper. Samper was wounded in the attack. The bodyguards seemed to be everywhere when you didn't need them and nowhere when you did.

One of the hardest areas to protect the UP was the capital, Bogotá, where offices and party leaders were spread throughout a city the size of New York. There the thankless job of organizing security for Bernardo and the UP fell to Sebastián González, the same FARC *político* who had set up *Juntas Patrióticas* in the coffee belt during the first days of the new party back in 1984. The FARC had sent Sebastián to Bogotá because of a leg condition— one of his calf muscles was atrophying. The orthodox revolutionary wasn't happy with the decision, but rebel leaders assured him he could do them more good in the city helping the new party. Eventually, he took on the job with the same gusto that he took to the bottle.

Sebastián began by assigning thirty guards every night to the party's headquarters in downtown Bogotá. They were a hodgepodge group—a mixture of trained UP bodyguards, FARC militia, and civilians. Their sheer mass made an attack on the headquarters difficult, and so they spent much of their spare moments finding ways to kill time. Between guarding the doors, the street corners, and the back alleys, they cooked huge stews for some early morning feasts and told dirty jokes.

Sebastián also gave out guns to the secretaries, administrators, and UP militants. The staff stashed these weapons in their desks or behind their file cabinets. When they mistakenly put them in their pocketbooks, he would scold them. "By the time you find that thing underneath all your cosmetics, you're dead," Sebastián would say to the frightened secretaries. He would also drill them. When they least expected it, he would arrive at the office and bust down the door. Sometimes he blew a whistle; sometimes he shot his gun in the air. The administrators would then pull out their weapons and take a defensive stance behind their file cabinets or next to a copy machine. "No, *compañera*," he would say during the drill. "Not *under* the desk."

The training didn't help. In fact, it made many of them more nervous. During one exercise, a visiting student intern dove for cover and broke her heels. During another, a secretary in the office pissed herself at the crack of Sebastián's gun. The place felt like a ticking time bomb, and the real harassment never ceased. There were constant rumors of a police raid, and every day there were threatening phone calls. The voice on the other end varied, but the message didn't: "We're going to cut out your tongues, you fuckin' guerrillas" was one of their favorites. They also sent letters that they signed "Death to Revolutionaries" or "Death to Communists." One time, an emboldened and angry UP member grabbed the phone from a secretary who was obviously fielding a nasty call and screamed, "How many are you, you fucker? Why don't you come down here and fight, you fucker?"

Bravado aside, the paramilitaries' tactics were working. Inside the office, no one stood by the windows. When a motorcycle—the assassins' vehicle of choice—drove by, people would dive to the floor. When they heard the motorcycle take a different route, they would breathe a sigh of relief. Outside the office, things were worse. UP members putting up campaign posters would establish a security ring. One party supporter told me that she and a group were plastering flyers on a wall when a person in the security ring let out a yell because she heard some motorcycles. Everyone dove into the bushes, she said. The caravan, however, turned out be a bunch of decommissioned motorcycles that the police were hauling to the stockyard.

The UP members tried to tough it out. "To hide meant you'd already lost, that they'd won," one former party supporter told me. "*Ni por el más, ni por el menos, ni por las putas retrocedemos*," or "Not in the good and not in the bad, not for anything, we will turn back," they would shout at marches. But the victims kept pouring in. Every day, there were more refugees from far-flung villages and visits from walking ghosts. One day, a UP militant would be there in the office talking to the administrators and politicians. The next day, he would be in the morgue, and the UP would be collecting money for his funeral. The office staff was a wreck; morale sunk. Workers would go to the cafés, smoke cigarettes, drink coffee, and commiserate for hours. At night, they would congregate in one of their apartments, look at photos of their dead colleagues, listen to Cuban *trova* from Pablo Milanés and Silvio Rodríguez, drink rum, and then cry. They were self-destructing.

Inevitably, the repression changed people's perceptions of the FARC. Many complained that the rebels weren't doing anything to stop the killing. "When they started murdering us," one UP militant told me later, "we all asked ourselves, 'Why didn't they give us military training?' and 'What are they doing? We're being killed, and what are they doing?' Nothing was the answer. It was like everyone was waiting for us to respond. People started to get angry with them [the rebels]. When the paramilitaries killed a mayor, people thought that we [the FARC] would take a town or have some kind of military response. 'Why don't they take care of the *compañeros* in the countryside?' we'd ask. 'They're getting killed and we don't do anything. And we're the ones putting up the dead.'"

Inevitably, the radical side of the party emerged with a solution. UP security coordinator Sebastián González and some others proposed killing ten "members of the establishment" for every one UP member killed. "If the enemy is in the political struggle, that's where we should be," he told me later. "If they're filling us with lead, we have to fill them with lead. The Christian thing about turn the other cheek doesn't work here." Sebastián told me the FARC should have taken out "a political leader, a military guy from their side, a representative of the church, and [one] of the economic conglomerate for every dead UP militant." He saw the rebels as the party's savior, the solution to the problem.

Not everyone agreed with Sebastián. Chief among them was UP president Bernardo Jaramillo.

It's difficult to say exactly what caused Bernardo to begin questioning his own beliefs with regard to the FARC and the Communist Party strategy of *la combinación de todas las formas de lucha*. Some of his colleagues and friends I spoke with pointed to his experience in Urabá. In the mid-1980s, the war in Urabá heated up quicker than in most other places in Colombia. The army stepped up its campaign to rid the area of the guerrillas. The FARC and the EPL responded in kind. Combat was frequent and bloody. Bernardo witnessed some of it.

"He was frustrated at the war," a friend of his explained to me later. "He mentioned a battle that left one person crippled for life with only the ability to speak. 'It makes me tired,' he said, 'to think that we're going to fight and all we're going to leave are people like her.' He woke up with nightmares. 'I know they're going to kill me,' he would say. He felt very old even though he was only thirty-three. He was resigned to his fate, though. He couldn't change his role. He couldn't go back."

After a while, Bernardo began to see the war and himself in a different light. The revolution and, more importantly, the revolutionaries weren't what he thought. In private, he started to question the guerrillas' methods: kidnappings, extortion, and executions. More essentially, he questioned their motives. It didn't happen immediately, but the militant FARC supporter was becoming more anti-war everyday.

While in congress, Bernardo met other senators and congressmen whose logic began to mesh with his own. He became less orthodox. He talked about inclusion, about forming a big party. For the first time, he didn't think of the UP as a tool but as an end, and he believed the new party could make a difference. Some of his colleagues did as well. They encouraged the new Bernardo to branch out, to look at other models, and to visit other countries.

In 1988, about a year after taking over as the UP president, Bernardo made a historic trip to Europe that would change his life forever. At the time, Mikhail Gorbachev had launched perestroika, and the Communist bloc was beginning to come apart. The statues were falling, as was the "truth" Communists had believed their whole lives. The old heroes—Lenin and Stalin, in particular—were the new villains across the Soviet Union and Eastern Europe. For the Communist Party in Colombia, this was hard to accept. In Colombian Communist Party circles, Lenin was a God and Stalin was his messenger; from Lenin, the party had deciphered its duplicitous strategy, *la combinación de todas las formas de lucha*, while Stalin had provided the party with structure and discipline.

Bernardo traveled to the Soviet Union, East Germany, Poland, Romania, and Czechoslovakia, where he saw these legends challenged in the streets, at the bars, and on television. He met with Communist dissidents and political reformers. They all told him the same thing: "Real Socialism," as they called it, was dead. At first, the UP president thought he might die with it. "When the things that we fight for and believe in, in what we've always believed in, dissolve into the reality of our world, men seem to find, almost happily, death," he wrote in his diary at the time. "Bolívar did it," he continued, conjuring up his favorite martyr again. "His deception about everything that was going on around him led him to a rapid death, although not a very easy one. We continue to hang on to life tenaciously even when she hides."

The reference to Bolívar's death troubled some of his friends, but Bernardo wasn't the type to stay depressed or suicidal. As he went from country to country, he met with leaders who drew hope from the situation. They didn't see theirs as the end, but as a new beginning. The discussions inspired Bernardo to return to the basics and search for what he was fighting for as well. "It's not that there's a crisis in the science that Marx taught us," he said later. "There's a crisis in the model that they wanted to sell us." Communism in Colombia *was* dead, he thought.

Following his trip to Europe, Bernardo was a different person. His needs as UP president were changing, and he was thinking long-term. As much as anything else, his relationship with Mariella symbolized his dramatic political shift. Just a year before, Mariella probably wouldn't have caught his attention. She was attractive, to be sure, with curly hair she put in a light perm that sometimes rose several inches above her head. But she was 100 percent *burguesía*, a lawyer from an upper-middle-class family in the coastal city of Barranquilla. In contrast, Bernardo's previous girlfriend was a staunch UP militant from the embattled banana-growing region of Urabá.

Although Mariella considered herself center-left, she had had no party affiliations prior to joining the UP. But she was the type of person the UP had drawn into its fold over the previous four years. They were young, energetic, and idealistic. Most of all, they were anti-war. It wasn't long before they clashed with the Stalinist sector of the Communist Party. This new group of outsiders questioned the hard-line, orthodox Communists and the way the Communist Party had tried to envelop the UP to make it its own. These new members pushed for a new movement that embraced the electoral process as a means for change, not simply as a tool in the larger guerrilla battle. *La combinación de todas las formas de lucha* didn't resonate with them; it was a poorly thought out and dangerous strategy, they believed. They were social democrats in the European style that Bernardo had seen in his recent trip. The perestroika within the UP began with them; then it touched Bernardo.

Internally, Bernardo slowly began to challenge the Communist Party's theories about the *combinación*. He wasn't alone. Several Communist Party and UP members, including the former FARC militia and UP propaganda chief Álvaro Salazar and the Communist Party stalwart turned UP senator Alberto Rojas Puyo, became some of his staunchest allies. Some of these allies, like Rojas Puyo, had questioned the *combinación* for years and would continue to do so at UP meetings and private Communist Party functions. Others, like Salazar, had come to the same conclusion as Rojas Puyo only after traveling with Bernardo to Europe, where the two saw the old Communist system challenged firsthand.

Soon the battle lines were drawn: The *Perestroikas*, as they became known, were Bernardo's clan; the *ortodoxos* or orthodox were the Communist Party hard-liners. For a while, combat between the two would take place in private meetings. But before long, the conflict would spill onto the pages of the newspapers.

The *Perestroikas* had a long road ahead of them. The base of the UP remained the Communist Party, and Communist leaders weren't happy with the shift in Bernardo's politics. In Urabá, for instance, Bernardo's old colleagues in the Communist Party told their militants to stop supporting the UP. In other areas, the Communist Party began openly defying UP leaders' orders. The Communist Party's position put UP leaders like Bernardo in a bind. If the *Perestroika* leaders like Bernardo alienated the Communist Party, they risked losing much of their organizational support network. If they didn't denounce the old strategy of the *combinación*, however, they risked losing the newer members—the Mariellas, the ones who made up the core of the growing *Perestroika* movement. What's more, Bernardo had a personal dilemma: He was in the executive committees of both the UP and the Communist Party.

At first Bernardo tried to persuade his counterparts to change. He met with the guerrilla leaders in Europe and asked them to reconsider their positions on kidnapping and bombing oil pipelines. Back at home, he fought with Communist Party leaders about their unwavering support of these actions, which he saw as antithetical to the fight to win the support of the masses. But when neither the FARC nor the Communist Party listened to Bernardo, he took his arguments to the public.

Bernardo's first outburst occurred in the city of Ibagué, in the province of Tolima, not far from where the FARC had fought off the army during its assault on the "independent republics" twenty-five years before. It was February 1989, only four months after Bernardo had given his own rousing pro-FARC speech over Jaime Pardo's grave. The UP leadership, which was a mixture of *Perestroikas* and *ortodoxos*, was attending a conference on peace. Behind closed doors, the two sides waged a fierce debate over kidnapping. Communist Party hard-liners still refused to condemn the guerrillas. They called kidnapping "retention" when they even admitted that it was occurring at all. The *Perestroikas* couldn't accept this position, and in perhaps his most famous public discourse, Bernardo let the hard-liners know it.

"The guerrilla movement must take definitive steps to improve the possibility of peace," he told the audience, which roared with applause. "We believe that attacks against pipelines, energy pylons, and various centers of production in this country do not contribute to peace for Colombians. We're also convinced that kidnapping and extortion aren't part of the political struggle, not here or any other place in Latin America."

The message was clear: Bernardo and the *Perestroikas* wanted a complete break from the FARC. Many thought the speech was a new dawning for the UP, an end to the dogmatic days, a "Prague Spring" in Colombia. But as in

Czechoslovakia in 1968, it was really the beginning of the fight. Communist Party hard-liners and FARC leaders were startled and hurt by Bernardo's comments and began scheming to bring his *Perestroika* movement to an end.

By the time the UP had its national convention a few months later, the fight between the *Perestroikas* and the *ortodoxos* was getting ugly. On the surface, the convention was a stirring success. Hundreds of delegates representing a wide range of movements attended. By an overwhelming margin, the party selected Bernardo as the UP's presidential candidate. But behind the scenes, the Communist Party's ire had turned to jealousy and anger, and party hard-liners were looking to bring the FARC into the squabble. Following the convention, Communist leaders passed messages to the FARC's supreme council, the Secretariat, about graft in the UP leadership. Soon the rebels were asking to speak to Guillermo Banguero, the ex-FARC who had become the UP's treasurer and, not coincidentally, a *Perestroika*.

Banguero traveled to the rebels' base in the cold, barren mountains of Sumapaz with only a vague idea of what his mission was. He was told that he was simply going to give the FARC leaders a report card on the UP's national convention. But the pudgy former rebel knew how the FARC operated. Like the Mafia, the guerrilla leadership would only "call for you" if it meant trouble. Banguero's UP comrades turned white when they heard the news. Still, Banguero was confident the rebels weren't going to do anything drastic. He had maintained a strong relationship with FARC leaders like Alfonso Cano, the "intellectual half-timer" commander. The two had joined the FARC around the same time and had a similar philosophical approach to the war. When Banguero arrived in Sumapaz, Cano let him stay for a couple of weeks at his small ranch. The two talked night and day and strengthened their bond while Banguero waited for FARC commander Jacobo Arenas to arrive.

It was a long wait. Arenas was far away and would take several weeks to get to Sumapuz. From his discussions with Cano over the next few days, Banguero found out that Arenas was angry with the UP. Surprisingly, the new party's unexpected success had put Arenas in a difficult position. The UP had been Arenas's baby, but the FARC commander no longer controlled the party. The *Perestroikas* put an exclamation point on this fact: They were chastising the guerrilla war, denouncing their former masters in public. They were also pushing the FARC to question their own fight against the state. Arenas knew that there was nothing more dangerous to a guerrilla group than a democratic revolt from within.

Since the new party had begun its rise in the polls, Arenas had also become jealous of the UP leaders' success, which sometimes came at a cost to his own popularity. Of the men that Arenas had sent from the FARC to help organize the new party, two major leaders had deserted the rebels: Banguero and Álvaro Salazar. It was the final slap in the face, and Arenas took out his anger on his former prodigy, Braulio Herrera. The results were catastrophic.

After the peace talks between the FARC and the government ended, a bitter and jealous Arenas had chastised Herrera in rebel gatherings in Sumapaz before sending him to do the impossible: reconquer the Middle Magdalena Valley. Paranoia, already a dominant feature in Herrera's life, became his centering force. When things got difficult in the Middle Magdalena Valley, he snapped and took on his entire unit. His pendulum, once a source of good, became a random determinant of life and death. One accusation led to another. Before long, news reports were surfacing that Herrera had killed more than one hundred of his own soldiers. Following the murders, the FARC Secretariat had called for Herrera, but with the Communist Party's help, the ex-congressman and UP leader had fled the country.

UP leader Guillermo Banguero, however, couldn't escape. He was already stuck in the camp and waiting for Arenas. The FARC commander soon arrived with an angry air about him. That afternoon, Banguero shyly entered Arenas's farmhouse and told him he was there to give him a report card on the UP's convention. "Who the fuck told you you were here to do that?" Arenas shot back. "You're here because of some problems with money." Banguero took a deep breath. Corruption was punishable by death in the FARC, so he tried to explain himself. When Banguero mentioned UP president Bernardo Jaramillo, Arenas snapped, "That son-of-a-bitch."

The rest of the meeting continued in the same tone—Banguero making motions to explain himself and Arenas shouting insults at him and the rest of the *Perestroikas*. Soon Banguero realized that the accusations were about more than missing money. Arenas didn't really care about the graft. For the FARC commander, the issue was much larger. Bernardo, Álvaro Salazar, and all the rest of the *Perestroikas* had committed the worst crime of all: treason.

As the notion dawned on him that he was really being held prisoner by his former rebel group, Banguero took a defiant attitude. After his meeting with Arenas, Banguero's friend, FARC commander Alfonso Cano—who he now suspected was the only person keeping him alive—tried to give him a way out by offering him "reeducation" and "retraining." But Banguero refused. He just waited for the verdict so he could die with dignity.

In Bogotá, the UP's wheels were spinning. When Banguero didn't return from his trip, Salazar suspected what was happening and went to the

Communist Party. Communist Party leaders told Salazar that "Banguero was a member of the FARC, and what the rebels did with him was their business." Salazar thought it through but saw no easy way out of the situation. He and the other *Perestroikas* were only now beginning to realize the consequences of their actions. The FARC was angry and, if necessary, was willing to attack the *Perestroikas*.

After a few weeks in captivity, Banguero sent a message to his wife telling her to vacate the apartment. Salazar, who lived with the couple, took that to mean that he was in danger as well. Indeed, the Communist Party hard-liners were themselves conferring and moving toward increasingly radical solutions to the *Perestroikas*. When one of them proposed killing Salazar, Sebastián González, the UP's security coordinator, volunteered for the job. The idea was eventually discarded, but the possibility lingered.

Meanwhile, Salazar sought to get his friend Banguero out of FARC confinement. In an act of desperation, he sent a letter to the country's largest daily, *El Tiempo*, explaining the situation. The newspaper printed the account, and the FARC was forced to release Banguero. Shortly thereafter, Salazar and Banguero fled the country.

It was a defining moment for the UP. What had begun as an internal battle for control over the party's direction and strategy had suddenly turned dangerous. Many, like UP president Bernardo Jaramillo, believed they could eventually win the internal battle. But the external battle, the one to convince the public and their enemies of their break with the FARC, would be much more difficult. To do this, Bernardo had to keep speaking out publicly against the rebels and against the Communist Party's strategy of *la combinación de todas las formas de lucha*. But the time to explain himself was running out, and not even his phalanx of bodyguards could protect him from what was to come. Bernardo was moving to the middle, the deadly middle.

CHAPTER 11

THE HOUSE OF CASTAÑO

During those first bloody years, the UP simply tried to survive the onslaught. But there was no clear strategy on how to deal with the attacks. The killings were happening so often that the party was left constantly off balance. Some party militants eventually took refuge, but many others stuck out their chests and waited for the bullets to come. Throughout, the party pressured the government to comply with the treaty it had signed with the FARC, the Uribe Agreement. "The Government, in accordance with the Constitution and the laws, will give the *Unión Patriótica* the guarantees and security it needs so that it can campaign as well as participate in elections in the same way other political parties do," the 1984 agreement read. "The government will use all the force of the law against any citizen or authority that inhibits these rights or denies, ignores, or refuses to recognize the rights that they [the members of the new party] have."

Of course, now that the peace process had ended, it wasn't clear whether this agreement was still valid. Still, the UP, in particular the burgeoning social democrats in the party, the so-called *Perestroikas*, made every effort to hold the government to its word. After all, the party remained legal, even if its former armed wing was now on the offensive against the state again.

During this time, UP president Bernardo Jaramillo and other party leaders met with members of the cabinet, military officers, diplomats, and anyone else they thought could slow the pace of the killing. Everyone shook hands, nodded heads, and said the right things: The government promised more protection; the army declared it would crack down on human rights abusers; and the diplomats said they would consider sanctions. But nothing ever happened. The UP kept falling, and the monster that was the paramilitaries kept growing. To slow the killing, the UP finally decided, someone else besides the government would have to stop these drug-financed death squads.

There were vicious paramilitaries in all parts of the country, but few could compare with those of José Gonzalo "*El Mejicano*" Rodríguez Gacha. The drug capo's power had risen steadily since he met with UP propaganda chief Álvaro Salazar in the Medellín hotel in 1986, and told Salazar the tale of the FARC attacks on his properties and business. Rodríguez Gacha boasted of an army of close to one thousand men now and saw no limits to the amount of wealth he could accumulate. By 1989, news outlets were saying he was the largest landowner in the country and that his men had murdered four hundred UP militants. The real number was probably much higher.

Bernardo Jaramillo figured there was only one man who could stop Rodríguez Gacha outside of the government, and that was Rodríguez Gacha's nominal boss, the mighty Pablo Escobar. Escobar was an enigma of sorts. The plump, curly-haired former car thief had become the biggest drug trafficker in the world due to a ruthless streak second only to that of Rodríguez Gacha's. But Escobar considered himself a leftist, a social democrat, much like Bernardo. Escobar's, however, was a piecemeal socialism; he was leftist in as much as it suited his needs. He handed out Christmas gifts to people in the small towns of the Middle Magdalena Valley, and he built soccer fields in the cities. But he was unpredictable. One month, he would give away hundreds of houses to poor Medellín families. The next month, he would set off a car bomb in the middle of a vibrant outdoor market or a bustling shopping mall. What's more, Escobar expected unquestioning loyalty in return for his favors. It was a dangerous bargain that put many innocent people on the firing line.

Still, given their political affinities, it was easy to set up an "encounter" between Bernardo and Escobar. They wanted to talk; maybe they could swap favors as well. Escobar eventually met with Bernardo at a large farmhouse just outside the city of Medellín in late 1988. Bernardo went with two bodyguards and a UP leader from Medellín. By all accounts, the meeting went from cordial to friendly in minutes. The two country boys felt at ease with one another. Escobar spoke Bernardo's leftist language; they were both "anti-oligarchy" and "anti-*gringo*," a fact that the drug dealer would try to use to his advantage. And they were both concerned about their safety.

Escobar was worried about being extradited to face trial on drug charges in the United States. In 1987, Colombian and U.S. officials had shipped Escobar's long time colleague, Carlos Lehder, to Miami, where Lehder received a life sentence. The kingpin's greatest fear was that he would rot in a jail cell right next to Lehder. In UP president Bernardo Jaramillo, Escobar had found an ally. The UP's position was clear: no extradition, because it compromised the country's sovereignty and made a mockery of the Colombian justice system.

In Escobar, Bernardo thought he'd found an ally as well, someone who could slow the slaughter of his political party. The UP president pushed the drug lord to mediate between the party and Rodríguez Gacha. The killing was draining the UP of the little life it had left, Bernardo told Escobar. And he needed the right wing to stop its killing so he could focus on battling the radical left wing of the UP, the orthodox faction of the Communist Party and the FARC. Escobar said he agreed with Bernardo—that the right wing needed to stop punishing the UP for the rebels' crimes—and said Rodríguez Gacha was being unreasonable. He would talk to Rodríguez Gacha, Escobar told Bernardo. At the end of the meeting, the two parted on what seemed like good terms.

But afterward, the killings of UP militants continued unabated, and the party continued to struggle with the paramilitary problem. Worse yet, it seemed that someone wanted to punish the UP for meeting with Escobar. In a curious case, Bernardo's own bodyguards disappeared as they drove from the Medellín encounter between Bernardo and Escobar. A paramilitary later testified that the two men were stopped along the road, pulled into the jungle, tortured, and cut into pieces before being thrown into a river. The UP politician who had accompanied Bernardo to the Escobar meeting was also killed—shot dead in Medellín shortly afterward. Suspicions rose about Escobar's possible involvement in both these murders, and when the drug kingpin called Bernardo to have another meeting, the UP president decided to send the experienced and battle-tested Álvaro Salazar in his place.

At the time, the UP propaganda chief was probably the only person qualified to meet with Escobar. Salazar was Bernardo's trusted ally in the UP as well as the party's unofficial mediator. He knew how the FARC, the Communist Party, and the UP worked. He had also been in touch with the conflict between the UP and the paramilitaries from the beginning. He had even met with the crazed Rodríguez Gacha in order to head off the fight before it started. Now, he would have another chance to slow the carnage.

In late 1989, about the time that the UP was declaring Bernardo its presidential candidate for the following year's elections, Salazar traveled to Puerto Triunfo, the dusty cattle town in the heart of the Middle Magdalena Valley where Escobar had his luxurious *Hacienda Napoles* and opulent zoo. There some heavily armed men picked Salazar up and drove him along the edge of the ranch toward the Magdalena River until they came to a small, simple farmhouse. After a few minutes, a beefy, beleaguered, and bearded Escobar showed up with about fifteen bodyguards.

Escobar and Salazar entered the farmhouse, where they talked until the early evening. They didn't drink or smoke marijuana—an Escobar trademark—but the drug trafficker was an amiable host. Escobar served his guest "*paisa*" food from Antioquia—sausages, eggs, *arepas*, and rice and beans—while the two discussed political parties, presidential candidates, the war on drugs, and the dirty war against the UP. As he did with Bernardo, the kingpin emphasized his left-wing credentials; he said he had been forced to take a right-wing attitude because of the government's position against him.

Then, Escobar told Salazar the truth about the UP's predicament: The party wouldn't have a problem with him, he insisted. The problem was with Rodríguez Gacha and Fidel Castaño. Fidel Castaño? Salazar inquired. Yes, Fidel Castaño. Escobar said he could convince Rodríguez Gacha to stop the war against the UP. Rodríguez Gacha's was an economic fight against the FARC because the rebel group had attacked him, Escobar said. The UP just happened to be an easier target. "But," Escobar warned, "Fidel is going to be a little tougher." It was only with time that Salazar understood what Escobar meant.

From the beginning, Fidel Castaño's fight was about more than money or drug routes or land. For Fidel, hatred of the UP began with a simple slip of paper. The year was 1980, four years before the FARC was to create its political party that would shock the country and challenge the traditional powers. Fidel's father, Jesús, had been kidnapped by the FARC rebels. The guerrillas were holding *Don* Jesús in the jungle near the Castaño's home in the mining village of Segovia. Some said they had tied the old man to a tree because he'd tried to escape.

Don Jesús was a stubborn Conservative, of the type only *La Violencia* could produce: Church and work were the house virtues; Liberals were the country's devil worshipers. The Castaño family head had built a modest cattle ranch on the backs of his twelve children. He had been nothing, if not a strong father and role model to his kids. "Our father was the town patriarch," Fidel's younger brother Carlos told me some years later when I met with him in his jungle hideout. "He was the judge at the cockfights. And if there was a problem between two people, he'd be the judge of that as well." *Don* Jesús was Carlos's hero, an example of integrity that Carlos would emulate. "He worked on the farm from six in the morning until five in the afternoon," Carlos told his biographer about his father. "The only thing he didn't do was pick up a machete."

Don Jesús made sure his oldest son, Fidel, understood the regime at the price of more than a few lashings. But in contrast to Carlos, Fidel didn't get along with his father. He was a rambunctious kid, a renegade who constantly irked *Don* Jesús and made it clear from an early age that he was going to live by his own rules. At sixteen, fed up with his father's authoritarian nature, Fidel left home. The next few years are somewhat of a mystery. By several accounts, Fidel went to Guyana and worked in the diamond mines. He also spent some time in Venezuela. He returned to Colombia some five years later, wealthier than his father. About this time, he also got involved in drug trafficking, emerald smuggling, and any other contraband he could easily transport in and out of the country. He was, as his younger brother Carlos later said, a first-rate entrepreneur, a businessman with a clear vision of what he wanted in life: money.

Now that he had it, though, he was forced to make a decision on how to use it. The FARC had been holding *Don* Jesús for several months. The rebels had asked for money once already, and Fidel had paid. They asked a second time, and he paid again. Now came the third time. A go-between slipped Fidel the piece of paper with the ransom notice, and Fidel exploded with rage.

"Fidel got us together," Carlos explained to me. "And he said, 'They're going to continue killing us.' And then I remember something very interesting that Fidel said. 'If you knew that after this we would have peace—well, what do you do? We figure it out and recover. But they're going to keep killing us; they're going to keep kidnapping us.'" Carlos paused. "War is horrible," he continued. "When it comes and knocks on your door, you have to confront it with whatever you have because when war isn't there, well, you have to have a little discussion: Do we go into it or do we not go into it? But when she's already come, and she's going to keep at it, not fighting it would be the worst mistake."

There would be no more ransoms, no more bullying, no more cowards. "Even if I had the money," Fidel wrote back, "I'd use it to fight you."

Don Jesús's body was never found.

So began the Castaño's endless war against the guerrillas, the Communist Party, and eventually the UP. Carlos, Fidel, and a handful of brothers and cousins—"The House of Castaño," as Carlos affectionately called it—became guides for the Colombian army. But when they located suspected guerrillas or collaborators, the army seemed to have little power to arrest or punish these people. So, Carlos explained to me, "We would get on our civilian clothes, grab our rifles or whatever, and—tan! tan! tan!—we would kill them." The Castaño cadre was relentless. The first to fall were *Don* Jesús's kidnappers, but the House of Castaño didn't stop there. One witness reported a weeklong killing spree in a neighboring province by men "dressed in ponchos, white hats and carrying new machetes, rifles, knives, pistols, and grenades." Dozens were killed, including women and children.

"The first year after they kidnapped my father, all I wanted was revenge," Carlos explained to me. "I wanted to destroy everything. At that time, the border between justice and vengeance was very difficult to decipher, very vague. . . . We killed a lot of civilians."

The Castaños' rampage had no end. Fidel, in particular, carried the family scourge to mythic levels that eventually earned him the nickname "Rambo," the Sylvester Stallone anti-hero of the Ronald Reagan era. Indeed, Fidel was the perfect Colombian warrior: a complicated blend of love and hate; a person who believed in God and revenge all at once; a loner whose battle against an unscrupulous enemy seemed as if it would never end. And when it came to the FARC and the UP, it didn't.

After the initial spate of vengeance, the family moved from the eastern foothills of Antioquia to the small, forgotten village of Valencia, in the coastal province of Córdoba. There, Fidel became the undisputed patriarch of the House of Castaño. In Valencia, Fidel moved easily in the rural setting, forged friendships quickly, and made an immediate impression on his neighbors. He was an "uncomplicated" person, the townspeople remembered when I visited them a number of years later, a man of the countryside. He owned a big ranch outside of town, but like them he dressed simply: a pair of jeans, boots, and a cowboy hat. He would greet everyone he saw on the roads with a smile and a strong handshake.

Fidel was about 5'10" and he was fit—built like a soldier with wide shoulders and a firm torso. He had a stern, serious face and kept his hair cropped short. His thin cheeks belied his age, and his soft eyes charmed the townspeople. "How are you?" he would say. "It's been a while." The locals glowed in his presence. He remembered their names and asked after their wives, their children, their businesses. "Whatever you need, you just come by the house," he always added at the end of the conversation. They didn't think of him as one of the country's biggest cattle ranchers, a drug trafficker, or a paramilitary chieftain. To them, he was simply "*Tío* Fidel."

Valencia is at the base of the Sinú Valley, a vast wetland that stretches up toward the mountains to the south and down toward the coast to the north. Aside from cattle ranchers like Fidel, the area was dirt poor. Valencia had a few dozen one-story houses and no paved roads. The local government was just putting in a plumbing system when I visited some years after Fidel had left the area. Two-foot-wide holes forced people to keep to the side of the road, while workers laid plastic tubes into the earth. A few donkeys roamed freely in the town market, and people walked the streets with the plodding pace of poverty.

To get to Valencia, I had to cross the torrential Sinú River in a rudimentary ferry that maintained its course only by attaching itself to two reinforced steel wires that stretched across the fast-moving muddy water. Fidel used to swim the river for exercise. A visitor once saw him dive into whirlpools that would suck the life from most. Fidel, of course, came up some twenty yards away and swam freestyle for another hour. He often complemented his swims with long jogs. And he was an avid chess player.

"He was always attacking, never on the defensive," one old compatriot who frequently played with Fidel told me. "And when he was waiting for me to move, he used to just sit there and say, 'I'm going to kill you. I'm going to kill you,' and tap the pieces on the table and whistle."

The two would play until Fidel had outmaneuvered his opponent in a sufficient number of matches. "Sometimes we'd play until eight or nine in the morning," his compatriot added. "He never lost."

Fidel's passion soon became land and the cattle that he put on it. He was part of an emerging class of nouveau riche in Colombia: drug traffickers who had found in land a perfect way to deposit their cash into something of value and, at the same time, achieve the social status that had eluded most of them. From the biggest to the smallest, the traffickers were buying land in vast quantities. It was the great narco-landgrab, and Fidel didn't miss any of it.

Following his move to Valencia in 1987, Fidel bought two large farms, which added to his holdings in the neighboring provinces of Chocó and Antioquia. Fidel's timing was impeccable. The municipality was controlled by leftist guerrillas. The mayor was from the UP. The other politicians and landowners did as the increasingly brash and aggressive guerrilla groups—the FARC and the Maoist-inspired EPL—said, paying an exorbitantly high tax to the "cause." Fidel's new neighbors were looking to sell their land at any price. Many had already fled the area. Sensing opportunity, Fidel bought more tracts of land, much of it in guerrilla-held territory. Then he went to work.

Fidel recruited a force of close to one hundred men and trained them on his farm, *Las Tangas*. The "*Tangueros*," as Fidel's force became known, eliminated suspected guerrillas and their supporters with startling efficiency. The UP mayor was killed in his ice-cream shop. Other dead began appearing on the sides of the road. When the shooting started on the streets, the neighbors would shut their doors and wait for it to end. Rumors swirled of a new regime, one without rebels and "guerrilla politicians" like the UP. Many welcomed the change. Those who didn't, left the region or died complaining about it. Valencia, once an area teeming with rebels, was "liberated" in months. The land value shot up, and the wise Fidel started to sell.

Fidel's genius for business and war was matched only by his lust for all things high-class. By the late 1980s, Fidel had started peddling black-market art, which he told an acquaintance was better than the illegal drug trade. He acquired only pieces he thought he could sell for at least a $50,000 profit. It wasn't hard. At the time, Colombia was a seller's market. Narcos longing for social acceptance were buying up expensive paintings, rare sculptures, and priceless statues, and Fidel quickly became their main supplier and most knowledgeable connoisseur.

Through art, Fidel also forged relationships with Colombia's and the world's cultural and economic elite. He learned English and French and traveled to galleries in New York and Paris, where he bought an apartment in a posh neighborhood. He had photographs of himself and Salvador Dalí, and he was said to own dozens of Fernando Botero's corpulent depictions of Colombians dancing, eating, and taking walks in the park. While abroad, he stayed in five-star hotels and dined at the best restaurants. Fidel was living a double life of the type only fictitious characters like Hannibal Lecter could match. One can imagine him splitting someone's head open with a machete one night and drinking a nice Chianti the next.

To be sure, Fidel remained a sizable drug trafficker and kingpin strongarm. And for a while, he brought some of his brothers in on his business deals. But things didn't always turn out as planned. In the early 1980s, bizarre reports surfaced that Klaus Barbie, the ex-Nazi turned narco, killed two of Fidel's brothers in Bolivia in a drug deal gone bad. Around the same time, Fidel's relationship with drugs changed. He may have dabbled a little in the illegal trade, but by the time he controlled Valencia in late 1980s, Fidel had outlawed cocaine-processing laboratories in his own territory. While he was happy to collect some of the proceeds, directly and indirectly, he didn't like the trouble that came with them: the police, the U.S. Drug Enforcement Administration, and the squabbles over money and drug routes. One of his fellow commanders told me that the few who disobeyed his order with regard to the labs paid for it with their lives. What's more, things were beginning to disintegrate around him, as were the *autodefensas*, or self-defense groups, and their drug financiers.

Inevitably, Escobar and Rodríguez Gacha's war against the government's extradition policy had become personal. In August 1989, narco-assassins gunned down the country's leading presidential candidate, the Liberal Party leader Luís Carlos Galán, as he was preparing to give a speech in a town just outside of Bogotá. Galán had been slowly tearing down the walls of Escobar's business and attacking the drug kingpin's legitimacy. The presidential hopeful had kicked Escobar out of his "New" Liberal Party in the early 1980s, and he was threatening to enforce an extradition order for him from the United States. UP militants had fallen in staggering rates over the previous three years. Hundreds of policemen, judges, and federal prosecutors had also been assassinated by the drug traffickers. Escobar had even killed a prominent newspaper editor and exploded a bomb in front of the paper's offices. But only with Galán's assassination did the country's elite finally take a stand against the narco-paramilitaries. Shortly after Galán was killed, President Virgilio Barco declared the *autodefensas* illegal and ordered the arrests of its top leaders.

Alonso de Jesús Baquero, better known as Black Vladimir, was one of the first major commanders to fall. In addition to his participation in the massacre of forty-three people in Segovia in 1988—most of them UP supporters—and a host of other heinous crimes, the hulking former FARC and his men, under orders from Rodríguez Gacha, had executed nine government investigators who were looking into a massacre in the Middle Magdalena Valley. Vladimir was captured shortly thereafter.

Other arrests followed, while the war between the government and the narcos picked up steam. "If total war must be waged," Escobar was quoted in the French newspaper *Libération* as saying, "we will do it until the end." Rodríguez Gacha's men placed a fifty-kiloton bomb in front of the headquarters of the presidential security guard, the *Departamento Administrativo de Seguridad* (DAS), in Bogotá. The entire face of the building was destroyed, but the intended target, the investigative unit's director, survived. The DAS bomb was but one of 150 drug traffickers exploded in the months following Galán's assassination. Another detonated on a commercial flight. One hundred seven people died when the plane crashed, and the entire country turned white with fear.

Internal rivalries were also beginning to tear the *autodefensas* apart. Rodríguez Gacha began fighting his former bosses in the emerald business. The "emerald war," as it became known, made for new alliances, and soon rival drug dealers began collaborating with the government to hunt down Rodríguez Gacha. With their help, police found and surrounded the drug capo at his hideout on the Atlantic Coast. During the ensuing chase, the police gunned down Rodríguez Gacha's son and surrounded *El Mejicano* in a wooden shack on the beach. The standoff didn't last long. Rather than surrender, Rodríguez Gacha kept fighting and was killed in a hail of police bullets. The UP's nemesis was dead. Unfortunately, its nightmare was not yet over.

Back in Valencia, "*Tío* Fidel" and his little brother Carlos continued to assassinate UP leaders in massive numbers. One of the nicknames Escobar gave

Fidel was "2000," for the number of UP members he'd allegedly killed. In his authorized biography, Carlos himself admits to killing "30 or 40 guerrillas outside of combat who were hidden in the UP." With the short work they were making of the guerrillas' fledgling political party, the two brothers were quickly emerging as the new leaders of the *autodefensas*. And surprisingly, it was Carlos, not Fidel, who was slowly becoming the head of the House of Castaño.

Carlos was a little guy, about 5'8", but a brutal warrior. He was only fourteen years old when his beloved father was killed by the FARC, and since then he had known nothing but war. Throughout the early years of the House of Castaño, Carlos worked for Fidel, mostly as a field operative. He was devastatingly effective, even in paramilitary terms. He assassinated people in their homes and on their way to work. When bullets were low, he buried people alive. Later he was trained by mercenaries in Israel in special ops. When he returned, he trained others in urban warfare. "I'm more agitated, more fiery, more vehement," Carlos said to me when I asked him to compare himself with his older brother some years later. When we spoke, Carlos squinted, sweated, gestured wildly with his hands, and talked with a raspy voice in a virtual scream.

"My brother was a lot more serene, a lot more calm without a doubt," Carlos continued. "He was cold in the way he thought. He wasn't as sensitive as me. He wasn't as spontaneous as me. He thought through things a lot more. He was very pragmatic. . . . In him, you would see more of the strategist who was at his desk with the plan, thinking of this, that, or the other. However, he wasn't a big student of the enemy—the culture, the idiosyncrasies of the enemy. Me, I look at the enemy: how he handles himself, where he comes from, where he was born, what he's like as a person. He was more a man of the countryside."

There were other differences. Fidel was a shadowy, secretive figure far more focused on protecting his ever-growing assets than on rescuing Colombia from the guerrillas' grip. Not surprisingly, it was Carlos who would transform the *autodefensas* into a large army and step forward as its public leader in later years. And it was Carlos who would relish the limelight, granting interviews, posing for photos, and being the protagonist in his own bestselling biography.

In the short term, however, Fidel remained the patriarch in the House of Castaño. While the narco-paramilitaries were fighting one another, Fidel and now his extended family from his farm, *Las Tangas*, tore through Valencia and parts of the banana-growing region of Urabá along the coast. In one particularly brutal massacre, the *Tangueros* sprayed a party with bullets, killing more than twenty people, many of them UP supporters. In another, one of his men told investigators, the *Tangueros* dragged some forty people from a neighboring village back to *Las Tangas*. There, they tortured them all night with crude instruments before shooting some and burying others alive.

Throughout his domain, Fidel inspired unparalleled loyalty. One man in the area, a political organizer for the paramilitaries who called himself "Churoto," told me Fidel would constantly challenge the people to defy the guerrillas: "'I need 150 men,' he would say. And sure enough, 150 men would arrive. Old men, teenagers, husbands, workers. They all came ready to fight.

"They should build a monument to Fidel," Churoto exclaimed. We'd had a few glasses of *aguardiente* at the bar where we were speaking. The bartender agreed, and everyone else around the table just nodded awkwardly.

Fidel ruled his fiefdom with an iron fist and a big heart. He gave away large tracts of land to local farmers and tried to establish cooperatives. Fidel also set up a grade school. When I visited, there was still a plaque outside the main entrance commemorating him as the school's founder. Inside the modern complex, the teachers taught physics, chemistry, and English. The school also had a library with a short wall full of books. It wasn't spectacular, but the school had more notebooks, test tubes, and basketballs than any school within a fifty-mile radius. More importantly, it tried to instill values, some of which Fidel could have used himself. Each classroom had a theme pasted above the door. "Love and Faithfulness," "Understanding," "Tolerance," and "Respect" were just a few.

"I should say that I had the honor to meet Fidel," a plump, jovial administrator named Lola Martínez told me as we walked into the library. "He was a great man, an intellectual. He was very nice and gave his life to humanitarian causes. He was one of those people who had a certain charisma." She paused, then added, "What did we learn from him? This sense of loving ourselves; this sense of feeling like we belong to something. And this is what we teach the kids at this school: the sense of belonging to this institution."

That institution was called The House of Castaño.

CHAPTER 12

THE *SUIZO*

Bernardo Jaramillo's assassin was a tall, lanky teenager named Andrés Arturo Gutiérrez. To commit his crime, Andrés assumed the name "Jaime Alberto Restrepo." His fake ID said he was born May 12, 1969, in the small rural village of Carolina, Antioquia. But Gutiérrez was sixteen, not twenty as his ID said. Far from a peasant farmer, he was a typical teen from a poor Medellín neighborhood who rarely left the city. Like his friends, he wore T-shirts and jeans just about every day. He had thick, overgrown lips and a thin mustache. Emulating the star soccer players of the time, he had a long mane of curly hair that stretched to his shoulders.

Andrés would carry the fake ID only once in his life. It was the one day he could be someone else—the one day he could escape from his own misery. Before that day, Andrés had dropped out of school and started caring for cars on the street. Later he had gotten work in a small factory, where he had earned minimum wage making chalk for pool sticks. Outside of work, he stayed active. He played soccer every Saturday. He also lifted weights, swam, and jogged at the park near his house. He dated a few girls and had a lot of friends. But Andrés was still unhappy. "He would come home with blisters on his hands," his father, Fabio de Jesús Gutiérrez, later testified. "But that's not what bothered him. What bothered him was how little money he made." *Don* Fabio was a poor ex-con whose lifestyle complicated his son's already tough circumstances. *Don* Fabio had served a few years in jail for falsifying documents and was unemployed. His wife worked, as did his eldest son, but *Don* Fabio always seemed to be angling for a new scheme to hustle his way through the day. He also liked the sauce. He admitted to investigators he enjoyed "eight or ten" drinks and a few cigarettes when he could.

Andrés's challenging habitat made him a perfect candidate for a "job," and the recruiters were ready to pounce. Some months before the assassination of Bernardo Jaramillo, Andrés was waiting for a friend, Yerry, in a Medellín cantina when a man unexpectedly approached him. "I recognize you," the encroacher said. "You don't know me," Andrés shot back. "I know you. I know your way of living," the older man continued. Andrés was confused. He had no idea who this person was. "I'm Joaquín," the man suddenly said. "I can see you come from a poor family," he continued. "Maybe you want to come work for me." "Doing what?" Andrés inquired. "It's easy work, and you can earn a lot of money," the man said to the youth. This, of course, piqued the teen's interest. "I'll have to think about it," Andrés said, trying to be cool. "Here. Take this. For a soda," Joaquín said, giving him some money. Andrés then passed him his phone number. A "*suizo*" was born.

Suizo was the term the narco-paramilitaries used for Colombia's version of a suicide bomber. As one paramilitary described it to me, *suizo* was derived from *suicidio*, which means "suicide." The *suizos* were mostly troubled teenagers who were lured into the Mafia by a short pep talk and the prospect of earning some fast money. They often had little idea of what they were getting into, but the kids were easy victims, lacking in supervision and self-esteem. "The [*suizo*] only thought about the money and how he was going to spend it," the same paramilitary explained. "He never thought he would die and not see a cent." Their new bosses understood the adolescents' pathology and worked on their weaknesses.

Narco-paramilitaries employed kids like the curly-haired Andrés Arturo Gutiérrez by the dozens. Pablo Escobar had an army of teens at his service. They killed rivals, policemen, judges, and whoever else stood in the kingpin's way. They were fearless. These kids were also cheap, bountiful, and best of all, disposable. Dead or alive, no one seemed to miss them enough to look for them. Yerry and Andrés were both *suizos*. They had been picked to do one job, and die doing it. Like many others who had joined the drug gangs, they didn't know their fate or were too poor to care.

Yerry and Andrés came from the same poor Medellín neighborhood. The city is a postcard. Towering mountains surround it on all sides, and slim valleys lead to long stretches of lush, green rolling hills. But unlike U.S. cities where the rich live on the periphery, in Colombia it's the poor who have the best views. Yerry and Andrés lived in shacks on the side of these mountains overlooking downtown. There the two scratched for odd jobs on the streets until the narco-paramilitaries recruited them for a "job."

Yerry had joined Joaquín's gang a few months earlier and had serendipitously set up the meeting between Andrés and Joaquín. Yerry and Andrés spent a lot of time together afterward. Andrés's relatives thought Yerry was a bad influence. Under Yerry's wing, Andrés started swearing more and got a BB gun. Andrés had only fired a gun once before in his life, but he was a good shot. "He could nail a cigarette butt from a long way away," his brother later told investigators. "One time, he . . . shot a neighbor's window from two blocks away. [And] the [other] neighbors made him pay for the lightbulbs he'd knocked out."

Following their short chat in the Medellín cantina, Joaquín and Andrés began meeting regularly. Andrés did simple errands at first, but after a while, Joaquín took the teen to the countryside. Andrés was ecstatic. Someone finally thought he was important enough to teach him something "useful." Joaquín recognized the youth's insecurities immediately and spoon-fed Andrés with "soda" money, encouragement, and false promises about the future. "One day, I'll take you to my ranch," he would tell the gullible teen, who soaked it up like a puppy dog.

The training went smoothly. In the countryside, the two shot at trees, thin boards, and tin cans. Andrés showed off his marksmanship, and Joaquín made every effort to compliment him. Joaquín and Andrés also traveled to Bogotá, where they drove around the big city getting ready for the "job." One time they stopped in at the Army's XIII Battalion on the north side of town. Andrés just figured Joaquín was part of the military but never asked too many questions.

They also visited the Bogotá airport, where Joaquín walked his student through the crime. "The target will be there," he would whisper pointing at the busy and heavily guarded entrance. "You will shoot him here," he continued, signaling an area just a few feet before the check-in desk. "Then you'll run into the waiting room, where I'll be," he said, trying to reassure the youth. Joaquín added that someone else would be shooting at the target as well, and the authorities would go after the other assassin, not Andrés. Andrés once asked Joaquín why the target had to die. "He's not good for this country," Joaquín told him before adding, "You wouldn't understand." *Suizos* weren't supposed to be bothered with the details. Andrés's gumption would later get him into trouble.

Despite the difficulties he was having with the Communist Party, UP president Bernardo Jaramillo was upbeat in those early days of March 1990. He had just been elected to the senate. And he was making inroads for a possible alliance with his former rivals from the M-19 guerrilla group.

In almost storybook fashion, the M-19 had signed a peace agreement with the government a year earlier. The peace process began unexpectedly when the rebels kidnapped Álvaro Gómez, the twice-defeated Conservative

candidate for president and ideologue of his traditional party. Gómez had
built his whole career on vilifying leftist movements, their guerrilla colleagues, and "soft" Conservatives who negotiated with them. He was the one
who coined the term "independent republics," referring to the Communist
strongholds just southwest of the capital city, Bogotá, in the early 1960s.
Gómez had also chastised President Belisario Betancur when he had sought
peace talks with the FARC. Yet during his captivity, Gómez and the M-19
spent long nights talking through the country's problems. Over time, the
two sides found a lot of common ground. The talks formed the basis of a
quick settlement once the M-19 released the politician a few months later.
Gómez and the rebel group later allied to push for a constitutional assem-
bly. In 1989, M-19 leaders posed for the TV cameras while they handed over
their guns.

The M-19 rapidly formed a new political party. Its presidential candidate was Carlos Pizarro. Pizarro was a perfect blend of guerrilla hero and
sensitive politician. He garnered immediate respect from the political establishment and leftists alike. His charisma and good looks also made him an
attractive choice for undecided voters. Suddenly, the Left had two formidable politicians. Both were young and handsome. If the UP's Bernardo
Jaramillo was the "*bizcocho*" or "sweetie," then Pizarro was the "*papito*" or
"cutie." Together, the UP and the M-19 represented a serious electoral challenge for the traditional parties.

More importantly, the two might have been a possible death sentence for
the FARC. By drawing Communists and other leftists toward social democracy, the new movement would tear the heart from the rebel organization. If
the Left could occupy a political space where there was some semblance of
democracy, the rebels would lose their principal justification for waging war
against the government. In other words, the new M-19/UP alliance was the
country's surest means toward peace. That is, if their enemies let it survive.

Contacts between the UP and the M-19 had begun in 1989. Leaders
from both groups held meetings and slowly inched toward an alliance. The
discussion centered on who would be the presidential candidate and who
would be the head of the new party. There was little progress because
Bernardo had already committed to being the UP's presidential candidate.
Still, the meetings caught the attention of the Communist Party.

Bernardo's stock in the Communist Party was already inching toward
zero even before he began flirting with the M-19. He had spent the last few
months of 1989 trying to get the UP a spot in the International Socialist. It
would have been the last step in making the UP what the reformists, the
Perestroikas, wanted to be: a social democratic alternative in Colombia.

Bernardo also continued to denounce the FARC and disregard the strategy of combining politics with guerilla warfare, *la combinación de todas las formas de lucha*. At a certain point, Bernardo even stopped going to Communist Party meetings, and the *Perestroikas* prepared to make their final break.

"Today more than ever, I'm willing to advance the Social-Democratic project," Bernardo wrote to one of his UP friends in exile in March 1990. "The decision is made. I want to pull other *compañeros* from the *PC* [Communist Party]." Bernardo went on to say that he would propose an emergency meeting of the Communist Party during which he wanted to debate *la combinación de todas las formas de lucha*, how the Communist Party made decisions, and the "type of socialism that we want and will defend." He then stated, "I'm going to propose that we publicly split from the *PC*."

For the Communist Party, the letter was tantamount to heresy, and when one of Bernardo's Communist bodyguards intercepted it, expulsion was all but assured. But Bernardo didn't care. He had traveled too far. He knew where he wanted to take what was quickly becoming his movement. He would run as the UP presidential candidate in this election. But afterward, he would break with the Communist Party to form an unprecedented coalition of leftist forces.

The coalition had the makings of a powerful third party, the likes of which the country had never seen. The two leaders, Carlos Pizarro and Bernardo Jaramillo, were both immensely popular, one because he had handed in his guns, the other because he had clamored for the other guerrilla groups to hand in theirs as well. It didn't hurt that both were charming, charismatic, and good-looking. The "*papito*" and "*bizcocho*" were getting ready to push the democratic left into a new era. Only a couple of teenage *suizos* stood in their way.

It was a typical balmy spring day in Medellín, just a few months before the presidential elections, when Joaquín called Andrés for the "job." The two met near Andrés's home. Joaquín gave Andrés a plane ticket, his fake ID, and some money, and told him to catch the noon flight to Bogotá. Andrés went home, packed his bags, and said goodbye to his mother; he told her he was going to a friend's cottage. He met with Joaquín again later that morning, and the boss gave him a suit and tie. Andrés then caught the plane and, as instructed, went straight to the Hotel San Diego, a rusty old *pensión* in the center of the city. That night Andrés went to a movie in the seedy neighborhood near the hotel and ate a couple of sandwiches. Joaquín later called Andrés in his room and told him to be at the airport at 7 A.M. wearing his new clothes.

At dawn the next day, Andrés arrived at the airport. Joaquín was there waiting for him. The two of them sat in the Presto hamburger joint staring out at the arriving passengers and had an orange juice. There they talked a bit about Joaquín's ranch again. Andrés knew Joaquín was telling him half-truths, but life was easier if he believed them. Like the fake ID, it was a trip into another world, away from his own miserable existence. Then, Joaquín pulled over a black suitcase. Inside was an airline ticket, a book titled *Legend and Myth of El Mejicano* about the recently slain drug capo José Gonzalo Rodríguez Gacha, a newspaper, and a Mini-Ingram 380 machine gun. "I didn't look at anything too closely," Andrés later told investigators. "I was petrified."

Joaquín pulled out the newspaper. "You're going to kill *this* man," he slowly explained, pointing at a photo of Bernardo Jaramillo in the newspaper. The UP presidential candidate looked kind of funny in the picture. He was tall, had curly hair, and showed a goofy smile. But seeing his face for the first time scared Andrés. Until then, it had been easy to think of shooting a man. Bernardo meant nothing to him and the UP even less. Governments, paramilitaries, guerrillas, and the army—they were all the same to the teen. But with a face, these things took on meaning. With a face, this victim had suddenly come to life, and Andrés started to get nervous.

"You will have someone there to help you," Joaquín reminded the now trembling teen, "and I'll be in the next room waiting for you." Andrés turned around and saw a man sitting in the seat where Joaquín said the man would be. "I didn't get a good look because I was so nervous," Andrés said later. Joaquín then told Andrés that once the job was done, he would give Andrés the $2,000 he'd promised him—the first $1,000 of which he had balked on paying already. "It's going to be just like we practiced," he reassured the worried boy. Then Andrés sat down amid the crowd and waited.

It was agonizing. Andrés watched television anxiously and occasionally glanced over his shoulder. But he didn't stare in any one direction very long. He was too afraid. He thought of running, but then thought of his family— they would be the real beneficiaries of his deed or, if he didn't do it, would suffer for his flight. He then started hoping that Bernardo Jaramillo's car would crash or have a flat tire. Or maybe the presidential candidate wouldn't walk by him. Maybe he wouldn't have to kill anybody. Maybe he could just go home and shoot BB guns into the neighbors' windows.

There were eleven government bodyguards from the president's elite guard, the *Departamento Administrativo de Seguridad* or DAS, on Bernardo Jaramillo's security detail that day. They were joined by two policemen and

two members of the UP. All but the UP men met at 7 A.M. at DAS headquarters in the city's industrial district. They then made their way to
Jaramillo's house in a posh neighborhood in northern Bogotá, where they
retrieved the UP leader, his wife, Mariella, and their UP bodyguards and
started toward the airport. It was a formidable caravan: two SUVs, an
armored jeep, a motorcycle, and a less than impressive Chevy Chevette (carrying the two UP soldiers). But they moved swiftly through the morning
ltraffic. Bernardo and Mariella were in the armored vehicle. Two DAS men
on the motorcycle had a radio and wove in and out of the caravan looking for
anything suspicious. The rest of the guards had Uzis and Berettas at the
ready.

Bernardo was excited. His political and personal life were coming
together. Gone were the days when he contemplated suicide. He was now at
ease with his ideology. It had taken a long time, but Bernardo could see exactly
where he wanted to go. It might take more time to get there this way, but he
was young, and he had all the support he could possibly hope for from his new
wife, Mariella. The couple was closer than ever. She campaigned with him
around the clock. He sought her advice and care. During the quiet times, they
talked about having a nice home with a cat and, of course, some children.

As Bernardo's caravan raced to catch the flight that morning, he and
Mariella were too distracted to think of the dangers ahead. The two sat in the
back and joked about how Mariella's breakfast was in her throat because of
the way the chauffeur drove. It didn't occur to them that perhaps they
shouldn't have told anyone their travel plans several days in advance or called
Mariella's sister to arrange for their arrival. They thought little, for instance,
of the fact that the DAS had sent two agents to the airport earlier that morning to check for anything suspicious.

Because of the mixture of people and confined areas, airports were tricky
places at which to provide security and arguably the most dangerous part of
these trips. Just a year earlier, assassins had gunned down Bernardo's
Communist ally and *Perestroika* confidant, José Antequera, as he prepared to
board a plane. The narcos followed this up by placing a bomb on a commercial
flight, which killed 107 people. Later, *El Tiempo* would report that there were
an astounding thirty-seven unprotected doors that led to the airport grounds.

It's not clear what the two DAS agents who went early to the airport did
that morning, but they didn't report anything out of the ordinary. Their own
behavior was perhaps the strangest of all. When the shooting that day hit its
high point, these two claimed to be having a soda in the Presto hamburger joint,
the same place where just a little earlier Joaquín had given Andrés the black suitcase with the plane ticket, the book, the newspaper, and the machine gun.

Still, Bernardo and Mariella seemed hardly bothered that day. These security questions were trivial concerns for paranoid politicians. The days of paranoia were over. Bernardo Jaramillo's—indeed, the entire party's—nemesis was dead. José Gonzalo *El Mejicano* Rodríguez Gacha's body was identified using about the only thing left from the bloodbath on the beach: his fingerprints. With "*El Mejicano*" in the morgue, Bernardo thought the worst of the war was over. He told his wife the UP should be relieved as well. Bernardo was so confident that he didn't even wear his bulletproof vest that day to the airport. His wife later said that it was bothering his back.

However, the UP leader should have been afraid. The other narco-paramilitary leaders—Henry Pérez, Pablo Escobar, Victor Carranza, and Fidel Castaño—were all still alive and remained at large. Fidel, above all, hadn't lost the bitter taste in his mouth following his father's death at the hands of the FARC, and he and his paramilitaries were swamping Bernardo's old political stomping grounds, Urabá. Just a month before Bernardo's trip, Fidel's men had gunned down Diana Cardona, a prominent UP mayor in the banana-growing region. The week before, Fidel's paramilitaries had killed six UP leaders in a neighboring municipality as the leftist politicians exited a political meeting. Following the death of Mayor Cardona, Bernardo had asked the DAS to increase security, and the DAS had complied.

For her part, Mariella knew of only one threat that Bernardo had received in the weeks leading up to the trip. "Leave in 24 hours," the note left in a hotel elevator in the city of Montería read. Montería was the capital of the province of Córdoba, the House of Castaño stronghold. Jaramillo did leave, but not because he was afraid, his wife would later testify. "He wasn't scared of anyone," she claimed.

Upon arriving in the airport that day, the DAS, the policemen, and the UP bodyguards got out of their cars first. Once they had secured the immediate area, Bernardo and his wife followed. The two grabbed their bags and hustled toward the entrance. They were walking very fast now. As always, the object was to get the candidate past the checkpoint and into the waiting room quickly, where he was easier to secure. They were surprised to see that one of the metal detectors was apparently not working. (The police manning the X-ray machine later said that it would work intermittently; a government investigator checked the apparatus the day of the assassination and found it to be working fine.) The UP bodyguards also noticed that there were just two policemen manning an entrance that normally had at least four. No matter, they were in the airport now and shuffling toward the waiting room.

It was very crowded. Passengers hustled to their early morning flights, while others lounged on the seats in front of some televisions mounted on eight-foot-high poles. Three DAS agents led the way. Behind them, Jaramillo and his wife walked arm in arm. Afraid her heels might cause her to fall, Mariella clung tightly to her husband's forearm. To her right was a police officer. Behind her was the DAS chief and a fellow agent. The rest followed closely in a semicircle. The crowds forced the bodyguards to separate perhaps farther than they might have otherwise.

Across the room, a nervous Andrés Arturo Gutiérrez rose from his chair and walked toward the UP leader. In his left hand, the *suizo* carried the newspaper with the goofy photo of the candidate; concealed in his right hand was the machine gun. In his pocket, he carried his fake ID. This was his day to be somebody else, anybody but himself. His palms were slippery with sweat, but Andrés moved fast, maybe too fast. He raised his machine gun and started firing at Bernardo and the phalanx of security guards. Andrés later said he missed his target, dropped the gun, and hit the floor. The guy who was sitting behind him, he said, was firing most of the shots. People scattered for cover.

After the first round of shooting from Andrés's side, the *suizo* said he felt a hail of gunfire. He lay in a fetal position taking bullets in various parts of his body and screaming, "Don't kill me! Don't kill me!" When the shooting slowed, a policeman approached the boy. "Bring me to the hospital, and I'll tell you everything," he said. "Just don't let me die!" Andrés was injured but would live, for the moment.

Across the linoleum floor, Bernardo was on his side writhing in pain. The UP presidential candidate rolled a little, then reached for some curtains to pull himself up, but he couldn't so he slumped back down on the floor again. "The sons-a-bitches have killed me, brother," he told one of his DAS bodyguards next to him. "I can't feel my legs." His wife lunged for him and cradled his head to her body. "They killed me, honey," he said to her. "The sons-a-bitches killed me." Then he fell unconscious.

Two DAS bodyguards got up from the floor, grabbed Bernardo by the arms, and carried the critically wounded leader toward the armored car at the entrance. They piled him into the backseat. Mariella jumped in behind her husband, and the car screeched away from the curb. Mariella was in shock but still coherent. She watched in horror as her husband turned red, then green, then yellow. It was too much for her to handle. All at once she started screaming, crying, and praying.

The DAS car wove through traffic at lightning speed to the nearest hospital and skidded to a halt at the emergency room entrance. The bodyguards pulled Bernardo into the clinic by his arms. Orderlies quickly supplied a bed, and then Mariella shouted to the attendants that her husband had "A-negative!" blood. The nurses moved to get the blood; the surgeons awaited them upstairs. But the elevator was slow. One of the DAS men pounded on the button to try and make it work faster. Over time, some of these agents had grown fond of the UP leader. Bernardo treated them much better than most political big shots. When he ate lunch, he invited them to join him. When he had a cup of coffee, they also got a *tinto* to go. "Fuckin' elevator," one DAS agent screamed. Bernardo was nearing death. They all knew it.

The doctors saw the bloodied UP president almost an hour after he was shot. He had no vital signs, but they tried to piece him back together anyway. They scrambled to pump blood into the wounded, limp body, clear out the bullets, and hook him up to a life-support system. But it was too late. After an hour, the doctors pronounced Bernardo Jaramillo dead.

Mariella knew it was the end before she got the news. She had slipped into a bathroom. She didn't want to see anyone, and when she did, she wanted to put on a brave face. In a way, she had been preparing for this since the first time the two met and talked of death on the beach, under the stars, with bodyguards looming in the shadows behind them. None of this was a surprise, but it didn't make it any easier.

The announcement that Bernardo was dead didn't surprise those already preparing to protest his killing either. When the news broke he was shot, UP supporters had erupted in pain and outrage across the country. In the coffee belt, Bernardo's home, party militants took over some government offices. In the city of Cali, professors walked out of schools and took to the streets with placards, while the more radical UP supporters burned cars. In the banana-growing region of Urabá, workers called a strike that eventually paralyzed the area for several days. In Medellín, protestors stormed the provincial government building.

Nowhere was the anger so apparent as in Bogotá. In UP strongholds, the protests turned bloody. In one neighborhood, one soldier died and two police officers were injured as they clashed with protesters. Downtown, militants burned buses and blocked the main avenues for hours. UP headquarters was in complete disarray. In front of the office, protesters and mourners alike stood shouting anti-government slogans. There was particular ire against Carlos Lemos, then interior minister. Lemos had recently publicly stated that the UP was "the political wing of the FARC." When so many people were dying for less, such talk could not be taken lightly. The people chanted, "Lemos-*asesino*" and "*Palacio Nariño* [Presidential Palace] killed Bernardo Jaramillo."

The clashes at the UP headquarters had a particularly eerie irony to them. People were burning tires and threatening to march on the palace, so the government dispatched the police to calm the disturbances. They approached the UP headquarters with extreme caution, using tear gas to disperse the crowds. The gas leaked into the UP offices. Party leaders and sympathizers grabbed for wet cloths and scrambled to put them on their faces so they could breathe. One member reached for a mop that he could use to filter out the gas. As he pulled it over to him, he popped open a ceiling tile, sending copies of the FARC's magazine, *Resistencia*, tumbling onto the floor. To avoid the embarrassment, he lit the magazines on fire before the police stormed the building. It was a fitting end to the brief history of the party: Even in death, the UP's contradictions came tumbling down on top of it.

No one could explain why the teenager Andrés Arturo Gutiérrez had shot and killed Bernardo Jaramillo. His grandmother was in tatters when she heard the news. "They must have brainwashed him," she told a television reporter the day Bernardo was shot. "Because . . . he never smoked marijuana, never did drugs, never drank. Nothing, nothing at all. . . . For all of us, for the family, his brothers and sisters, this is a huge blow, a mortal blow. . . . I feel like I'm dead and can't come back. It's like death will always be with us."

Others were in shock. "He was good kid, a good worker," his former boss at the chalk-making factory told investigators. He was responsible, got to work on time, and finished what he started, he added. "I have no explanations," he said when investigators asked why such a boy would shoot the UP's presidential candidate.

Andrés's father, *Don* Fabio, seemed to take the news the hardest. "He was my friend and my son at the same time," he explained to investigators. "We talked all the time. He told me about work, about his girlfriends, and whatnot. Sometimes we'd have little fights over how high he put his music and things like that. He'd get mad, but then a few minutes later, he'd be fine." Like the others, the elderly and broken *Don* Fabio looked for answers that weren't there. "Maybe I'm all mixed up because I'm his father, but I can't believe it. As the father of this kid, I can't believe that he had so much time on his hands that they could train him like you say [they did]. I can't believe it. I swear to God, I can't believe it."

Investigators sought to find out whether Andrés had changed in the weeks preceding the shooting, but little stood out. His father said he had begun to use swear words like "faggot." His brother said he had brought home new music and listened to it on his "*wolman*." He also began shooting his BB gun more often. But there were no indications he would attempt to shoot a presidential candidate. He had no prior record, and Andrés had never even mentioned Bernardo Jaramillo to anyone. It was also likely the first time the family had talked about the UP leader among themselves as well.

The only major change that had come was his friendship with Yerry. His relatives, it turns out, were right about his new friend. While investigators interrogated Andrés, Yerry was getting the final instructions for his "job." His trainer was none other than Carlos Castaño, Fidel's younger brother. And his target was the other half of the nascent left-wing political alliance between the UP and the M-19. Like Andrés and Joaquín, Yerry and Carlos practiced on ranches just outside Medellín. "I laid out plastic seats as if they were in an airplane," Carlos later recounted to his biographer. "Then I had him stand up, walk back, and shoot at the target. We used hundreds of bullets."

Just a little over a month after Bernardo Jaramillo's assassination, M-19 presidential candidate Carlos Pizarro and two of his DAS bodyguards boarded an airplane bound for the coastal city of Barranquilla. Two paramilitaries and Yerry boarded the airplane as well. Carlos later said he was in the airport on the same day, anxiously waiting for the results of the "job." Yerry, whose real name was Germán Gutiérrez Uribe, was even more deluded than Andrés. He thought his employers were going to hijack the airplane and land it at a remote airstrip where a getaway car would be waiting. Carlos Castaño even perpetuated this myth in his biography.

Shortly after takeoff, Yerry got up from his seat and went to the bathroom. There, he removed a Mini-Ingram 380, the same type of machine gun that Andrés had used to kill Bernardo Jaramillo. Yerry flushed the toilet, took a few steps out of the bathroom, and fired several rounds at the back of Carlos Pizarro's seat. Thirteen bullets lodged into the M-19 leader's head, chest, and arm. The candidate slumped over, bleeding from half his body. The DAS bodyguards turned and shot Yerry dead on the spot. During the melee, a stray bullet entered but did not break a window, perhaps sparing dozens more lives. "When I saw the plane coming back," a relieved Carlos Castaño told his biographer, "my soul returned to my body and I thanked God." Pizarro, meanwhile, died on the plane. Yerry had proven himself to be the ultimate *suizo*. Colombian authorities later said he acted on the "absolute conviction that he would be killed after committing the assassination."

Andrés's saga, however, still had one more chapter. As a minor, authorities sent the *suizo* to a boarding school in Bogotá. Two years later, he was transferred to another school in Medellín so he could visit his family. During one of these visits, he and his father left the house, "to do an errand," they told Andrés's mother. The two were later found in a parking lot shot dead.

Some investigators believe that Andrés and his father may have tried to extort money from the criminals who had hired him.

Andrés's mission was over. He was dead, as was the UP.

Following Bernardo's assassination, there was a massive exodus from the UP. With Bernardo's death, it was painfully apparent that the *Perestroika* reform hadn't worked; public criticism of the FARC hadn't convinced the UP's enemies that the party was anything other than a tool of the rebels. Perhaps if Bernardo had made the formal break from the Communist Party, there would have been a chance. But his enemies didn't let him. It was a mistake that Carlos Castaño himself would admit to me later. At the time, though, for the House of Castaño, the "democratic left" was still the same as the guerrillas. For those who didn't want to fall into that category or the morgue, there was nothing else to do but leave the party.

Worse yet for the UP was the sinking sensation that even with the death of the drug capo José Gonzalo *"El Mejicano"* Rodríguez Gacha, the nightmare hadn't ended. "They say this is over because Rodríguez Gacha is dead, *if* he's dead," an exasperated Mariella told a television news reporter following her husband's death. "Now who's killing the UP members?"

For the public at large, the answer to Mariella's question was Pablo Escobar. The government had immediately blamed the drug kingpin for Bernardo's death. Escobar was a convenient scapegoat for most political murders at the time. But even UP leaders had their doubts that he was responsible. Most of the party accused Fidel Castaño of hatching the scheme and carrying out the plan with the help of some military and DAS personnel. But there was little proof, and Escobar was more visible than Fidel and so remained an easy cover for the government's dirty work.

Longtime Communist Party members, like the hopeful and stubborn Alberto Rojas Puyo, left both the UP and the Communist Party following Bernardo's assassination. Other non-Communist UP members like Mariella followed. Some of them briefly shifted allegiance to the M-19. The M-19 was now under the direction of Antonio Navarro Wolff, a frail-looking ex-commander who had overcome his slurring style of speech and homely face to become an effective, albeit less attractive, party leader. Navarro rode a wave of pro-Pizarro/Bernardo sentiment to the polls, where the M-19 made a magical showing by garnering over 800,000 votes. But emotion alone wasn't enough to sustain the movement. Its base was weak, its politics more center than left, and its victories caused unwanted attention. Paramilitaries began picking off M-19 leaders, and the new party quickly folded under the pressure. The lesson of the UP had been clear; no one waited too long to go into hiding.

The end of the UP was really the end of center-left politics in Colombia. UP militants dispersed into other political organizations and the guerrillas, or they disappeared altogether. The FARC, meanwhile, had the perfect excuse to hang on to its guns forever, and the Communist Party had another martyr. Despite the difficult relationship between the UP and the Communist Party and the likelihood that Bernardo Jaramillo would have eventually defected from its ranks, the Communist Party worked hard to make Bernardo its own again. Rifts were forgotten, and words of praise have been passed around for "*compañero* Jaramillo" ever since.

With the departure of the *Perestroikas*, the Communist Party and the FARC could also maintain their strategy of *la combinación de todas las formas de lucha*. The weaklings, the social democrats, were gone. Control of policy was theirs again. What was left of the UP would also return to its former status: a tool in the rebels' long march toward power. Militants like the lawyer Josué Giraldo, the beleaguered district attorney political activist and human rights defender who inspired me to write this book, stayed with the Communist Party and the UP. Theirs became a struggle to pave the way for the final "revolutionary" victory. But they would die for less.

For all their electoral and moral victories, the most important one had eluded Bernardo and the *Perestroikas*. They realized early on that theirs was a fight of degrees, a struggle to celebrate the simple things in life. After a while, they weren't talking about campaigns or democracy or peace. They were talking about life. No one said it better than Bernardo Jaramillo himself. "The ability to walk the streets without armed guards," Jaramillo explained to a reporter, "without people recognizing me or pointing at me with their finger, 'There goes the UP.' The ability to enter an ice cream shop and have an ice cream cone; sit down in a park and give corn to the pigeons; read a magazine, a newspaper; go to the movies. I think this is my greatest dream, and I hope I can fulfil it one day."

PART THREE

CHAPTER 13

FARC-*LANDIA*

It was an overcast day in Colombia's southern jungles, and the lush, grassy hills that roll toward the mountains in the west seemed covered in rebels. Their tents stretched for miles, and guerrillas clad in dark green fatigues and assault rifles draped over their shoulders milled about with the casual flair of family members on vacation. Some lay in the grass, staring at the sky. Others poked sticks into the ground that held the ponchos above their heads and protected them from the incessant rain. Some of the fighters were in their thirties, others in their early teens. They all had the dry look that you frequently see on guerrillas' faces: tired of the sun beating down on them, the rain dripping overhead, the jungle leaves scratching their cheeks, the mosquitoes biting their necks, the lack of sleep, and the boredom. There were no smiles for me as I passed by them on the dirt road, leaving dust on their scant belongings. They were bored, and they were angry.

It was April 2000, ten years after Bernardo Jaramillo had been assassinated in the Bogotá airport. The UP was dead, but the FARC was thriving. The rebels had become something no one, except perhaps themselves, dreamed possible: an army. They had gotten it done in a subtle way, but evidence of their evolution was everywhere. Down the road were some signs posted on a fence reminding all of the guerrillas' quasi political control in the area: "Don't litter—FARC-EP"; "Take care of the trees—FARC-EP."

The EP, or "army of the people"—so ambitiously made part of the name in the rebels' historic VII Conference in 1982—was now a reality. One wooden plaque pegged to a tree called for locals to "Join the FARC-EP." It was a tempting offer for many, considering the country's ongoing economic crisis and the government's tragic ineptitude. Half the population languished in poverty, a good portion of them living in substandard conditions in crowded cities and run-down villages. The chaos and economic despair had meshed perfectly with the FARC's strategy to build its army; some 18,000 Colombians had become guerrilla soldiers—most of them during the decade since Bernardo Jaramillo's assassination and the disintegration of the UP. Countless others were part of a vast support network that was employing at least another 35,000 people.

The FARC was by far the largest, best-equipped rebel force in the hemisphere, and it was striking fear in the hearts of politicians in Washington, D.C. At the time, the U.S. government was in the midst of sending $1.3 billion to Colombia to fight the "drug war," which Washington would later expand to include the battle against the guerrillas. In reality, U.S. money was part of a modern-day rehash of the "bullets and beans" concept that the Kennedy administration had tried in the early 1960s. Colombia's old *Plan Lazo* was replaced by *Plan Colombia*, an ambitious social, economic, and military strategy. But as it was during the Kennedy years, Colombia would get more "bullets" than "beans." Most of the U.S. money for *Plan Colombia* was going toward helicopter-gunships, training, and intelligence equipment, although Washington put a cap on the number of U.S. soldiers who could be deployed at four hundred. The money made Colombia the third largest recipient of U.S. aid in the world, behind only Egypt and Israel. Colombia, it seemed, had become a priority in Washington, and the Communist rebels had once again become the U.S. government's principal concern.

To be sure, these rebels were a different bunch from the ones who'd set up the "independent republics" in Tolima in the 1960s. Their "army of the people" threatened the stability of Colombia's government. And more than anything else, it was the slaughter of the UP that had pushed the FARC in this decidedly military direction. Since Bernardo Jaramillo's assassination, rebel leaders had stiffened their rhetoric. Anytime anyone mentioned disarmament, the FARC said the words *Unión Patriótica*. There was no response. The massacre of its political party gave the FARC the perfect justification to fight forever. To prove they just might, the guerrillas had spread across half of the country's thirty-two provinces. Small and large rebel columns, using sophisticated weaponry and increasingly younger soldiers, moved easily through the mountainous and uncharted terrain. Along the way, they attacked police and military installations, extorted money, and kidnapped Colombians and foreigners to obtain healthy ransom payments.

The FARC's ability to consistently put the Colombian military on its heels had forced the government to take it more seriously than ever. Just over a year before I rolled through these jungles, the government had removed the police and the army from the area in an attempt to make room for a peace process with the FARC. It was thirty-six years since the military had stormed toward the mountainous province of Tolima. Thousands of troops and dozens of airplanes with napalm stashed in their hulls hunted down forty-two Communists in the "independent republics." Now, the government had evacuated a much larger area to accommodate these "bandits." This war had traveled well beyond irony.

The military's and paramilitary's physical annihilation of the UP had certainly accelerated this process. Hundreds, if not thousands, of party militants had filtered into the FARC, most of them after the slaughter of their UP colleagues and the assassinations of party leaders like Jaime Pardo Leal and Bernardo Jaramillo. They had given up hope that the UP was a viable way to reach peace. In contrast to what the army and paramilitary leaders believed, destroying the guerrillas' political party had proved to be a horrible long-term strategy. The demolition of the UP made the civil conflict a zero-sum game. Neither side was willing to give an inch now. The war would be won on the battlefield, not at the polls.

The government furthered the rebels' resolve when in 1991 it launched a full-scale offensive against *Casa Verde*, the old home of the FARC commanders and where peace talks had taken place with the Belisario Betancur government just a few years before. The bombings lasted for days. Army troops followed the airplanes' devastation and set up a military base at the foot of the cold, barren Sumapaz mountains in La Uribe, the place where Jacobo Arenas had come up with the idea of creating the UP. The government called it a major victory, but the rebels looked at it as another betrayal. Guerrilla leaders placed it alongside General Rojas Pinilla's "peace talks" in the 1950s, after which the general killed dozens of rebel leaders; the army's full-scale attacks on the "independent republics" in the 1960s; the failed negotiations with Presidents Betancur and Virgilio Barco in the 1980s; and, most importantly, the "political genocide" of the UP. It was a long list that made peace seem that much more remote.

Following the government's offensive at *Casa Verde*, the FARC recruited thousands of new soldiers. Thirty Fronts were soon forty-five, then sixty. The guerrillas had also added fourteen mobile columns, nineteen smaller mobile companies, and four urban fronts. It had taken longer than the eight years the FARC's VII Conference had predicted, but the rebels were growing into an army that could fight and hold territory. The FARC began to engage the Colombian military for long periods instead of relying on traditional hit-and-run tactics. New homemade weapons, like propane gas canisters fashioned into bombs, destroyed entire police stations and broke through once impenetrable walls of military garrisons. The rebels coordinated these assaults with a precision and timing that left the military looking flat-footed and completely overmatched. The culmination of these efforts resulted in three decisive battles in the mid-1990s. Hundreds of army troops were dead, hundreds of others in rebel captivity. Hamstrung, the government had to negotiate. The result was the creation of what came to be known as the "Demilitarized Zone" or DMZ, where the government and the rebels would hold peace talks and through which I was traveling on that overcast day.

When I went past the guerrillas in the DMZ, they looked as fearsome as ever. They had amassed perhaps the largest military show of force in their 36-year history. Over three thousand troops were camped out near a small farming settlement. Another two thousand were in other parts of the DMZ training or resting. These FARC didn't look like the ragged guerrillas of the past that had organized the UP. Many of them wore new uniforms now, spoke to their comrades through sophisticated radio systems, and never relinquished their Galil rifles. They were definitely an army, a long way from the politicking days of the UP.

The story of the UP didn't end when the party died. In fact, in death the UP may have been more important than in life. For the FARC, the UP was certainly as useful. The party was the rebels' energy, their heart and soul. The UP meant defiance, courage, love, and even might. The UP was the guerrillas' way of reminding people they weren't dead and they weren't going away. It was a way of saying, "You can kill us, but you can never defeat us."

Nowhere was this more evident than in the DMZ. Early in its existence, journalists dubbed the DMZ "FARC-*landia*," or "FARC-land," a play on a country that could be. And why not? In 1999, the government withdrew all of its representatives from the DMZ except the ombudsman's office, elected officials, and those who were going to work on the peace process. There were no international monitors allowed in the zone aside from the International Red Cross. In all, the FARC formally controlled an astounding sixteen thousand square miles, an area the size of Switzerland, where it only occasionally negotiated with its beleaguered counterpart. The rest of the time, the rebels prepared for more war.

As in the UP era, the FARC was using peace talks to expand its military power. The guerrillas spent much of their time in FARC-*landia* building roads and bridges to be able to transport troops quickly to future battlefronts. Some said the rebels were digging tunnels like the Vietcong did to fight the United States in the 1960s. The FARC was also using the DMZ as a docking station for the cocaine-for-guns trade the rebels had developed in the years since they had first begun collecting taxes. The guerrillas were also holding kidnap victims and stockpiling weapons in the zone. And the FARC was launching attacks from the DMZ on neighboring towns and then using the zone as a safe haven for its retreating troops.

Rebel control settled quickly over the DMZ. The FARC designated San Vicente, a dusty cattle village, as its capital from which it would govern. There was a token visible presence in the town's central park—two or three guerrilla soldiers flirting with the girls walking to school—while rebel leaders drove Toyota pickups at top speeds through the streets. Some soldiers walked the beat, peeking into the bread stores and feed shops that lined the roads. Others gathered at an office in the old "cultural center," where the rebels hung a tricolor FARC flag with an outline of Colombia and two rifles crossed in front of it.

The rebels ran a "justice system" with a small courtroom on the outskirts of San Vicente. There, beneath a rudimentary tent, the FARC meted out punishments that included sweeping streets and digging ditches for minor infractions like public drunkenness. The guerrillas also expelled thieves and "enemies." About six months into the life of the DMZ, the rebels killed several suspected paramilitaries, causing an international uproar. But overall crime in the zone dropped to next to zero, and few complained of the frequent curfews the guerrillas imposed to keep military control over the area.

By the time I first visited in June 1999, six months after the DMZ had begun, the area had started to take on the patterns of a small country. International diplomats, local politicians, and well-known academics had already gone through the area to see rebel leaders. Local officials said the Canadian and Swedish embassies had sent letters to them saying they would finance development projects in the DMZ. The Iranian government later signed the first international economic agreement in the zone to build a meatpacking plant (a deal that the U.S. government pressured the Colombian government to block). Perhaps the greatest vindication for the FARC was when Richard Grasso, then president of the New York Stock Exchange, visited the DMZ. There he met with FARC leaders for over an hour to talk about Colombia's problems and its economic potential. When Grasso left, he hugged his FARC host and invited him for a stroll around Wall Street sometime.

Powerful Colombians also vindicated the FARC's rising power. On my first trip to the DMZ, the country's biggest and wealthiest entertainer, Jorge Barón, was hosting his variety program, *The Show of the Stars*, in San Vicente. Barón is a multimillionaire but spends much of his time bringing entertainers to the forgotten parts of Colombia. Over ten thousand spectators crammed San Vicente's center square to see their favorite musicians, many of whom reluctantly agreed to be on the show for fear of being kidnapped.

Surrounding the stage were hundreds of armed guerrillas—looking only slightly less menacing than the Hell's Angels motorcycle gang did when it provided security for the Rolling Stones concert at Altamont. Some of the rebels carried cameras instead of rifles and filmed the event from special platforms in the middle of the sweating audience. Meanwhile, Jorge Baron's legendary water cannons drenched the overheating spectators, taking special care not to wet the guerrillas.

Although some of the rebels showed little emotion during the concert besides an occasional smile, other guerrillas basked in their newfound fame. *Comandante* Jairo, the head of FARC security in San Vicente, shook hands with anyone he could reach and posed for pictures with little children. He then danced his way in front of the crowd and urged it to join him in a salsa spin while he pumped his AK-47 over his head. "Some people got here at seven in the morning," Jairo told me later. "And they were here from seven in the morning until seven at night. Twelve hours of continuous salsa, rhythm, and flavor," he added laughing.

Even Barón got an emotional charge from the concert. At one point, the middle-age, white-suited showman invited *Comandante* Jairo to join him on stage, where he presented the FARC commander with a small white flag and asked the guerrilla leader to give the country the gift of peace. "We want peace," Jairo responded to Barón. "And we can see it through your beautiful programs. And whenever circumstances permit, there you will find us in front of the television watching your show."

Inside the FARC's "cultural center" the guerrillas put up posters of the Argentinean revolutionary Ernesto "Che" Guevara and pictures of FARC leaders Manuel "Sureshot" Marulanda and Jacobo Arenas. Arenas had died of natural causes in 1990, just a few months after Bernardo Jaramillo was shot in the airport. Sureshot was still alive and maintained order with the troops, but Arenas's death left the guerrilla group without any clear political direction. Alfonso Cano, the thick-bearded former Communist Party scholar, was Arenas's nominal replacement. But Cano had a hard time gaining the support of the troops or the FARC hard-liners, who continued to call him an "intellectual half-timer" because of his scant military experience. Without Bernardo to challenge them on the outside and without Arenas to guide them from the inside, the FARC had a huge void to fill. But the guerrillas never filled it. While the war marched on in the decade following Bernardo's assassination and Arenas's death, politics was relegated to the sideline. In the post-UP and post-Arenas era, charisma was less important than raw power, politics less important than warmongering.

The symbol of the military-minded FARC was a pudgy, round-faced commander named Jorge Briceño, a.k.a. Mono Jojoy. The *mono* or "monkey" in his alias refers to his light skin that resembles the pale monkeys roaming the Colombian jungles. Mono Jojoy headed up the FARC's military wing, and he was steering the rebels' efforts to control large swaths of territory in unscrupulous ways. In addition to using teenage soldiers to overrun government troops, he was thought to be responsible for the practice of mass kidnapping—whereby guerrillas would stop cars along the highways and take people in tens and twenties—and "law 002," a rebel tax on all people with assets reaching $1 million. Under Mono Jojoy's watch, the FARC was making an estimated $200 million per year froom kidnapping. Critics also blamed the commander for pushing the FARC closer to the category of drug trafficker, a process that brought in ever-larger profits for the guerrillas to expand their arsenal and, in turn, their war. Taxing drug traffickers and, in some cases, trafficking drugs netted close to $500 million per year for the rebel group. The U.S. government eventually indicted three members of the FARC for drug smuggling. None of these criticisms or legal problems made any difference to the FARC. Mono Jojoy was the heir-apparent to Sureshot.

Even when the guerrillas did offer an olive branch, it was hard to tell if the FARC was being sincere. About a year into the life of the DMZ, the rebels launched a "clandestine" political party. They called it the Bolivarian Movement, drawing from the legend of Simón Bolívar, the South American "Liberator" who had become the Left's substitute for Jesus Christ. Like the UP, the party was billed as a way the guerrillas could eventually enter mainstream politics. But few took the FARC seriously when it hinted at the end of the war. Once again, it looked as if the guerrillas were lining up a sacrificial battalion.

The Bolivarian Movement's members were certainly martyrs in the making. Rebels said their political ideals would be spread by using "Bolivarian cells" in the towns where they operated. Members of the cells could hold political positions or simply voice the movement's position without identifying their affiliation with the FARC. Except for the name of the party, it was *la combinación de todas las formas de lucha*—the old Communist strategy of combining legal and illegal activities to topple the government—all over again.

On the morning of the Bolivarian Movement's first political rally, I walked with the new party's supposed peasant supporters from San Vicente toward the main event. It was the rainy season, but the sun beamed down for the first time in days. A rebel stood on the railing of the footbridge leading out of town, greeting the families on their way to the event. His AK-47 hung from his shoulder, and his freshly washed olive green uniform shone in the morning light. He wore a black beret stuck with a small Che Guevara pin at the tip. He was in a jovial mood, as was the rest of the FARC. "Good morning!" he shouted to the people passing by. "Good morning," some of them responded. "Long live the Bolivarian Movement!" the rebel said loudly. "*Qué viva!*" a few marchers returned.

Visibly worn from their journey, the *campesinos* moved like a herd of cows along the dirt road. Some mothers dragged their children. Large groups of young men trudged behind the old school buses and cattle cars, slowly making their way to the event. One FARC leader had told me the day before that the rally would be "transcendental." I had my doubts, so I asked some of those in tow how they felt. Not surprisingly, most of the participants didn't want to speak to me—a blond foreigner with tightly cropped hair and a microphone in his hand. "It's dangerous to talk," an elderly peasant farmer finally said to me looking around, "because they forced us to come here."

As we inched near the cow pasture where the Bolivarian Movement's rally would be held, rebels were still making last minute arrangements. On the pasture was a wide stage with a forty-foot-high canopy. Four stories of speakers were stacked on both sides. Rebels on stage were arranging chairs and adjusting microphones. Young men and women soldiers wearing brown *Movimiento Bolivariano* visors patted the *campesinos* and their families down for weapons as they stepped through the wooden fence that led to the stage. Inside, some female guerrillas offered the people a sandwich and a Colombian soft drink. Looking like rows of newly planted trees, rebel soldiers stood guard on the hills surrounding the rally. FARC leaders, several of them with pens in their shirt pockets, were gathered backstage, conversing among themselves.

To commence the rally, midlevel FARC commanders climbed on the stage and began shouting party slogans. Almost on cue, the movement's faithful started to wave their homemade banners bearing the name of their municipality and their support for the FARC's new party. "With Bolívar . . . with Manuel . . . with the people . . . we'll take power," the commanders screamed. Rebel soldiers lined in a square around the stage replied to the slogans. No one else knew what to say, and few really seemed interested in learning. Still, the people were present; more than twenty thousand of them had filtered onto the settlement and were beginning to sit down on the wet field.

Next to the stage, the FARC paid homage to its heroes. On one side was a ten-foot-high painting of dead FARC leader Jacobo Arenas. On the other was an equally large painting of slain UP leader Jaime Pardo Leal. UP spirit was everywhere. So were the walking ghosts. I found a group of young would-be martyrs gathering their sandwiches from the rebel soldiers at the gate—three of them between the ages of eighteen and twenty-five. One of them wore a Nike hat that read "No Fear." "I would be more afraid if I were alone," the eighteen -year-old told me when I asked why he would risk being a part of such a movement. "But they can't kill us all." It was an ominous sign: The words echoed what UP leaders had proclaimed just fifteen years earlier.

A short while later, the FARC's top command, the Secretariat, climbed onto the stage. Some in the audience clapped. Most of the crowd simply inched closer to the barricade of soldiers in front of them. For security reasons, no one was allowed to get within ninety feet of the speakers, so people stood on their toes or climbed on the men's shoulders to get a peek at the leaders they had heard so much about, especially Manuel "Sureshot" Marulanda.

It was worth a look. The sixty-something FARC leader—who'd begun his life as a shopowner in the coffee belt—had fought off the government for fifty years without losing a limb or his revolutionary edge. To think that he had never slipped up in battle, that his neighbors had never turned him in, that he'd outsmarted dozens of officers who undoubtedly said when they had entered the academy that they were going to be the ones who got Sureshot; yet there he stood, slightly hunched over in the middle of the Secretariat, wearing a new camouflage uniform and matching baseball hat. He also wore thick-rimmed, square glasses, presumably to do what many people thought he couldn't: read. He was like the grand wizard presiding over his own, never-ending rebel fairy tale.

Those who have spent time with him say the FARC commander is as humble as his past. He does not talk about his great battles or his renowned marksmanship. He is a man of few words who goes to great lengths to avoid saying "I." He prefers the Spanish third person construction, 'my person.' "He's incredibly serene, but at the same time a powerful force," one person that met him said. "Make no mistake, he's a warrior." Through half a century of fighting Marulanda has become the undisputed symbol of Colombia's current war of attrition. With little flash he has created the largest rebel army in the hemisphere; most of his troops emulate his sturdy lead-by-example tradition. Like their leader, they seem to be saying they do not seek fame, just a small plot of land.

Sureshot Marulanda barely moved until FARC leaders called on him to speak twenty minutes later. Then he shuffled forward. Some of the crowd clapped lightly, while most of the others strained their necks to see. Rebel troops then pointed their guns toward the sky and shouted "HO!" to welcome their maximum *comandante*. He glanced up, acknowledging their salute, then settled behind the microphone. Like most of the people there, I was anxious to hear what, if anything, the ancient warrior would say. He rarely spoke in public, and even when he did, it was usually in a deep, threatening tone. This time, he pulled a piece of paper out of his pocket, unfolded it, and read in a slow methodical manner, pausing to catch his breath between each phrase.

"We must make changes to the government through the Bolivarian Movement in cities and the countryside with the help of the FARC to avoid what happened to the UP," he said before pushing his glasses back to his face. "This forces us to act clandestinely in the entire country until the political conditions allow us to participate on equal footing with the traditional political parties. This rally is going to make history in Colombia because a new movement [has arrived] in which all political races or creeds can come together to promote their social and economic interests with the knowledge that we are opening ways for a new democracy without fear of being assassinated by the government."

The words came out dry, like a fourth-grader reading an essay. But with so many UP comrades in their graves, they rang true to many people in the crowd. The FARC's original experiment with Colombian democracy had failed; the UP was destroyed, and the FARC would have to act clandestinely. In a way, the rebels were the victims, and hearing Sureshot say it made the point even more powerful. But I knew there was more to the story, and so did many Colombians.

The rally ended, but the new debate had already begun. Even before the Bolivarian Movement had finished its first call for new members, people had started to ask the question that had plagued me about the UP for years. In the days leading up to the rally, the army claimed it had intercepted a conversation between Mono Jojoy and another FARC commander during which Mono Jojoy allegedly said that the Bolivarian Movement was another "party of war." That's what they said about the UP, I thought.

As the guerrillas herded the people toward San Vicente again, I wondered if Colombia was bracing itself for another slaughter. The front lines, of course, wouldn't be anywhere near the DMZ or the FARC's camps. They would be where they've always been in Colombia: in people's houses and their front yards; in the parks and the cafés. And the frontline soldiers wouldn't be the guerrillas. They would be eighteen-year-old boys with Nike hats that read "No Fear" and who believed in myths that only someone like Sureshot Marulanda could inspire.

The FARC's void of political leaders was like a gaping hole in a roof. During the UP years, the rebels had gathered huge crowds just by dropping in for breakfast. Guerrillas like Braulio Herrera became national voices. Their opinions were heard on the radio, in congress, even in the backroom political powwows. The day the FARC launched the Bolivarian Movement, however, it seemed more like May Day in Moscow than the UP's national convention. The rebels' show of arms was more convincing than their speeches. They didn't mingle among the people, and it was clear they had coerced most of them into going to the rally. A local teacher standing in the muddy field listening to the rebel leaders yell over the loudspeakers told me that the FARC levied fines on those who didn't attend the event. "In this difficult economic crisis," he said, smiling, "it's easier to get involved than pay."

If it was all a show, what was left of the FARC's politics? It was a tough question to answer, so the next day, I met with the proclaimed leader of the Bolivarian Movement, Alfonso Cano, at a small farmhouse in the DMZ to try. Unfortunately, Cano wasn't in a good mood, nor were his FARC comrades. What was supposed to be a great moment for the FARC felt like a wake. In front of us, rebel soldiers were cleaning up the debris on the muddy field, midlevel commanders were having solemn conversations among themselves, and Cano was grumbling at anyone who came within an arm's length. You would have thought that tragedy had befallen the group.

But once he sat down with me, Cano worked hard to give the appearance of an upbeat political leader. He was one of the few FARC commanders who didn't carry a rifle around at all times. Except for the fatigues, he looked much like the professor he would have been were it not for the war. He had a furry beard that was graying and glasses as thick as a windshield. The subject was the Bolivarian Movement. But both of us knew that there was a larger theme at hand: Does the FARC really have a political agenda? Of course, the rebel group had issued a political platform at its VIII Conference in 1993, which included a promise to dedicate 50 percent of the budget to social programs, make the state the principal owner of all natural resources, and create a unicameral system. But that wasn't what made a political movement, and both he and I knew it.

Not surprisingly, Cano began by trying to convince me that the rebels had a lot more political support than it seemed. "There are a ton of people," he said, "a ton. You can't even imagine how many there are who are telling us, 'Organize me. Put me to work but not working with you guys because I'm no good with guns, bombs, explosives. No. No . . . I'm not the one who is going to assassinate someone. I don't want to have anything to do with that. I'm interested in your political proposals.' So we're working with these people, the ones with political needs."

Cano was charismatic in his own way. His voice had a fever pitch to it and a sense of urgency. Yet he seemed agitated like other Communist hard-liners I had met. From the first moment, I felt like I was wasting his time, especially as I started criticizing the FARC's strategy. With the Bolivarian Movement, the enemy now had more targets to shoot at, I told him. "For us, what the enemy thinks is never a point of reference," Cano fired back. "We think about what we have, and we analyze what's happening, and what could happen, and then we make decisions."

But, I pressed on, the enemy is going to kill unarmed people and simply say they were with the Bolivarian Movement. Doesn't this seem dangerous to you? "They're going to do it anyway, with or without the movement," he responded, a little peeved now. "The government's policy is to use terror to wipe out anything that doesn't adhere or sympathize with what it's doing. What I mean is that we can't let what the government is doing determine what we do."

The army, I pointed out, declared that the Bolivarian Movement was a "party of war," just like the UP. But Cano denied that Mono Jojoy was one of the recorded voices who spoke of the "party of war." Then he added, "We're building an organization so that we can reach political power. The conditions under which we struggle are imposed on us. By principle, we want the road to be a civilized one, peaceful. But they won't let us. . . . Since 1983, they've been saying: 'The FARC's tactic is to increase its capacity for war.' No! No! This is not the final objective. So then what is it? Whatever they let us do. In the case of the Bolivarian Movement, it's to see if they'll let us campaign. If this movement starts to win political space, then it might reduce the need for military confrontation. But what happens is that our enemies want us to dis-appear. . . . They're the problem."

I reminded him of what happened to the UP. He paused, then assured me that the same thing wasn't going to happen to the Bolivarian Movement: "We're not going to be that stupid again. Sure, it's going to be more difficult working in secret. . . . But we can't do the UP thing again. This has to be something much more serious, and we have to take all the necessary security precautions."

Cano was, it was said, the country's best hope for peace. If anyone in the FARC was going to convince the hard-line rebels that they needed to hand over their guns, it was him. Yet Cano was hardly a peace lover or even a prag-matist. When I asked him what the FARC's long-term plans were, he didn't hesitate. "We've got that all worked out," he said. "We're going to be in power."

CHAPTER 14

JUSTICE AS A MEMORY

Colombia's politics has been called "the politics of anesthesia." There is so much death that people simply turn it off; they stop feeling. You see it in politicians who disregard death threats. You see it in wealthy city dwellers who ignore the increasing poverty and murder in the countryside. You see it in the newspapers who bury the constant reports of massacres, bombings, and combat. The anesthesia only wears off when they're directly affected by the war or when someone prods them with a stick. I would get berated by Colombians who thought international journalists were "only showing the bad side." What other side was there? I would ask. But then, after a while, I understood why they had gotten angry with me. What choice do they have? This is their country, and the easiest way to deal with the everyday violence is simply to ignore it.

Such was the case with the *Unión Patriótica*. By the late 1990s, the *Unión Patriótica* was more a political tool than a political party, more a fading memory than a reality. The FARC used the destruction of the UP to justify its neverending war against the government. The Communist Party used the UP to explain its demise in Colombian politics. But few people I spoke to outside of leftist circles even knew the UP still existed. Some of them, mostly the younger Colombians, stared blankly at me when I mentioned the party's name. To them, the UP was little more than an asterisk in a book, a brief mention in a newspaper article, a segue in a lecture. And it had only been a decade since Bernardo Jaramillo's spectacular murder by a teenage *suizo* in the Bogotá airport.

What was left of the party's political capital was being put into reviving this memory, understanding the UP's importance in the current conflict. It wasn't easy. So many people were still dying in Colombia. In most countries, a politically motivated assassination would have been front-page news. But in

Colombia, it hardly got more than a brief mention. Witness the death of Josué Giraldo, the lawyer I met early in my stay in Colombia. On October 14, 1996, the day after Josué was assassinated, the country's second largest newspaper, *El Espectador*, buried a two hundred-word story on page 6A; the country's most powerful newspaper, *El Tiempo*, carried a slightly longer version of the murder on page 12A.

To be fair, Josué's murder was smothered by a sea of homicides. During that same month, at least sixty-eight other people were killed for political reasons, while another twenty-three were "disappeared." Peasant farmers, small businessmen, students, Indians, and blue-collar workers all figured on the list. Most died in a style similar to Josué: tracked down by anonymous gunmen at their home or office, stopped at a roadblock, or caught in a bar. Throughout the 1990s, there were nearly four thousand politically motivated murders per year in Colombia; each seemed to carry its own insignia. The day after Josué was killed, for instance, right-wing death squads forced a child to show them where their victims were having a drink before dragging them away to their deaths in front of the tiny, unwitting informant.

Still, what was left of the UP sought to sift through this endless barrage of death. UP leaders fought for protection for their surviving members, and indemnity for the victims' relatives. They wrote reports and wriggled their way into human rights commissions to get their voices heard. Most of all, they sought justice. In this struggle for justice, there were a few brave people leading the UP's efforts. One of them was Iván Cepeda.

I met Iván in New York City years before I began investigating the UP. He was giving lectures on the destruction of the party. We kept in touch after I moved to Colombia and occasionally shot pool together in the dusty billiard halls in downtown Bogotá. Iván was a tender person, the type you couldn't imagine being involved in anything nefarious or risky. He was more mischief than real trouble. His corpulent body, thick glasses, and curly, black hair made him look like the philosophy professor that he was. But he took life about as seriously as a clown in a circus, and his black humor sometimes made me squinch.

Iván's struggle for justice centered on his father, Manuel Cepeda. For Colombian Communists, Manuel was an icon. He was the director of the Communist Party weekly, *Voz*, for years before running and winning a congressional post for the UP in 1992 and a senate position in 1994. He had a revolutionary spirit that members of the party revered. He didn't seek fame; it found him. To youngsters in the Communist Party, Manuel was the working man's artiste, the blue-collar bohemian. Manuel organized theater groups. They performed original plays at marches and in poor neighborhoods. He put together artists and writers who would give dramatic readings of revolutionary poetry in cafés and bars. With Manuel, they spread the word through compassion, not rhetoric. He also instructed them to challenge authority through subtle directives, not blaring megaphones. "He taught us that the artist should be committed to the people," one of his former Communist Party students told me. "He taught us to be honest revolutionaries. 'The revolution begins with us,' he would say. 'In our houses.'"

At the office, Manuel was the vertebrae of the Communist Party; the ideologue, the one who set the tone for the discussions. But he never put himself in front of others. He preferred the backroom debate to the speech at the podium, the printed word to the public argument. In part, he sought a lower profile for his own safety. "He wanted to go out and eat ice cream," the same former student told me, echoing the needs of other slain party members like Bernardo Jaramillo. "He never played with this idea of threats. He was never self-important."

By the early 1990s, most of Manuel's closest colleagues were dead or hiding, and he was forced to take center stage. It didn't take him long to adjust. He was not a politician by trade but strutted through congress like he had always been a member. He attacked the UP's critics and denounced its repressors. Manuel mentioned army officers by name, including the man who many believe would later order his killing, Colonel Rodolfo Herrera Luna. "They're all powerful commanders of military battalions," he told the senate just before he was murdered, "who oppose negotiations and distinguish themselves for their professional anti-communism and their connections to paramilitary groups."

Manuel's frankness and very public outrage eventually caught up to him, as did his famously pro-FARC stance. Manuel was a well-known "orthodox" Communist. First, he shut out social democrats like the old Communist Party stalwart Alberto Rojas Puyo as they challenged the party's strategies. Then he battled *Perestroikas* like Bernardo Jaramillo. *La combinación de todas las formas de lucha*—the Communists' longtime use of legal and illegal methods simultaneously to overthrow the government—was Manuel's credo, and as part of the Communist Party's Executive Committee, he had responsibilities that included maintaining contact with the FARC. Manuel was not a martyr like other Communists, but he also wasn't a pragmatist. His indiscretions cost him his life.

Four months after Manuel became a senator, he was killed. Assassins riding double on a motorcycle shot him dead as he drove through Bogotá in his car with a bodyguard. The two men accused of shooting Manuel were army personnel. Paramilitary chief Carlos Castaño was being tried in absentia for masterminding the murder. Iván had been pushing the case for years, and his persistence had paid dividends. Manuel's was one of the few UP cases to ever reach a judge, and Iván was seeing it through to the end despite the possible repercussions.

I visited Iván as the judge was nearing a decision on his father's case. Iván lived with his wife, Claudia, in a tiny two-room apartment on the edge of Bogotá. It was clean but overrun with books and artifacts from around the world. Whenever I turned, I risked knocking over a nineteenth-century clock from Russia or a hand-carved bowl from Hungary that Manuel had collected while he was in exile with his family in Eastern Europe. Manuel left Colombia many times because of the constant threats and legal actions taken against him. He almost always took his family with him. His time in Europe gave him an appreciation for the high culture he had missed while trying to survive in Colombia. Manuel took up painting and sculpture. After his father's death, Iván collected all the memories. Manuel's dark, abstract portraits hung along Iván's single narrow hallway.

Iván was thirty-eight years old when we met that day, but he had the tired feel of someone in his fifties. He walked slowly around the dining room table where I was sitting and pulled a chair out for himself. His bushy beard had a few strands of gray amid his dark complexion. He was a little chubby but on the verge of becoming a new man, he said, "by starving myself." He and Claudia were in the middle of a grueling diet that left him weak. Still, as always, he was in good spirits. "If we don't lose twenty pounds by the end of the month, then we lose a bet with our cousins," Iván said, giving a nice pat to his belly. "I've already lost five in about three months, so I figure I'll just accelerate the program a little bit."

I nibbled on the sweet bread he had on the table, while Iván looked at me with his eyes springing from underneath his thick, square-rimmed glasses. Claudia was in the kitchen scrambling some eggs with onions and tomato to make me the Colombian breakfast standby, *huevos pericos*. Neither of them could eat the bread or the eggs. They simply ogled the possibilities.

Iván and I spoke that day as we had since we met five years earlier in New York: with a light touch and dark humor sneaking through about every other sentence. "My father had a penchant for clocks and keys," he explained to me about the abundance of artifacts in the apartment. "He had a liking for antiques. He would see something on the street, and he would buy it. "

Then Iván launched into one of his many quirky stories about his father. After finding what looked like a bone in a parking lot one day, Iván said, Manuel dragged the family into an excavation project. "And when the police came to check it out," he continued, "they didn't know what all the rocks were doing there laying in the middle of this parking lot." Fittingly, Iván said, the family had found an old, buried cemetery.

Since his father's death, Iván had created a foundation in Manuel's name. He used the foundation to revive his father's spirit and push people to think about the UP's legacy. Iván and his wife drew together disparate pieces of the leftist community at the foundation's events, where, like Manuel, Iván tried to combine art with politics. During one event at Bogotá's planetarium that I attended, Iván presented a slide show about the UP in between the stars on the ceiling. He followed it up by having someone paint a portrait to the sound of a cello.

Later, he and Claudia compiled a book called *Memoria frente a los crímenes de lesa humanidad* (Memory Against the Crimes Against Humanity). In it, authors from a broad spectrum reflected on the politics of anesthesia. "There's a psycho-social amnesia," the two wrote in one chapter, "that comes from the traumatic experiences in life." They didn't specify which experiences, but the couple went on to indict the army, the government, and the entire ruling class for the extermination of the UP. "The newspaper *El Tiempo* [the most influential in Colombia]," they wrote, "frequently insinuates, suggests or explicitly says that because of the actions of the guerrillas, the representatives of the legal opposition can be Objects of Extermination."

In his father's case, Iván was only slightly hopeful that he would eventually get true justice. Case files showed that Colonel Herrera Luna organized the killing following the death of one of his colleagues at the hands of the FARC. Officers like Herrera Luna never made the distinction between FARC commanders and UP politicians. In this case, the colonel believed that Manuel Cepeda worked for the FARC, and so he organized the hit as a kind of tit for tat. He selected two members of the intelligence unit, who coordinated the job with paramilitary leader Carlos Castaño. Using vehicles from the XX Brigade, the army's intelligence headquarters, the two men snuck up on Cepeda as he left his house for the senate and filled him with several rounds.

The two hitmen's bravado set the investigation in motion. They bragged to another member of the intelligence unit about how they'd killed the senator on orders from Herrera Luna who had since become a general. The listener subsequently provided this evidence to investigators. It was also easy to trace the gun that killed Manuel back to the military. But there were always snags when investigations got too close to high-ranking military officials. The witness's wife disappeared, and the ballistics division destroyed one of the bullets that fatally wounded Manuel. "It isn't logical or normal," Iván's lawyers wrote in a brief, "that evidence handed over to the authorities, which was so essential to this case, be handled so irresponsibly."

Not normal or perfectly logical? Iván understood the situation. "There's a very complex system of impunity in place," he told me while I ate the *huevos pericos* that Claudia had prepared for me. "They pay the paramilitaries, and when they realize everything's coming out in public, they start to cover their tracks: threatening the witnesses, covering up the assassination. Then they have their own disciplinary code; it's like a legal wall that's impossible to get through. . . . It's incredible that we've gotten so many details about how the crime was committed. I mean we've gotten past the part that no one ever gets past. And now we have the proof so that the perpetrators can be found guilty. We can show how they work with paramilitary groups, what role the para-military groups play, and what role the army plays. This is a huge step toward justice, right?"

I stared at him blankly. Iván knew the answer. General Rodolfo Herrera Luna—the subject of his father's public scorn in the senate and the one who had most likely ordered his father's death—had died during the investigation. What's more, the two soldiers who had committed the crime remained on active duty until just days before I met with Iván and Claudia. Iván was frus-trated but not surprised. "What this shows is that there's a very sophisticated system of impunity in place," he reiterated. "For their part, the paramilitaries killed all the other guys involved in the crime. And up to this point, [para-military leader Carlos] Castaño has been untouchable. These guys in jail [the two men accused of assassination], I'm sure they're going to be killed too, don't you think?"

With every word, Iván was growing more weary and pessimistic. But he liked to treat these things as academic questions, not the life-and-death issues they were. It somehow made it easier if he was dealing with sociology rather than his father. "In the army, there are always groups of military per-sonnel who know each other and would never let anything happen to one another," he continued. "How these groups relate to the rest of the govern-ment is an interesting question, right? And how do these groups work within society? I'd say these people are just going to continue doing whatever they want. That's the system that's in place. That's what everybody wants. What's different about this is that we've gotten so far with our case. That's the crazy thing."

On the heels of an international statement by Human Rights Watch, the military had reluctantly suspended the two army soldiers accused of the mur-der of Iván's father. They had been working for military intelligence even while being investigated for Manuel's murder. As Iván said, the officers were protecting their own at all costs. Still, Iván and Claudia pushed ahead. That afternoon, they were meeting with Colombia's defense minister about Manuel's case. They hoped to convince the minister that he needed to purge the military. (The minister would later force more than three hundred personnel into retirement; paramilitary leader Carlos Castaño told the *Washington Post* in an interview that some 30 of those who were purged ended up working for him.) It was part of the larger battle those from the UP could still play in Colombia. The party was dead, but the fight to alter the system continued.

As expected, his father's case also brought Iván and Claudia unwanted attention. The two received death threats over the telephone, one of which they still had on tape. Iván took out the tape, put it in the answering machine, and hit play. Claudia's voice came on announcing the telephone number and the "please leave a message after the beep." What followed was incomprehensible babble; the static from what apparently was a radio telephone virtually drowned out the message. Although I could tell the voice was deep and disturbing, I couldn't understand anything, so Iván explained it to me.

"Look," he said with a smile creeping into the corner of his mouth. "This is more or less a rap song. First it says, 'Yes, why not,' or 'Tell me why not.' Then there's some part that says, 'Little bitch, you better take care. I'm going to kill you as well.'" Iván imitated the scratchy voice of the man on the tape and repeated, "'And you as well.'" Then he laughed. "It's not Gloria Estefan," Iván joked. "But what can you do?"

Iván was realistic. The odds of obtaining justice in Colombia are slim. Legal watchdog groups say that 97 percent of all crimes in Colombia go unpunished. The government says what it calls "judicial impunity" is really closer to 40 percent. In either case, murderers who escape the scene of the crime rarely have to face a judge. When they do, they can often bribe or intimidate their way out of jail time.

The irony is that Colombia is full of attorneys, progressive laws, and a plethora of government bodies designed to process legal problems. According to the government, Colombia has over 100,000 lawyers—about one in every four hundred people—and a growing number of law schools and aspiring JDs. In 1991, Colombia also adopted a new constitution. This constitution affords indigenous and black communities some of the most generous allowances in the world. Both minority groups can obtain collective land titles, and in the case of indigenous groups, they can apply their own laws. The constitution calls for the government to protect minorities' interests and promote the education of their cultures. It ensures housing, health, and education. It has antidiscriminatory acts that relate to sex and ethnicity, and it provides the legal framework to keep false accusations from leading to jail time. The constitution also added the ombudsman's office and attorney general's office, two bodies designed to assist in bringing justice to Colombian citizens. Together with the inspector general, the comptroller, and the military penal system, the government has five entities receiving complaints and filing cases.

Still, this attempt to beef up the already meaty judicial system means very little in real life. Murderers walk free. White-collar crime continues uninterrupted. Corruption runs rampant. Few people believe the new laws, new government bodies, and new constitution have changed anything. And why should they? The government made similar piecemeal efforts just as the FARC was launching the UP.

"The Government, in accordance with the Constitution and the laws, will give the *Unión Patriótica* the guarantees and security it needs so that it can campaign as well as participate in elections in the same way other political parties do," the 1984 cease-fire agreement between the government and the FARC read. "The government will use all the force of the law against any citizen or authority that inhibits these rights or denies, ignores, or refuses to recognize the rights that they [the members of the new party] have. The government will also guarantee security and liberty to the FARC during the process of incorporating its members into political activity."

With the UP long since destroyed and virtually no one in jail for killing its members, party leaders sought to hold the government to the 1984 agreement. Fittingly, they sought justice outside of Colombia. In 1997, UP leaders went to the Organization of American States's (OAS) Inter-American Tribunal and filed a complaint charging the government with political "genocide" of the UP. The OAS's tribunal had little judicial sway and even less independent investigative power. I once mentioned the name José Gonzalo "*El Mejicano*" Rodríguez Gacha to one of the OAS lawyers working on the UP case, and she asked me, "Who's he?" Still, the tribunal had some symbolic and economic power. Condemnation from the OAS could lead to economic sanctions or, at the very least, continued diplomatic pressure to improve the government's human rights record.

In the end, the case didn't go well for the UP, but a larger battle has resulted from it. "Genocide," the OAS judges decided, did not include the elimination of an entire political party, as the UP lawyers contended. The OAS judges, however, did try to mediate between the sides. An arbitration resulted in a "friendly" agreement: The government would reopen the cases that had been shelved or "archived," as they say in Colombia; the plaintiffs would gather a working list of all the victims. In this way, relatives of the victims would get indemnified, and the government didn't have to accept that it was guilty of "political genocide."

To push the OAS case forward, the UP formed a nongovernmental organization, which it called *Reiniciar* or "New Beginnings." The person in charge was a stunning and stylish woman in her mid-forties named Jahel Quiroga. Jahel was an ex-UP militant who came from outside the Communist Party. Like few others, she could deal with peasant UP militants as well as she could deal with high government officials. She had learned most of her tricks during the UP wars in the blue-collar city of Barrancabermeja in the late 1980s. It was, as she told me, a "complicated" story.

"There was a whole bunch of us who were always picking up the dead," she explained one day in the *Reiniciar* office. "So we just said, 'Hey. Why don't we form a committee?' And that's how CREDHOS got started." CREDHOS stands for *Comité Regional de Derechos Humanos* or "Regional Human Rights Committee." Beginning with the UP, the group chronicled the paramilitaries' and militaries' destruction of the party and the region. Then the committee itself was targeted. Three CREDHOS leaders were murdered. After a couple attempts on her own life, Jahel had to flee to Bogotá. She and several other Barrancabermeja refugees then started *Reiniciar*.

When I saw Jahel in her Bogotá office, she was swamped as usual. The office was in a cramped eleventh-story apartment overlooking downtown. It had four rooms packed with old computers and rickety wooden file cabinets. It was more than a decade since Bernardo Jaramillo had been killed, but *Reiniciar*'s office was flooded with victims. They came from every corner of the country, and they looked as if they had been walking in the desert for weeks.

It was in the *Reiniciar* office that I had met María Carmen de Cañón, the widow of Julio Cañón, the UP mayor who died along a road in the Eastern Plains that he wanted so much to pave. When I met her, living was a burden María Carmen could barely stand. She had survived. Most of the rest of her family and friends had died. And then she was being reminded of it in the worst kind of way. Like most of the others in the office, she had come to see Jahel because she was under threat. A man had telephoned her and said he was a paramilitary commander from San Martín, a small village in the Eastern Plains. "Remember your husband and your kids," he had said to her menacingly. He wanted her to be an informant, and María Carmen could barely contain herself. As she told me the story, her eyes widened, she rubbed her knees, and then María confessed, "I'm so tense. My legs hurt. I'm sick in the heart. I'm psychologically sick. . . . My only crime was that my husband was from the Communist Party and the UP. I've been denouncing this. I've been a victim of the UP."

There were countless others who sought out Jahel for the same reason: They were victims of the UP. On that same day that I saw María Carmen, a former UP supporter from the coffee belt came into the office. His brother had been shot the week before by paramilitaries. The gunman thought his brother was him. The man was devastated that someone had died in his place. "My brother wasn't part of any political party," he told me, holding back the tears. "He was just a teacher."

Others told similarly horrifying stories. There's not enough room in one book to write them down.

Jahel herself could barely keep up with the demand. A few weeks later, while I was in the office, a dozen UP militants arrived one day from La Uribe, the old home to the FARC's *Casa Verde* headquarters and one of the municipalities forming part of the current FARC stronghold, the DMZ, where the rebels were negotiating peace with the government. The people had heard the paramilitaries had a death list with their names on it. As they mingled in the *Reiniciar* office, Jahel drafted a letter to the government asking for the state to "guarantee their safety." She then signed, sealed, and sent it, knowing full well that it read exactly as had the cease-fire agreement signed between the FARC and the government in 1984. It was the kind of empty promise that she was constantly forced to make as the head of the organization. Most UP victims sought exile. Others would settle for peace and tranquility. Jahel had a hard time delivering either.

Still, *Reiniciar* chugged along. People came in presenting new cases every day. And when I last visited, the organization had cataloged 1,163 murders, 123 "disappearances," and 225 threats against UP members. There were also forty-three UP survivors of attempted murders. Jahel insisted there were "many, many" more cases to be found, perhaps as many as three thousand. When I asked her how she knew, she shrugged. "We know there were deaths that weren't registered and others that didn't want to say that their dead relatives were from the UP for fear of what might happen," she told me. "This investigation is hard. People are hiding; others are in exile. No one wants to talk."

Jahel had a team of lawyers and investigators helping her, but they had just begun the real work of going town by town looking for victims. "Besides," she added, "this is the attorney general's job." Yet by the time I met with Jahel, the one-year-old agreement between the UP and the government to dig up archived cases was already hitting snags. The attorney general's office worked overtime on the UP cases in Bogotá. They also moved to reopen archived investigations across the country. But things were moving slowly, and Jahel was frustrated. She complained to the government, the OAS, the diplomatic community, and me. She even accused one of the investigators of being a paramilitary supporter. When I saw the investigator, he could barely hold back his contempt for *Reiniciar*'s leader. "I spent all of my spare time reading these files, reconstructing cases, calling people, and then she says that about me," he said. "I don't need this." He excused himself from double duty soon after Jahel made the accusation.

There was also the question of guilt. For many government investigators, the UP militants were simply rebels disguised as politicians. These investigators were not paramilitary supporters. But they were also not keen on reopening investigations into "guerrilla" deaths, and when they did, they often treated the victims' relatives and friends as if they were guilty of a crime as well, no matter what their connection to the FARC. "They aggressively interrogate witnesses," Jahel said of the government investigators. "They ask about UP 'commanders.'" Jahel claimed the attitude made it seem as if murdering a UP militant was justified. "Aside from killing them," she added, "they're stigmatizing them for life."

In the meantime, Jahel said her team was trying to recover the "real truth." "Not the judicial truth," she explained, "you know, what the attorney general and inspector general are going to get. We want to show them the value of the truth because they said we were guerrillas." Like Iván, Jahel was fighting more for memory than justice. "We just want the victims to feel some dignity again," she said. "The punishment for the crime is relative. . . . We're going to condemn them with the truth."

Throughout the investigations into UP deaths, the government continued to argue that it wasn't to blame. Authorities insisted that drug traffickers like José Gonzalo "*El Mejicano*" Rodríguez Gacha were responsible for the majority of UP murders. In 1992, the ombudsman's office issued a report stating that the FARC had robbed Rodríguez Gacha one too many times, and the UP had "picked up the tab." The ombudsman's office drew similar conclusions from the FARC's kidnapping and killing of *Don* Jesús Castaño, Fidel and Carlos's father. "This was the best the party could hope for," one government lawyer assured me, handing over a copy of the amicable settlement between the sides that called for the opening of archived cases.

But the frustrations continued. While the attorney general's office and *Reiniciar* worked to unearth the "real truth," other cases against UP killers came apart. An investigation into the November 11, 1988, massacre in Segovia linked several policemen and a lieutenant colonel to the threats and subsequent killings. But the police were absolved from any responsibility, even though it was clear they had avoided confronting the paramilitaries' caravan of death as it killed forty-three people that day. Authorities also tied the "Codfish" Liberal congressman César Pérez to the slaughter but never gathered enough evidence to try him for his participation. For his part, the lieutenant colonel had appealed the guilty verdict, and the case was at the Supreme Court awaiting its determination.

Cases in the Eastern Plains followed suit. One of the most infamous paramilitary leaders, Victor Carranza, spent over four years in custody for his participation in the murders of dozens of leftist militants and UP supporters. Investigators even unearthed mass graves on one of his properties in the Eastern Plains. The sixty-year-old "emerald czar" seemed unfazed by the charges when I visited with him at a DAS training facility just outside Bogotá where he was being held. He told me that people confused him with a paramilitary leader because he spent his time with a lot of friends.

"If we're going to leave the area, we'll call some others," he explained to me. "And say, 'We're going tomorrow.' And they'll say, 'Why don't we go together?' And then we'll have a whole bunch of us going at the same time. This is a big group. There are four, sometimes five cars. We all leave together. And then where are we going to eat breakfast? Anywhere where there's a restaurant on the side of the road. So we go, and we have the five or six cars from the ranch. And when we all arrive, sometimes we have ten cars, and the people get scared. They say we're paramilitaries. . . . But we're just people. It's just a coincidence that we get together on the side of the road, and we have a lot of cars. It's the same if we're going to eat lunch. There are thirty or forty people, the majority of them with revolvers, and the people say we're paramilitaries."

Carranza was in custody but maintained control over his business interests during that time. He was a powerful man with powerful contacts. For a while, he was even able to wash his image. In 1995, before he was arrested, U.S. embassy representatives visited the legendary emerald czar at one of his Boyacá emerald mines to talk about the latest developments in the industry. Local press got wind of the visit and of a thank-you note from the embassy to Carranza. "It was an unexpected pleasure for us to see Victor Carranza in action in the mines scratching away at the mountain in search of more emeralds," one of the U.S. officials wrote. The official added that the embassy would encourage the U.S. emerald mining company Kennecott or any other interested U.S. company to form a partnership with Carranza's *Tecminas*. "We'll never forget the experience," he ended the letter. The embassy later issued a statement saying the employees didn't know who Carranza was.

Not long after I saw him, Carranza was released. A judge had determined that the time limit of the investigation had expired. Another judge
appealed the decision, but in the meantime, the emerald czar was free to go.
He kept a very low profile thereafter. I tried several times to track him down,
but they always told me he was working in his mines.

The pattern was repeated in other cases. While I was doing my investigation, one of the few UP killers ever to be convicted for murdering party
militants was about to be released from prison. When I saw the huge ex-
FARC turned paramilitary assassin in the high-security prison near Cali,
Alonso de Jesús Baquero, better known as Black Vladimir, had been in jail for
12 years. He wouldn't tell me the details of what he had done, he said,
because he was waiting for someone to buy the rights to his horrifying tale.
In his mind, the money would be to compensate for his suffering. "They say
you have a son when you're with them between the ages of one and ten," he
told me, referring to his second child. "After that, you're just friends. Well,
I've missed the better part of both of my children's lives." I thought about his
eight hundred or so victims; he continued. "I was in the war for a long time.
First, I fought for the people. Then, I fought," he paused, "for individual
interests. This last fight is for me and my family."

During his time in jail, Vladimir had used the system to his advantage.
His original jail sentence was Colombia's maximum, thirty years. This fell to
twenty because he confessed to his crimes. He had studied and worked for
about forty months, which had dropped his sentence a comparable time. He
had given up a lot of his friends and colleagues, which further lowered his
sentence. When I saw him, he was hoping to get out after two more years.
Fourteen years, I thought, was a small price for killing more than eight hundred people.

But other cases didn't even get as far as the one against Vladimir. Despite
the mountain of evidence to convict all those charged, the Manuel Cepeda
case against paramilitary leader Carlos Castaño ended pretty much the way
Iván Cepeda had predicted. The two soldiers took all the blame. The
deceased General Herrera Luna was never investigated. And the judge exon-
erated Carlos Castaño, who walked away from the case laughing at the
Colombian justice system. "How ironic! How sad is this justice [system]!?"
Castaño told his biographer. "The court absolved me from all responsibility
of the crime, and I didn't even assign a lawyer to defend me." Castaño admitted to the author that he "directed" the killing of Manuel. Castaño was angry,
he claimed, because the FARC had detonated a bomb that killed an army
general in the days prior.

"Manuel Cepeda was part of the FARC," Castaño said. "And if anyone has any doubt about it, verify the name of the urban front of the guerrillas in Bogotá: *Frente Manuel Cepeda Vargas*. I reacted swiftly after the death of [General] Carlos Julio Gil Colorado because Manuel Cepeda worked for the FARC as a legal representative. I was always watching him. I intercepted his calls and listened to his conversations. I was always watching him so I could catch him in his dirty game, retain him, and exchange him for an important kidnap victim. Manuel Cepeda didn't have a position in the FARC, but he was one of its important people. He founded the Communist Youth [JUCO] and taught the most important guerrilla leaders."

Shortly after the verdict in his father's case, Iván and Claudia fled to Paris on an academic scholarship. They were, of course, disappointed at the judge's decision, but at least they were still alive. They sent me an e-mail a little while later. They hadn't given up, they insisted. They just needed a break. "We're safe and learning new things," Iván wrote, "like French."

CHAPTER 15

THE GREAT ESCAPE

It was a blistering hot, sunny day in the small cattle town of Puerto Berrío when I realized that the right-wing paramilitary leader Carlos Castaño thought he would escape prosecution for terminating the FARC's political party, the *Unión Patriótica*. He believed he could escape because he was a popular man who had fought all the battles no one else would in Colombia. He believed it because he was powerful, commanding an army of close to ten thousand well-trained troops who regularly took on the guerrillas in their strongholds in order to wrench the country back into the hands of the government and the country's elite. Most of all, Carlos believed he would escape prosecution because he thought that punishing the FARC by killing off the UP was justified. Getting off free was his reward.

To see Carlos Castaño in Puerto Berrío that day, Scott Wilson, the *Washington Post* correspondent, and I went through an elaborate maze. First we flew over the central mountain range from Bogotá to Medellín. As instructed, we went straight to a chicken fingers place in the airport, where we rendezvoused with some of Carlos's assistants. One of them then led us downstairs and onto the Medellín airport tarmac, where we boarded a four-seat Cessna. Soon we were over the mountains, heading for Puerto Berrío.

It was a clear day, and the scenery below us was stunning. A patch of lakes surrounded by mountains reflected the sun. A resort town sat along the edge of one of the shorelines. Pieces of the mainland spread into the water; steep precipices and jagged rocks encircled it. There was a tall, smooth, oval-shaped boulder resembling *pão de azucar*, the famous rock steeped on the waterfront in Rio de Jainero. The area would have been a paradise like Rio, but there wasn't anyone left to enjoy it. Dirt roads led to abandoned vacation homes and barren docks. No one risked traveling too far from the big cities anymore. The war had swallowed Colombians' courage.

In the back of the airplane, I read furiously. The book was Carlos Castaño's second. But as opposed to his first, which just reprinted things he had written in press releases, this one had all the characters and plots of a great spy novel: politicians, military officials, drug traffickers, and guerrillas all vying for our hero's head; and Carlos excitedly explaining to the author how he had managed to escape from the clutches of the enemy again and again until he created his army of ten thousand men. These men now formed part of the United "Self-Defense" Groups of Colombia or *Autodefensas Unidas de Colombia* (AUC). They were an expanded version of Fidel's *Tangueros*, the private army Carlos's brother had used to wipe out guerrillas, their suspected collaborators, and the UP just a decade earlier. What was left of the *Tangueros* had filtered into the AUC, which was now run by Carlos.

Fidel, meanwhile, had simply disappeared.

Like Carlos, Fidel had fought the dirty war for the government against the FARC and its political party, the UP. Significantly, Fidel and Carlos had also organized a vigilante group—the PEPES or *Perseguidos por Pablo Escobar* (People Persecuted by Pablo Escobar)—that helped the government hunt down and finally kill the mighty drug lord. Before then, Escobar was holding the government hostage—detonating car bombs in the middle of major cities and kidnapping prominent Colombians—so he wouldn't get extradited to the United States. In the four years since Escobar had begun his war against the Colombian government, his men had exploded four hundred bombs, killing more than one thousand people, including one bomb that killed sixty-seven people in Bogotá. Extradition, meanwhile was outlawed.

The destruction wasn't limited to Colombia. "When a kid smokes crack," *People* magazine declared at the time, "there's Pablo. When Miami cops bust a dealer, there's Pablo. When . . . a baby [is] born addicted to drugs in New York City or another celeb [is] booked into rehab, there's Pablo too." The thought that one man could have such a negative impact on the United States infuriated the U.S. government, which began calling for a war without quarter. The vigilante group led by The House of Castaño began waging it.

The PEPES bombed Escobar's houses and burned his relatives' and associates' offices; they threatened, harassed, and assassinated dozens of Escobar's friends, relatives, and business partners. Escobar hit back with more terror, but Fidel and Carlos thwarted some of the attacks and led authorities to safe houses and to drug and weapon depots. They acted as chiefs and guardians for the police. On one particular raid, several policemen fell into a river they were crossing. Fidel jumped into the rapids and pulled one of the officers to safety. Two others died, but Fidel's allegiance to them—and theirs to him—had become as unquestioned as his leadership.

The U.S. government knew all about the PEPES's dirty war against Escobar. Both the Drug Enforcement Administration (DEA) and the Central Intelligence Agency (CIA) worked closely with the police in the Escobar manhunt. A 1993 memo written by the U.S. ambassador shows that the agencies knew the PEPES were running the show. Another government document indicates that the DEA had at least one direct contact with close associates of the Castaño brothers. The agencies couldn't claim ignorance about whom they were dealing with. A May 1990 U.S. embassy memo read: "Authorities now believe that [Fidel] Castaño was responsible for many of the most notorious of the massacres of rural inhabitants which have plagued Colombia over the past several years." Other memos detailed Fidel Castaño's role in assassinations, massacres, and mass graves throughout the north of the country. But the U.S. agents didn't complain. They wanted Escobar too much.

The chase continued for months. Escobar deftly eluded authorities, but his associates kept falling, and his scramble to find a safe place to hide his family from the PEPES kept drawing him into the open. By now, the PEPES had destroyed Escobar's organization, leaving him desperate and isolated. On December 2, 1993, Colombian government agents tracked Escobar to one of his Medellín safe houses. When Pablo fled across the tin roofs of some ramshackle huts, police gunfire cut through his beefy body. A dramatic photo of Escobar doubled over like a slain lion proved once again that Fidel Castaño had no rivals.

The campaign against Pablo Escobar would be Fidel's last public battle. He was tired of war, but he was even more tired of not getting his due. Nothing irked him more than the lack of respect. "I don't need forgiveness from anyone," Fidel told some guests on his farm once. "I saved this country from communism." He had also saved it from Escobar, he thought. But neither victory seemed to bring him any closer to what he really wanted: a way out.

Fidel was under investigation by the Colombian government for multiple assassinations of UP leaders, massacres of Communist supporters and suspected guerrilla sympathizers, and his involvement with the PEPES. In the early 1990s, other paramilitaries had made deals with the government to avoid being prosecuted as drug traffickers and murderers. They had managed to win some of the same legal protections as the guerrillas who were treated as political combatants rather than common criminals. Now Fidel, too, wanted political recognition, which could eventually lead to amnesty. He sent letters to Colombian officials, but they were mute. The government had stopped talking about deals for paramilitaries; it was talking about jail. And Fidel wasn't going to find out what that meant for him. "If I can't resolve my legal situation," he told the guests on his farm, "I can live in Europe or Israel. I'm not bound to this land."

Just a little more than a month after Pablo Escobar was gunned down in Medellín, Fidel vanished. Carlos told varying tales of how Fidel was "swallowed by the jungle" and, later, how Fidel was felled by a "shot right to the heart" from guerrillas and died shortly thereafter. But the rumors and sightings of him have yet to die away. In May 1994, five months after Carlos said Fidel died, the U.S. State Department's Bureau of Intelligence and Research produced a dossier titled "Profile of Fidel Castaño, Super Drug-Thug," which treated its subject as very much alive.

In Colombia, the attorney general's office continued to charge Fidel with crimes long after he disappeared. In 1998, four years after "the shot right to the heart," the office indicted him and Carlos for the 1997 murder of two human rights activists in Bogotá, one of them a former Jesuit priest. One ex–government investigator told me he had good reason to believe Fidel was living in Medellín as late as 1997. That impression was reinforced by a later encounter with a paramilitary assassin, who told the investigator that "Professor Yarumo," one of Fidel's aliases, had sent him to kill the ex-priest in Bogotá. An internal investigation by the attorney general's office in 1997 said Fidel was running the paramilitaries in the province of Antioquia.

Other leads continued to come in. A London source told me Fidel did finally make his way to Israel, where he bought some land. A former Colombian security agent said that Fidel was in Portugal, buying and selling black-market art. Sightings also included Madrid and Paris, his old stomping grounds while he posed as a posh art dealer and connoisseur. In Córdoba Province, along the coast where Fidel had his home during his last public years, a security agent told me that high-level politicians talked openly about Fidel as if he were alive. And in Valencia, the poverty-stricken cattle town where Fidel's legend stood the tallest, few people believed he was dead. "If the guerrillas had really killed him," an elderly shop owner asked me incredulously when I visited, "don't you think they would have said something?"

Whatever the truth, Fidel was gone. And while he left Carlos with the beginnings of a mighty army, he also straddled him with a rap sheet and the legal burden of the sins of the House of Castaño. But by all appearances, Carlos wasn't going to disappear like Fidel. His was a different strategy, because Carlos was a different paramilitary fighter. While Fidel protected his ever-growing assets, Carlos transformed the paramilitaries into a large army and stepped forward as its public leader. While Fidel stayed away from the press, Carlos relished the limelight, granting interviews, posing for photos, and writing a best-seller. *Mi confesión: Carlos Castaño revela sus secretos*, (My Confession: Carlos Castaño Reveals His Secrets), the paramilitary leader's authorized biography (the book is copywritten by both the author and Castaño) that I was frantically reading in the back of the Cessna on my way to Puerto Berrío, had sold close to 100,000 copies in Colombia. Carlos hoped to use this fame and the political legitimacy that came with it to escape prosecution, just as his older brother had. Only Carlos would face his accusers and dare them to send him to jail.

After an hour over the Andean mountains, we landed in Puerto Berrío on the burning plains of the Middle Magdalena Valley. The pilot smiled and popped open the doors for us. We piled out, and the heat of the valley hit me like a wave. The airport was tiny. There were no police or government security anywhere in sight, and the transition to our next vehicle was swift. We greeted some new guides, hopped into a shiny Toyota Landcruiser, and were off again.

For the first few minutes of the next leg, I just watched the town go by. Puerto Berrío was more than the heart of the Middle Magdalena Valley, it was the headquarters of destruction, the place from where the *Unión Patriótica* and the peace process between the government and the FARC were shattered into pieces. The angry General Fernando Landazábal had launched the XIV Brigade in Puerto Berrío in 1983, and countless anti-UP operations drew intelligence and logistic support from the brigade. What's more, Pablo Escobar and José Gonzalo "El Mejicano" Rodríguez Gacha owned land near Puerto Berrío and trained their soldiers, including the hulking ex-FARC turned paramilitary, Black Vladimir, in the region. Indeed, Vladimir's trucks of death that rode through Segovia on that fateful November 11, 1988, killing forty-three people—most of them UP supporters—left from Puerto Berrío and arrived to a party here after they had finished their macabre "errand."

In what some might call poetic justice, Escobar, Rodríguez Gacha, and Landazábal had all been killed themselves. Escobar and *"El Mejicano"* died at the hands of the police, Landazábal most likely at the hands of his own corrupt military. Just a few months after I spoke to him, the retired general was gunned down by a single assassin as he walked from his home to his office in northern Bogotá. Many theorize that a radical right-wing group within the army was responsible. But his assassin was never found, and the case remains shrouded in mystery.

Given its history, I expected Puerto Berrío to be a lot bigger than it was. But like so many other Colombian towns, Puerto Berrío seemed to be stranded in time. Bicycles and horse-drawn wagons occasionally crossed our path. Peasant farmers scurried along the streets. Our SUV must have looked like a spaceship compared with the rest of the dusty vehicles on the road. Over the years, the paramilitary project had proved that it was more a deep-freeze machine than an engine of economic growth. Change, especially when it involved modernizing an agrarian society based on cattle ranching and drug trafficking, was not part of the narco-paramilitary plan. Colombia, it seemed, remained stuck in the past because of the guerrillas' penchant to destroy things and the paramilitaries' tendency to thwart any change at all.

We exited on the other side of Puerto Berrío onto a smooth, level high-way. The air conditioner was on full blast, but the sun beaming through the window made me sweat. A conversation about guerrillas inevitably began. They had "lost their ideals"; they were "barbarous"; they had "no respect for human life," our hosts told us. The *autodefensas*, on the other hand, didn't kill civilians. "The press and *la Huoomen Raaghs* groups lie," they insisted.

After crossing through a few cow pastures and being waved by armed guards past some wooden fences, we arrived at a house that looked something like a small Swiss chalet. Several armed men in civilian garb lingered on the side porch. In the distance along the hills were some of Carlos Castaño's personal bodyguards, ring after ring of defense manned mostly by ex-guerrillas in fatigues. Our driver led us to the backyard, where there was a sparkling pool with white marble siding and a fountain.

Carlos was there waiting in a full camouflage outfit. He reached out his hand and said, "Steve." Then he greeted Scott, who congratulated him on his recent marriage to the daughter of a prominent cattle rancher. "Ah, *gracias, gracias*," the raspy-voiced commander responded. "And congratulations on your book," Scott continued. "*Gracias*," Castaño said. "But you know, there are more secrets," the paramilitary commander added shyly, referring to the title. "There are things people should know and things they shouldn't."

The three of us, plus Carlos's political attaché and one of his regional commanders, sat beneath a thatched-roof kiosk next to the pool. It was only 10:30 A.M., but the heat was unbearable. Two beautiful, scantily clad women brought us a constant flow of liquid—cola, coffee, water—to quell the torridity, while the paramilitary commander spoke with his characteristic flair. His arms sprang up and down. He reached for the sky and clenched his fists. He pinched at his pants while his eyes darted back and forth. He almost knocked my microphone out of my hands a few times. All the while, he never skipped a beat, stopped for a thought, or paused to consider what he was saying. He talked about congressmen, presidents, and diplomats; guerrillas, paramilitaries, and drug traffickers; politics, economics, and war; fame, family, and women. He was a machine who spoke incessantly about any subject. Well, almost any subject.

Just a year before we met in Puerto Berrío, Carlos's popularity had never been higher. His war against the guerrillas was proceeding at a faster pace than even he expected. The AUC, the organization he created following the disappearance of his brother Fidel, was growing exponentially. His territorial reach had increased as well. The $1.3 billion U.S. aid package for the Colombian government seemed to be helping his forces. Carlos understood that his war against the guerrillas and the U.S. war against the guerrillas were at their roots the same war. It was a mutually beneficial relationship, something that Carlos would try and use in his favor.

In the previous two years, U.S. special ops had trained three thousand Colombian army troops to fight illegal drug trafficking and the rebel groups. In the southern province of Putumayo and in the northern province of Arauca—both FARC bastions for years and centers of coca production in Colombia—paramilitaries arrived just ahead of the U.S.-trained anti-drug forces. And just after the Colombian government deployed its new specially trained troops, paramilitary leaders were spied in Putumayo suspiciously eating U.S. Army–supplied rations and bragging to reporters that they were spearheading the fight to retake the area. "The U.S. policy with regard to Colombia is good," Carlos had said to me point-blank during our first meeting.

Paramilitary leaders also told me on several occasions they were protecting business interests in Colombia, including international companies. The AUC had a strong presence near British Petroleum's oil fields in the Eastern province of Casanare, just south of Arauca. They controlled the Urabá region near the Panamanian border, where Dole and Chiquita had extensive banana plantations. In the northeastern corner of Colombia the paramilitaries had troops around a coal mine owned by Alabama-based Drummond. Throughout the country, they had established bases near Coca-Cola bottling factories.

By working closely with U.S.-trained troops and protecting U.S. business interests, Castaño seemed to be sending a message to what he liked to call "our neighbors to the north." He loved the United States. After Colombia, it was his favorite country. He dreamt of living there and studying sociology. He also admired the way the United States took charge of its own security. "I've always considered the U.S. as a nation that has worked as the police of the world, that keeps an eye out so nothing happens to it," he had told me that first time we spoke. It was a feeling that many Colombians shared. Surveys showed a majority favored more U.S. involvement to resolve the country's four-decades-old civil war. Carlos felt he was doing his part by helping U.S.-trained forces.

Colombians rewarded Carlos for what they saw as his patriotism. Polls showed that he had become a hero to many Colombians who believed that the AUC, under Castaño, was the only solution to the seemingly endless war in their country. Ten years before, José Gonzalo "*El Mejicano*" Rodríguez Gacha, Pablo Escobar, Black Vladimir, and Carlos's brother Fidel had run the *autodefensas'* image into the ground. But Carlos, without his brother around to remind people of the paramilitaries' sordid past, had rehabilitated it.

In 1999, in a much-publicized interview for prime-time television, Carlos showed his face in public and quickly emerged as the short-haired, clean-shaven, wide-eyed handsome leader of the new *autodefensas*. He had worn a suit, but his lawyerly look was partially offset by his agitated mannerisms. In a second interview, he had shown a softer side by sporting a yellow V-necked sweater and speaking to a female journalist on a windswept mountain. He had done many interviews since, and his popularity had risen along with his possibilities of negotiating his way out of the war and escaping prosecution for crimes against the UP. But as I found out, even with his rising popularity, the UP remained one of his biggest obstacles to freedom and one of the only things Carlos refused to talk about.

As the heat pounded down on us under the kiosk in Puerto Berrío, Carlos continued his rant about Colombian politics. He felt comfortable with Scott and me. It was the second time that each of us had interviewed him. He was laughing and joking about the presidential candidates. He even poked holes in his own, former designs to be a politician. "Carlos Castaño can be loved by a large percentage of the Colombian population," he said. "But another percentage won't like him. It's hard to get the immense majority to love warriors."

After about an hour, I finally turned the conversation to the UP. In his book, Carlos had admitted to killing "30 or 40" UP militants. And in my previous interview with him, he blamed most of the murders on *El Mejicano* Rodríguez Gacha. But he also admitted that he and his disappeared brother, Fidel, made some errors in judgement when it came to the democratic left. "The ignorance was so much for us that anything that looked like a guerrilla," Carlos had said in the closest thing to an actual "confession" that he ever made to me, "anything that seemed from the left, and anything that was communist, was for us the same thing, including unions. This was our biggest mistake. If we had had the slightest education that taught us at least what the democratic left was, what the radical left was, what communism was, what the FARC was, what the ELN was, what Maoism was, we wouldn't have committed so many mistakes and maybe we would be a legal 'self-defense' group even today. But the ignorance was so much that whatever was on the Left was [part of] the same thing. We started to learn while we were doing it, learning by our mistakes."

In Puerto Berrío, I went a step further. I wanted details about a UP murder. I wanted Carlos to tell me how they decided who they killed and why. I wanted to understand the logic behind eliminating an entire political party. Who sent the teenage *suizo* to murder UP leader Bernardo Jaramillo? I asked. My question lingered in the hot Puerto Berrío air for a moment while Carlos gave an uncharacteristic pause.

If the UP was an obstacle to freedom, then the assassination of Bernardo Jaramillo was the biggest brick in that wall. In other cases, Carlos didn't mind being linked to a political murder; he even took pride in it sometimes, as in the cases of UP leader Manuel Cepeda and M-19 presidential candidate Carlos Pizarro. But Bernardo Jaramillo was different. The UP presidential candidate was part of Carlos's attempts to show that he had gone beyond his brother Fidel's indiscriminate war, that he made a distinction between the "democratic left" and the "revolutionary left."

In his book *Mi confesión*, Carlos says, "I was there when they made the decision [to kill Bernardo], and said I didn't agree. . . . I said, 'I don't want any part of this deed.'" He also admitted to his biographer that he trained the teenage boy who shot Pizarro. The two murders were so similar in style and intent that it was hard to believe he had nothing to do with Bernardo's assassination. And few did.

Just days before my trip to see Carlos in Puerto Berrío, a judge in Bogotá had found Carlos and Fidel guilty of "conspiring to murder" Bernardo. The judge put particular stock in the testimony of a former assassin in the Pablo Escobar gang. "I made friends with Carlos Castaño," the former assassin testified before his grandfather, two uncles, and lawyer were gunned down, presumably by the House of Castaño. "He told me what 'jobs' he'd done and what 'jobs' he might do; he said that these were 'jobs' all done with the same modus operandi during which leftists had tragically died." The former assassin also made reference to Andrés Arturo Gutiérrez, the *suizo* who killed UP leader Bernardo Jaramillo, "The Jaramillo Ossa [job was] just like the [M-19 leader Carlos] Pizarro one, but the *suizo* lived so later they had to kill him with his father."

Other testimony from former paramilitaries and drug-trafficking assassins bolstered the state's case against Carlos and Fidel. One was an ex-M-19 member's testimony whose colleague infiltrated the paramilitaries. "He [the ex–guerrilla infiltrator] asked them [the paramilitaries] about the Bernardo Jaramillo Ossa assassination," the ex-guerilla said, "and with pride they admitted they'd done it. . . , which coincides with what Fidel Castaño told me: that he had been responsible or was the principle protagonist in almost all of the extermination of the *Unión Patriótica*."

Deep down Carlos knew that the murder of Bernardo Jaramillo might have done more harm than good. He couldn't take responsibility not so much because he wasn't guilty, but because it was an error for which he would never forgive himself. Carlos was an intelligent person. He knew that a democratic left was as effective at combating the FARC as his paramilitary forces were, perhaps even more effective. The question was about more than guilt or innocence, it was about getting at the heart of a flawed right-wing belief that "political genocide" against leftists would eventually mean an end to the war, the mistaken notion that killing the UP militants meant the death of the ideas they espoused.

"Jaramillo was a mistake," he finally said looking right at me. "Let's take a break," he added before standing up. It was the last time I ever asked him about the UP.

If it were up to Colombians, they would probably give Carlos Castaño full amnesty. Even if you made a list of Carlos's crimes and showed it to them, they would probably defend him. Carlos's own defense has always been that he was attacked first by the FARC. Colombians can relate to this. What's more, his ability to admit his own mistakes appeals to them, even if he sometimes applies a strange logic to his mea culpas. After telling me that killing "Jaramillo was a mistake," he reiterated that M-19 leader Carlos "Pizarro had to die."

There are many others who agree with this twisted logic. A few days before I saw Carlos under the kiosk in Puerto Berrío, I went to see the judge of the Jaramillo case, Julio Ballén. I found Ballén in his Bogotá office alone, looking through some papers. Ballén was a gentle man and had a soft manner of explaining himself. He never struck me as particularly courageous, but he was also the only man I knew who had ever sentenced Carlos to jail. Why do you think they killed Bernardo Jaramillo? I asked him. "Because he was from the Left," Judge Ballén stated matter-of-factly. "They killed all the leaders of the UP because they were the political wing of the FARC.

"In any case," he added, elevator music playing softly behind him, "the guerrillas are much worse. They're bloodsucking bastards. Not like the others [the paramilitaries]. At least they have some ideals. They're fighting the guerrillas. Yeah, sometimes they do some things they shouldn't. But whatever."

This seemed to be Carlos's forte: Even when he was guilty, Carlos seemed to find a way to get a victory for his cause. Unlike Fidel, Carlos had convinced Colombians that his war against the guerrillas and their "collaborators" in political parties like the UP was necessary and just. The details didn't seem to matter, even to intelligent, educated people like Judge Ballén.

But the details were becoming an issue for some powerful people outside of Colombia. In September 2001, the U.S. State Department put the AUC on its list of international terrorists. The paramilitaries joined the FARC and the ELN on the list, and Carlos was put on alert that some of his crimes crossed borders. "We're not stupid," he explained to Scott and me under the kiosk in Puerto Berrío. "So what we're doing is trying to convince the American government we're not terrorists. . . . We're trying to prevent, as much as we can, all massacres. If we know there are thirty guerrilla collaborators out there, we kill ten or eleven, the leaders, and try not to kill those that help the guerrillas just because they're forced to. We're trying to arrange a strict hierarchy of our organization; train our people—soldiers and commanders—in international humanitarian law; and close off the AUC to drug dealers."

It was the "drug dealers" who worried the U.S. government more than the human rights abusers. While he had managed to lay his brother's soiled image to rest, Carlos could never completely break from the narcos' grip. In his second television interview, Carlos admitted that taxes from drug traffickers provided about 70 percent of the financing for his organization. However, dozens of large drug traffickers hadn't just contributed—they had filtered into the AUC's ranks. They didn't have high profiles like Pablo Escobar and José Gonzalo Rodríguez Gacha, but they were equally wealthy and perhaps even more powerful than their predecessors. As it was in the beginning with the *autodefensas* in the Middle Magdalena Valley, some of these traffickers had also subverted the AUC's interests to their own. "I accept that we tax the big coca producers," Carlos had said in our first meeting. "But collect taxes from those that process it with alkaloids, never; get involved in exporting the drugs from an airport, I can never accept that; accept that someone helps someone else export cocaine, never. I can't. . . . This is how the majority of the 'self-defense' commanders think. . . . But this is also where we began to split."

About a year before we met under the kiosk in Puerto Berrío, the fissures in the AUC over drugs started to become public. First, the attorney general's investigators raided some AUC supporters' offices in the House of Castaño stronghold in the coastal province of Córdoba. Around the same time, a prominent drug dealer and paramilitary leader on the coast had begun openly defying Carlos. Gun battles between the two groups had erupted on the streets of the coastal city of Santa Marta. The fight, one *autodefensa* leader told me, was over drugs. In Puerto Berrío, Carlos calmly told Scott and me that the defiant narco-paramilitary leader "would give up, or he had to die." Other battles followed. One group of three thousand paramilitaries eventually declared themselves independent from Castaño's AUC. This breakaway group controlled huge swaths of coca fields in the central and southern parts of the country. The fight was revealing because it showed the AUC for what it was: a bunch of drug-dealing fiefdoms that fought guerrillas as much for their own personal gain as for the "good" of the country.

This internal strife would have made most people uneasy. A few of these drug traffickers' earnings were said to dwarf even Pablo Escobar's at his height. But Carlos was a crafty character. Where others saw doom, he saw opportunity. While many in the AUC worried the rifts might lead to jail, Carlos saw them as a chance to finally escape prosecution for all his murders and massacres and for his destruction of the UP. As he made clear in his autobiography, he was a Houdini. And this would be his Great Escape.

In Puerto Berrío, Carlos leaned forward and gave Scott and me a serious look. "We have a plan," he said. He then told us that he was engineering the single largest criminal handover in history: fifteen of the biggest drug traffickers in the country (and perhaps the world) had "agreed" to turn themselves in as a group to U.S. authorities. Some of the traffickers on this list were members of the AUC. The country's cocaine industry would shrink to nothing, he added. There would be no one for the FARC to tax, and the rebels would be forced to negotiate with the government. "I can end drug trafficking," he said. "I can hurt the FARC." But won't new traffickers just emerge in their place? we asked. "We'll take care of that," he explained. We could only guess what he meant. The Great Escape was in motion.

The Great Escape had several facets to it, the most important of which was winning over the U.S. government. Like Fidel, Carlos knew that the United States held the keys to his freedom. He could convince Colombians to give him amnesty because of his "patriotic" war against the FARC and the UP. But he hadn't yet convinced the United States. Fidel had tried to win favor with the *gringos* by helping track down Pablo Escobar. When Fidel found out that a dead Escobar wasn't enough to get him freedom, he disappeared. Carlos had decided to up the ante. He would offer not one dead Pablo Escobar but fifteen live Pablo Escobars. "We know that sooner or later," Carlos's attaché had told me on several occasions, "all roads lead to the United States."

By giving the U.S. government these traffickers and putting an "end" to drug trafficking, Carlos believed he would gain favor in Washington. He also thought he would smoothen the path toward dialogue with the Colombian government. This was the second facet of the plan: A negotiation with the government would mean a possible amnesty for the murders of countless UP militants, unionists, student activists, journalists, peasant organizers, and human rights workers.

By allying themselves with the AUC, many drug traffickers thought they could take part in the Great Escape as well. Some of these would stay in Colombia and negotiate with the Colombian government. As Carlos's attaché once told me, "They want to be judged for their fighting in the war, not for their role in drug trafficking." By doing so, the drug traffickers hoped to enjoy what they had accumulated during the war, which included vast amounts of land and cattle. These narco-paramilitaries also hoped for an amnesty for the crimes they had committed in their fight against the guerrillas and the rebel "collaborators" in the UP.

There was some precedent for Carlos's handover. In 1996, drug traffickers began brokering deals with the DEA. They provided information or became informants in return for lenient sentences. Some got out on bond. Others got between thirty-four and ninety months. All of them got the promise that they could keep most of their houses, land, cattle, swimming pools, discotheques, hotels, and so on. The traffickers on Castaño's list expected the same leniency. It wasn't altogether clear they would get it. The DEA agents who had brokered some of the earlier deals—deals that Carlos apparently helped administer—had been suspended. And the main go-between in the United States, a flamboyant Colombian fashion photographer who was doubling as an FBI informant, had been charged with obstruction of justice and tax evasion. The legal troubles had temporarily shut down the pipeline.

As we sat under the kiosk in Puerto Berrío getting the details of his plan, Carlos didn't paint this picture for us. Instead, he presented his plan as a goodwill gesture, a means by which he could suck the "oxygen" from the war by eliminating drug trafficking. He also thought he could debilitate the FARC, and put the government in a much better position to negotiate a peace settlement with the rebel group. He didn't mention legalizing land and cattle he had accumulated during the war or his fellow narco-commanders doing the same. He didn't say anything about amnesty for the murders of UP leaders like Bernardo Jaramillo and Manuel Cepeda or about the destruction of a political party and, in turn, a peace process. Carlos was portraying himself as a victim, a sacrificial lamb. "I'm very aware of my duties," he told us. "And I know I'm doing them the best I can."

In the months to come, the Great Escape would hit some snags. Many of the drug traffickers dropped out of the plan at the last minute when they saw the

AUC leaders weren't participating in the handover. To salvage the deal, Castaño offered to hand himself over and dared U.S. officials to try him as a drug trafficker. But the drug traffickers on the original list didn't return to the negotiating table. Subsequently, the AUC suffered more splits. In the biggest blow to the plan, Carlos and two fellow paramilitaries were indicted by the U.S. Justice Department for trafficking seventeen tons of cocaine to the United States. The indictment appeared to be a message from Washington that the game was over. And Carlos himself was frazzled by the U.S. decision to attack him directly. Scott and I saw him just a few days after the indictment. He was holed up in a jungle hideout, struggling to maintain his grip on the AUC and—unlike the earlier pledge he made to the drug traffickers— giving mixed signals about whether he would surrender to U.S. authorities. His greatest fear, he confided to me, was of being thrown into a U.S. jail "without any light, without any access to anyone."

But Carlos quickly regained his balance. As predicted, the Colombian government announced its intention to negotiate a settlement with the AUC, and the two sides gingerly began talking "peace." Amnesty seemed like it was on the horizon again. More importantly, the United States seemed to be changing its plans as well. Castaño's attaché told me that shortly after the indictment was handed down, the Castaño camp was approached by U.S. embassy officials who wanted to negotiate Carlos's handover. With the U.S. officials there was no mention of crimes against humanity or destruction of a political party known as the UP. The charges were drug trafficking. It sounded like a rehash of the plea bargains that the earlier drug traffickers had copped with the DEA. For Carlos, a deal with the United States was perfect, and he sent his Miami-based lawyer snooping around for people who would bargain. For the UP and so many others who had died at the hands of the House of Castaño, it seemed like another chapter in the book of impunity.

Like so many Colombians, the United States seemed to be missing the larger point when it came to the House of Castaño. More than a drug trial or a trial for the murder of one UP leader like Bernardo Jaramillo, Carlos and Fidel should have been on trial for killing the country's chances at peace. As one former paramilitary said about the Castaño brothers in his interrogation, "The important part [of their strategy] is that . . . if they keep killing leftist candidates, if the government isn't capable of controlling this, then there's no peace, and a democratic process that involves opposition forces isn't possible."

Instead, Carlos was making plans for his Great Escape. Whether it worked or not, it was clear that soon Carlos would either be studying sociology in the United States or joining his brother in obscurity.

CHAPTER 16

SHADES OF JAIME

Even if the *Unión Patriótica* was dead politically, somehow its spirit lingered. Despite the obstacles—the lack of money, the dangers, the wee prestige, the small hope of self-benefit, the dim chances of helping others—people still volunteered to be leftist politicians. Even stranger, there was a group of Colombians who hung on to the idea that a leftist political coalition was possible. They created what they called the *Frente Social y Político*. (For many, it was just a long-winded way of saying martyrs.) These included what was left of the UP, the Communist Party, and the M-19—the rebel group turned political party. There were others who tagged themselves as "independents," but they couldn't hide. It was the 2002 election, fifteen years after assassins had riddled UP presidential candidate Jaime Pardo Leal with bullets in the mountains outside of Bogotá, but little had changed. To be a politician in Colombia was an adventure. To be a leftist politician in Colombia was a death wish.

The elections brought a typical swirl of turmoil and fear. The threats came from all sides, and everyone took cover. Machine politics still dominated Colombia, but it was under heavy protection. Liberal and Conservative politicians crisscrossed their regions behind phalanxes of security guards. One presidential candidate had seventy bodyguards with him at all times. Meanwhile, leftist politicians from the *Frente* on shoestring budgets slid from appointment to appointment and tried hard to strike a balance between getting to their supporters and not drawing too much attention to their campaigns. All politicians limited their public appearances. Some of them ran their campaigns from their homes, making phone calls and sending out flyers; others politicked over the television and radio. It was a virtual election without the modern equipment.

During my investigation into the UP, I had always wondered what it was like to campaign amid the threats, the bodyguards, and the guns. So during the last week of the 2002 elections, I spent a day with Wilson Borja, a *Frente* candidate for congress. Wilson was a charismatic character in the mold of Jaime Pardo: a unionist, a Marxist, and a former UP militant who was as threatened as anyone in the country. A little over a year before the elections, gunmen intercepted him as he left his home in Bogotá. His two bodyguards fired back. One was shot in the head and died. The other got it in the hand. Wilson took a bullet each in the shoulder and the leg. Another grazed his head. He was lucky. When I saw him he was out of the wheelchair and was hoping to get the pins removed from his leg in a few years.

One of the assassins was shot and critically wounded. His hitmen colleagues pulled him into the car. But when they saw how bad off he was, they killed him and dumped his body in the street. Stupidly, they forgot to remove his cellular phone. When investigators located the phone, they found that the most recent call received was from a colonel at the army's XIII Brigade. Nevertheless, Carlos Castaño took credit for the attack. Wilson laughed at the paramilitary leader's mea culpa. Carlos was just doing his job, Wilson later told me, by covering up for the military.

The assassination attempt had backfired. Wilson had run for congress in 1998 but had gotten just 12,000 votes, a few thousand below the cut-off point for that year. He was known more for his trilby than his politics. He never let his hat stray far from his head, in part to hide his balding noggin, in part to keep an image. Opponents would say things like "my little hatted-friend, Wilson Borja," and Wilson would smile. But since military and paramilitary forces had tried to kill him, his crutches had become as much a symbol of his personality as his hat. He wasn't just the leftist with the trilby. Now he was the cripple with the trilby—the true image of a crime fighter in a twisted nation. More importantly, he was inching closer to the 25,000 votes he needed to become a congressman.

I saw Wilson in the final days of his campaign. Despite his condition, he was on a torrid pace. He started the morning with a radio interview from his house at 6:30 A.M. Then he went to three meetings, one of them a strategy session, the others small "unofficial" campaign rallies. (Colombian law forbids rallies during the last week before elections.) We met at a gas station after lunch, where I hopped into his armored SUV to get out of a heavy Bogotá downpour.

Wilson's hat sat lightly on his head, and his left leg was propped up on the footrest between the two front seats. He had a muscular upper body that was hidden by a thin layer of girth. He wore an intense look on his face that went well with his black suit, light crimson shirt, and red paisley tie. He also had a button on his lapel that read "No to *Plan Colombia*," the U.S.-funded anti-drug and counterinsurgency strategy.

Despite its bold projections that it would simultaneously wipe out the drug crops and provide jobs, the multi-billion-dollar *Plan Colombia* had brought the country little relief. Although a massive aerial eradication campaign had destroyed thousands of acres of coca fields, these fields had been replaced by new ones in other, more ecologically fragile areas. Colombia supplied 80 percent of the cocaine consumed in the United States before *Plan Colombia*, and there was nothing to show that had changed since the implementation of the plan. The only winners seemed to be the guerrillas. Hundreds, if not thousands, of displaced and out-of-work peasants had joined the FARC since the U.S.-financed anti-drug effort had begun.

Wilson's leg obviously made him uncomfortable. The suit pants were cut down the seam so as not to interfere with the shiny metal pins sticking out at a right angle. The pins were partially covered by a black cloth that fit snuggly around both the bottom and top ends of his calf. His foot had a stocking on it but I could tell it was noticeably scarred and looked as if it had sat idle for years. As we drove south down the bumpy Bogotá streets toward his next appointment, his pants slipped down, revealing the atrophied muscles in his thigh. He said he was in rehabilitation—weights, leg lifts, and flexing exercises. But it would be a while before he could walk again without the aid of crutches.

We arrived at a state-run notary's office where Wilson was to address some of the union members about the current contract negotiations with the government. He was a *Frente* candidate, but he was also still a union boss. We circled the office through some tight streets. Cars were packed on both sides. The sidewalks were thick with people. There were two big avenues that crossed on either side of the office entrance, which would make for nice escape routes. The car had suddenly turned quiet. These were the danger zones. There was little control over the environment, and to make matters worse, no one seemed to know exactly where the entrance was. After circling the office for a third time, Wilson got fed up and asked to get out. "Maybe they don't see me," he told his armed men. "That's why they haven't come out to meet us."

We double-parked. I exited the car first and moved to the sidewalk. Wilson's bodyguards got out of the pickup, then the armored car. Everyone faced away from the vehicles positioning themselves for a possible attack. One of his bodyguards handed Wilson his crutches as he slipped out of the SUV, and they all moved towards where I was standing. Wilson was cupped between them, and they were spread out like linemen protecting a running back on a screen pass. As they approached me, I maintained my buffer zone.

The most logical place to wait was at the entrance to a small floor-paneling showroom. The showroom was open to the street like a garage. Wilson inched in beside me, and we looked out onto the cars splashing their way down the road. There was an assortment of bathroom tiles mounted on the walls next to us. Inside, some people sat around a square table and discussed a deal. In front of us, just inside the door, three bodyguards stood in a line facing the street. The others remained on the sidewalk.

Wilson had been a marked man for a long time. He said he was such a target that the threats stopped coming after a while. "But it's not like you aren't on their list," he added. "You just know who's supposed to die." Wilson said he started out with one bodyguard, which was financed by the Communist Party. "I had to pay his bus fare," he told me, laughing. As the threat level rose, it went to two. "We drove around in an old pickup, the three of us crammed in the cabin," he said. He had moved to three body-guards by the time the paramilitaries tried to shoot him. Thereafter the government financed an armored car and agreed to pay for ten bodyguards. Each bodyguard was trained by the government's security agency, the *Departamento Administrativo de Seguridad* or DAS, the same agency who had trained the UP bodyguards. But none of Wilson's bodyguards was a government employee. Wilson had selected them individually. "They each came with strong recommendations," he said. "I needed to know they were trustworthy."

Still, as I found out, they weren't always the quickest guards. After about five minutes, a car parked illegally in front of us. The owner of the car exited the vehicle and went into one of the stores along the street. Wilson then got a call on his cellular from a journalist. While he was speaking on the phone, two policemen on motorcycles began eyeing the illegally parked car. One of the policemen—a short, stocky fellow with a fat face that barely fit into his helmet—got off his motorcycle and walked toward us. Then he nonchalantly lowered his sawed-off shotgun from his shoulder and pointed it at Wilson. My heart stopped. The bodyguards reached into their jackets. Wilson simply screamed in one long spurt of emotion, "Put-that-gun-down-I'm-Wilson-Borja!" Startled, the policeman did a double take, then raised his gun to his shoulder again. "Do you have any idea what these guys will do to you?" Wilson continued.

There was a long silence. "Is this your car?" the policeman stupidly asked. "No. This has nothing to do with us," Wilson was yelling at him now. "You can't approach people like that. You know that any one of these guys could pull a gun on you."

"But I have a uniform on," the policeman responded.

"Paramilitaries also wear uniforms!" Wilson replied. After the policeman walked away, Wilson laughed. "I have no idea why I even have bodyguards sometimes. You guys have to be more alert," he scolded them. Then he turned to me. "Now you have a little story to tell," he said giggling. I just shook.

When he was nine years old, Wilson started working at a fish market in the coastal city of Cartagena. It had moved a few times since he worked there, but remnants of it still existed when I visited the city a few weeks before. Small wooden shacks lined the street and spread into a lot behind it. The fishermen brought in their catch, which they laid on some long tables. The salesmen descaled it with lengthy knives they called *champetas*. The knife was also a popular weapon among gangs, whose members brandished it enough during parties that they had named a new indigenous music after it.

Wilson worked for a few years at the market to pay for his studies at a local university. Although he never finished his systems engineering degree, he did manage to get a job in a government-run farm bureau, where he worked until he became a "professional" union leader in 1990. The union was still paying him about $650 a month when I met with him. But he told me it hadn't cut him a check in weeks.

In college, Wilson joined the Marxist-Leninist Communist Party or PCML. The PCML was Maoist and worked in clandestinity. Their members didn't believe in *la combinación de todas las formas de lucha*—the Communist Party's strategy of combining legal and illegal struggles at the same time to topple the government—although many of Wilson's colleagues later filtered into the PCML's guerrilla group, the Popular Liberation Army (EPL). Wilson left the PCML after a few years, and by the early 1980s, he had permanently switched to the Communist Party.

Throughout his early years in the Communist Party, Wilson followed the Jaime Pardo tradition. Like Pardo, Wilson was his own man and tried not to take the Communist Party or himself too seriously. He was not a member of the Central Committee and was always a little late on his dues. He also didn't seem to hang around with Communist Party members much and didn't feed his arguments through the Communist filter. Although dedicated to the Communist Party's ideology, he also believed his own ideas were important. Leninism was a proposal, he reasoned, not a way of life.

He openly told me there was constant turmoil in the Communist Party, especially with regard to armed insurrection and the long-time Colombian Communist strategy, the *combinación*. "When Lenin said armed struggle is superior, he wasn't saying it in the middle of a war. He was trying to convince an army to turn back to protecting the people," Wilson said as we sipped some cold oatmeal at a coffee shop after his meeting at the notary office. "When we made the strategy, we wanted to forget historical reality. It's clear that no one form [of struggle] is better than the others. The guerrillas don't accept this. They think the armed struggle is superior. But there's no doubt in my mind that the people make the revolution. When the people rise up, that's the revolution."

Wilson met Jaime Pardo when the boisterous former UP presidential candidate was still the head of the judges' union. Both served on the board of directors of Fenaltrase, the labor federation that Wilson would later run. In addition to being Wilson's drinking partner, Jaime Pardo was as close to a mentor as Wilson had in the Communist Party. "Our bond went beyond work or the Communist Party," Wilson told me. "He had a solid ideological background, but he wasn't so strict. The rules didn't matter as much to him. In that way, we were a lot alike."

Unlike many of his colleagues, Wilson was a student of Marxism. In a strange way, this made him less orthodox than some of the others. "Marxism is a method," he said. "It's not a dogma." He was leaning on his crutches as he spoke. His guards had brought him to a café without any chairs. "I don't negate the validity of the armed struggle, especially in Colombia," he began again. "What I'm saying is that the world won't allow an armed socialist revolution. The fight is much more ideological. With the unipolar world, how do you struggle? That's the problem. . . . Lenin said the highest form of struggle is the armed struggle. But today's world has to resolve things at the negotiating table."

Wilson was a staunch UP militant during the hard times. He had ducked when the bullets were flying, and he had lived through the fights between the *Perestroikas* and the *ortodoxos*. I got the impression he had learned something from the process. Yet it wasn't enough to push him away from the Communist Party. "In the end we all ended up *Perestroikas*," he told me. "This was the problem—not because we were *Perestroikas*, but because we ended up as followers, not leaders."

Many of these followers had ended up dead, so I asked Wilson if being a martyr was part of that same psychology. He sighed. "I don't think there was a martyr complex. We just didn't know what the enemy was capable of. And our measly status didn't give us the possibility to really assess the dangers." And was *la combinación de todas las formas de lucha* an adequate strategy given the unequal distribution of forces? I pressed him. "In your scenario," he explained, "the government is a tiger, and we're tied up like a mule. The mule's job is very difficult. But the *combinación* is real and can work. It's just that the government applies it much better."

After the adventure with the policeman at the notary office, the rest of the day seemed uneventful. Every time we stopped, the men would perform the same routine: The guards in the rear vehicle would get out first, then the men in the lead vehicle, then Wilson. After three or four times, I no longer maintained my buffer zone, and I was no longer shaking. I was becoming an easy target.

To change things up toward the end of the day, Wilson shoved me into the back of the trail vehicle. It was a small four-door pickup truck. Despite the lack of bulletproof windows, the atmosphere was a little more relaxed. I slid into the backseat and sat on a mini-Uzi. Luckily, these guns don't discharge easily. The bodyguards laughed at my carelessness. As we took off, the guard to my left gathered up the Uzi, and the one to my right pulled out his 9mm Beretta. The two in front both had pistols. In all, the six bodyguards on duty that day carried four handguns and two submachine guns. And they never seemed to take their fingers from the triggers.

The trip was made more terrifying by the need to transport Wilson through the city at incredible speeds. And when I got into the trail car, it was the afternoon rush hour and getting dark. The driver in the lead car never paused to see if we were following him, so it was up to our driver to keep up. We wove in and out of traffic going at least fifty miles per hour. Buses and taxis flew in front of us. We veered around them into oncoming traffic or hugged the edge of the road on either side just to stay close. Occasionally, to make sure we could sneak in behind the lead vehicle, one of the guards would flash his weapon to other drivers. The message usually got through.

No one had any statistics, but bodyguards for people like Wilson got killed at a rate comparable to the people they were protecting. Wilson's bodyguards had been working for him for about five months when I accompanied them. All but two of them were married. One of them said his wife hated the job but understood that he needed the work. "Every morning, my wife says, 'God bless you.' 'Be ready.' And 'Come home soon,'" he said, holding his pistol with two hands just below the window line. The government paid them each about $600 a month, a hefty sum for most Colombians. I asked them how they dealt with the stress. "It's just like any other job," one said to me unconvincingly. "You get up and you gotta work somewhere." Then the driver suddenly chimed in, "I love it when my grandmother says, 'God bless you.'" The rest of them just nodded and continued peering into the darkness.

There were a lot of politicians with more bodyguards, but few more threatened than Wilson Borja. After he was shot, Wilson had gotten treatment in Cuba. He returned despite warnings that he was still a major target. In fact, he had become more of a target since he left. The investigation into his shooting implicated the head of the armed forces, the commander of the II Division, a commander in the army's intelligence unit, a police captain, and the paramilitary leader Carlos Castaño. One of the accused assassins had worked for José Gonzalo "*El Mejicano*" Rodríguez Gacha and was trained by Israeli mercenaries. Another was an army major. After the arrests started, so did the irregularities. Most of the accused were released shortly after they were taken into custody. The man thought to be behind the planning and execution of the attack on Wilson, an army major, was fined "100 minimum salaries" by the inspector general's office and released. He then appealed and got the fine lowered to "40 minimum salaries." Under heavy pressure from the international community, he was rearrested.

"I've got good information," Wilson told me on a number of occasions that day. So good, in fact, that even the *gringos* were worried about his safety. Just a couple months before I met with him, the U.S. embassy called Wilson and said it had arranged for him to leave the country for one month. He left the next day. After I returned to his car from the trail car, I asked him if he thought about staying abroad, but he brushed it off like most former exiles do. "Whenever I'm abroad, I'm always thinking about Colombia," he said. "Besides, here I'm everything. Outside of my country, I'm nothing."

This was evident all day. Wherever he went, Wilson was a cult hero. He took in ovations wherever he spoke as well as the occasional spontaneous cries of "Wilson!" on the streets. Like Josué Giraldo, the UP lawyer I met when I first came to Colombia, Wilson was a walking ghost. People talked to him like they would their grandfather who had lived through a world war. They smiled gently when he spoke and listened intently. It was clear why he had wanted to return to this civil war: He was alive in Colombia and dead anywhere else. But he was just waiting for the next hail of bullets.

As election day neared, the tension grew. The FARC threatened to boycott, and candidates—especially in remote areas—were beginning to drop from the race. Since the destruction of the UP, threats and boycotts had become a regular part of the FARC's strategy. The rebels also abducted dozens of politicians, including five congressmen and one presidential candidate, who they hoped to swap for guerrillas being held in Colombian prisons. Democracy in Colombia was in "checkmate," the pundits declared.

To better understand the rebels' political position, I drove in my jeep with two colleagues to the cold, barren mountains of Sumapaz, where we hoped to find some FARC commanders. Sumapaz always seemed to hold the keys to the rebels' thoughts. It was where FARC commanders Jacobo Arenas and Alfonso Cano had dreamt up the UP in the early 1980s. It was where the

Communist stalwart Alberto Rojas Puyo had shared cognac with the rebel leaders Arenas and Cano as the three of them imagined the possibilities for the party during their historic all-night gab session. On the other hand, it was where the guerrilla leaders had constructed the plan to become an army at any cost during the VII Conference in 1982. The FARC command then began its steady march toward the big cities, while the carnage of the UP grew.

So many things had changed since the Rojas Puyo–FARC meetings. Peace was a distant proposition. The latest peace talks between the FARC and the government in the sixteen thousand-square-mile area known as the DMZ had folded just a month before the congressional elections. Each side blamed the other, but the end result was the same: Full-scale war had returned to Colombia. The road that Rojas Puyo had taken to see the FARC leaders in the early 1980s had also changed. It was now known as the "kidnap trail" because the rebels used it so often to transport kidnap victims through the rugged terrain to what would most likely be a long period of captivity. At the time, the guerrillas were making an estimated $200 million a year on kidnapping, another $500 million by taxing proceeds from the illegal drug business. Big war was big business.

Reminders of the rebels' distorted values followed us everywhere on our journey. We drove to a place where we knew we would find them, a small town called Nazareth. There, in the central park, on a grassy knoll next to a basketball court, FARC commanders in dark green fatigues were talking softly to a group of civilians. It was a picturesque scene of civility tainted only by the fact they were negotiating ransoms for kidnappings.

I knew one of them. I had met him while he was in jail. He had gotten out because a judge decided he was trustworthy enough to go on furlough while awaiting sentencing. The day after the judge let him go, he was in the mountains scheming with his fellow commanders to attack the government again. Newspaper reports later said this same guerrilla was responsible for sending several mortar bombs hurtling toward the Presidential Palace and congress during the president's inauguration. The explosions missed their intended target and killed more than twenty people in a run-down neighborhood a few blocks from the palace.

For me, this commander had another plan. "Steven," he said with a smile on his face, "how would you like to do a 'self-kidnapping' and share the ransom?" A self-kidnapping is when you let yourself be kidnapped and collect some of the proceeds. I froze while my colleagues quickly changed the subject. Luckily, the commander didn't persist. He simply went with the new conversation, while I reflected on just how far the guerrillas had gone astray.

After some cajoling, we convinced a skinny, pudgy-faced commander nicknamed "Omar" to speak to us on camera and for radio. Omar was the commander of the 51st Front and was typical of the hard-liners of the FARC. He had joined the rebels when he was seventeen. The largest city he had ever visited was Villavicencio, which has a population of just over 250,000. When we asked about his politics, he shied away from us. But when we talked about war, he brightened with pride. He told us he had taken part in the rebels' famous ambush of an army mobile brigade in the south of the country, which had left more than eighty soldiers dead and dozens more in FARC "prisons."

But Omar was awkward when it came to talking about things like elections. His political training consisted of what he had read in rebel camps and while guarding army soldiers in captivity. What's more, he was not a good public relations representative. When asked to speak, Omar found it difficult to improvise, think on his feet. He even bumbled through a statement that he and some other commanders had written specifically for the elections, which called for people to "abstain" from voting. Finally, he shied away from taking any firm political position aside from the standard, "The politicians only hope to increase the size of their wallets."

Omar had joined the FARC just as the UP was formed. And his political knowledge was limited to what he knew of that era and what the rebels had learned from that experience. It was perfect for the new FARC, the apolitical FARC, the "army of the people." It didn't involve any profound analysis on Omar's part. Indeed, it mostly required memorization of the facts, which he sometimes flubbed up anyway.

"There have never been democratic elections in Colombia," he told us. "We don't need to go far back in history. For example, during the electoral campaign of 1987 [it was 1986], in which there were leftist candidates like [Jaime] Pardo Leal. There wasn't a democracy. There was gunfire, you know? They killed this *caudillo*, this popular leader who was one of the most important people of Colombia, and they killed him because of this. So we're not waiting for democratic changes, political changes. We're not waiting for anything like that to happen anymore."

What was the impact of the death of Pardo Leal on you? I asked. "The impact wasn't just personal, it was on a national level," he responded. "The people felt the pain in their own bodies. . . . A lot of people [then] joined the struggle. A lot [of] people are carrying the flag of that leader, of that man who not only had a great impact on the guerrillas' thinking but also on the popular movements: in the unions, in the universities, and in national and international organizations. Obviously, people were going to follow his example."

As fate would have it, Omar's 51st Front was also called the "Jaime Pardo Leal." He hadn't decided the name, but it was a perfect fit. When Pardo was killed, Omar and some of his fellow rebels wrote a poem dedicated to the former UP presidential candidate and Pedro Nel Jiménez, the senator from the province of Meta who had been gunned down by Rodríguez Gacha's men just a few months after he was elected. Omar had memorized the poem, and he recited it for us:

Everyday we wake up
And relive the memory of Pedro Nel

Everyday in the afternoon
In our minds Pardo Leal is reborn

They were fighters
We could tell

Tireless revolutionaries
Who will never die

The fascists killed them
So they couldn't complain

About the other leaders
That they were going to kill

But if we go to battle
We're always going to take you with us

They will be reborn in the countryside
And also in the city

And the history of our martyrs
Revolutionaries they will always be

"We have a political philosophy," he concluded. "Through a revolutionary process, we will change the actual power from the ground up. We've always said that through elections we'll never reach power because the same thing [that happened to the UP] is going happen to us every time. The only way to struggle and reach political power in Colombia is with guns, through the guerrilla war, because the conditions are there, and they will continue to be there. This process is long and hard, but it's the only way."

On election day, there were reports of sporadic violence. The military said it killed eight FARC rebels in two separate skirmishes. The guerrillas also burned ballots in fifteen municipalities. Many people voted in darkness due to widespread blackouts. Most of them simply didn't vote at all. Abstention was close to 80 percent in rebel strongholds and high nationwide: Just 10 million of the 24 million eligible voters cast a ballot.

In Bogotá, people went to the polls. Some even waited in line to vote. The results were to be expected. Traditional candidates from the traditional parties won their traditional posts, and congress remained largely the same. The big surprise was the *Frente Social y Político:* one ex-judge turned politician won a senate seat for the party, and Wilson Borja a congressional seat. The *Frente's* other congressional candidate, Daniel García-Peña, entered as a substitute for a leading vote getter, Gustavo Petro.

The price on each of their heads leapt following the elections. Petro had to flee the city for a while. Wilson stayed but seemed to be waiting for the inevitable. Everyone called his substitute "The Widow," and Wilson hadn't even been killed yet. Still, in true Jaime Pardo fashion, Wilson took it well. As congress was set to convene, Wilson told me he was going to wear an army helmet to the ceremonies.

CHAPTER 17

LEFTOVERS

By the time I started investigating the *Unión Patriótica*, the party was on the endangered species list. There was virtually no formal political component left. The UP had about thirty municipal council reps, a couple of mayors, and a half-dozen provincial assemblymen. The rest were dead or hiding or, if they were smart, had taken refuge from politics altogether. The last UP senator fled the country in 1997, shortly after armed men entered his house while he was having lunch with his wife and daughters and told him he would leave the country or die. Other lesser-known party members went into exile as well, one of them after paramilitaries shot a rocket at her car as she drove down one of Bogotá's main thoroughfares toward the city council building where she was a councilmember. She survived. A man in another vehicle was injured.

Meanwhile, the death toll kept rising. The paramilitaries never forgot who was with the UP. Their goal was the complete extermination of the political party, and they were well on their way to achieving it. "With this dirty war, it's impossible to draw people to the UP," the chain-smoking party president Mario Upegui told me when I visited him in his Bogotá office. "No one wants to join a party whose leaders are still getting assassinated."

It was the first time I spoke to Upegui. The gray-haired and wrinkled UP president looked as if the war and the cigarettes were sucking the life from him. He had a pack of Marlboro Lights tucked away in his gray suit and another lying on his disorderly desk. He only seemed to take in fresh air for about two seconds at a time between puffs. His small work space in Bogotá's city council building filled quickly with smoke, as did the slim passageway lined with aides and supporters.

Upegui had seen it all from beginning to end. Like so many others, he had started with hope, with the belief that the UP could put a dent into the traditional parties' stranglehold on power. But reality had settled in quickly, and these days Upegui had nothing left but the memories of the dozens of dead comrades he hoped to avenge. "Our objective is to clarify the facts, to look for the truth," he told me, referring to the case of "political genocide" the UP had brought against the government, "to show that the state is guilty so that there's a [financial] solution for the families, the orphans, the widows; and a [political] solution for the party."

Upegui was surprised to see me waiting for him that morning. No one cared about the UP anymore. The party didn't put up candidates for national offices and at the time was joining the *Frente Social y Político*, the leftist political coalition. The UP was a cog in a larger machine now. Perhaps it could hide better from its enemies, I thought. But Upegui had other ideas. "Ideally, we'd form a huge party that would bring together all the democratic sectors of the left," he explained to me, harking back to the glory years of the UP. "We've got a television program, a radio program, a few headquarters," he added. "We're not going to just give up this space that we have, that we've conquered."

But Upegui could only fake so much enthusiasm. He was tired and defeated. It was like he had been in a car crash and was still trying to figure out what happened. He had retained his ability to articulate his political positions, but they came out empty. The murders—and the smoking—had completely sapped him of his energy. All he could give was himself, which he would have, if they gave him an opportunity. Like so many others before him—Josué Giraldo and Pedro Nel Jiménez, Jaime Pardo Leal and Bernardo Jaramillo, Julio Cañón and Manuel Cepeda—Upegui was ready and willing to die for this, an admittedly lost cause. He was a walking ghost. The only way to live was to prepare for death. "We've always been in danger since they began the dirty war," he said to me in his scratchy voice. "All of us have been in danger. But in our case, we're willing to take those risks."

He took another drag on his cigarette.

This sense of martyrdom never ceased to perplex me. And I wasn't alone. In Villavicencio, I met a priest named Omar García. García was a short, skinny man with a pockmarked face. He was full of energy, almost hyperactive. And he spoke in these short bursts that often surprised me. "I still sympathize with the UP," he said with a straight face. But García was never a UP militant. He was more of a witness to the leftover UP militants' quest to die with dignity. It was painful for him to watch. After the assassination of Bernardo Jaramillo in 1990, the UP was effectively done. But militants like Josué Giraldo, the man who inspired me to write this book, held on for reasons that were never very clear to García.

García met Josué shortly after the UP leader joined a human rights committee that García then helped run. The two worked closely together during the last years of the UP leader's life. The priest observed closely as the pressure and the paranoia slowly destroyed his friend. García said that Josué saw things that may or may not have been there: mysterious men in a red flower van watching him; another one with a newspaper under his arm following him; still another posing as a telephone repairman monitoring all his calls. Yet the priest was impressed by Josué's commitment and amused by the UP leader's attitude. García told me that Josué always claimed he didn't want any ties with the church; the priest didn't believe him. "He said he wasn't religious," García said, a smile crossing his face, "that when he was a kid and a priest came to his house, he would hide underneath the bed. . . . [But] human rights was his way of working with the church."

Josué's parents were staunch Catholics. His father woke the kids for mass every day and invited church leaders over for meals. Although somewhat overbearing, the father's religious push paid dividends. Two of Josué's brothers became priests, and one sister became a nun. Josué shunned Catholicism in public, but, García told me, the UP leader carried his faith to his grave. "This is something that I've thought about for a long time," García said. "I'm not sure if it was ideological or personal. I sense that it was a question of martyrdom." Martyrdom? I asked. "He says he wasn't religious," García continued, "but look at the religious discourse he was using: anti-corruption, the struggle, a willingness to give up your life. This is a religious commitment."

García said the same was true for other UP members. They pretended to disregard the church, but their struggle closely paralleled their belief that their sacrifice would be rewarded. Within the party, it was. García said that the UP functioned using a strange honor code. "To be threatened was to get more prestige," he explained. "That's why they took risks. Risk is what gave them importance. The one who was the most threatened would be the most important. . . . I don't know what it was—sympathy for death; sympathy for martyrdom." Josué's virtually unprotected house, García said, was a perfect indication of his attitude. "Me, with a rifle, I never would have missed," the priest added. "They could have killed him whenever they wanted."

It was as if the ones who lived weren't as virtuous as the ones who died. And it wasn't just the main leaders who were afflicted by this belief. On the margins were dozens who tortured themselves over what had happened and probably wished they were dead as well. Some of them seemed to be looking for a way to prove that they were more UP than the next, more militant, more willing to die no matter how small the cause had become. Like Josué, they were walking ghosts.

Others simply slipped into depression. One former UP worked at *Voz*, the Communist Party newspaper. While I was doing research there, he would wander around the office drunk, sometimes talking about the dead to himself. Then he'd enter the editor's small, windowless office (when the editor wasn't there), and speak to a large picture of Lenin. On his days off, his colleagues told me, he would go to the cemetery downtown and speak to Jaime Pardo's grave. Unfortunately, he wasn't alone in his grief. Others hid in their homes and drank or stayed in bed depressed. The death of the UP had done more than destroy a political movement—it had fractured the psyche of an entire generation. As one former militant told me, "We're like Vietnam veterans."

Sebastián González, the former FARC and UP militant who had organized *Juntas Patrióticas* and later security for the party, was a typical UP veteran. He spent most of his days drinking and reminiscing. When I met him, he was out of work and living in a tiny one-room apartment with his second wife and his ten-year-old son from his first marriage. To make a little money, he was trying to sell miniature replicas of famous Colombian churches that his neighbor made from clay. But it just wasn't enough; his new wife was the one bringing in the money and helping him support his son. To make matters worse, the UP had kicked Sebastián out of the party. One of the last times I saw him, he told me he was suing the UP. "They say that I'm alcoholic," he told me, during one of the few times we didn't put back a six-pack each. "They say I'm very aggressive."

Are you an alcoholic? I asked him. He thought for a moment. "I like to drink a lot," he answered. "According to the doctors, I'm a dipsomaniac. I've been drinking, uuufff," he paused, "even before. . . . When I was with the bottling company, we drank every week. Culturally, it's what you do in this country. Besides, the ones that accuse me of being an alcoholic are also alcoholics. Who do you think I drink with?"

Out of the party he loved so much and low on drinking partners, Sebastián seemed to be searching desperately for other ways to die. He talked to me incessantly about the betrayal of the FARC. "When things were good, people would say, '*los compañeros de las FARC*,'" he said. "But when they started to attack us, they'd say, 'We have nothing to do with the FARC.' This position of *vai bene*, of the pendulum, was never convenient for us."

Then he grabbed a book from a shelf next to him and handed it to me. The cover had a picture of a couple walking through a flowery field. "Look at the table of contents," he instructed me. I leafed through it. It was an urban guerrilla manual. "We're working on an updated version," he told me with a big smile on his face.

"I've always defended the FARC," he continued. "And of all the people who started with the UP, I was the last one who came directly from the

FARC. But I'm from the UP. I'm from the UP a lot more than many of those fuckers left. When I was at the thirty fifth anniversary of the FARC, I met up with some *compañeros*, and I told them, 'I'm from the UP.' And I started telling them the story: 'Fifteen years ago, a little girl was born dressed in green and yellow, and she was baptized the UP. But in birth she was born bloody, and they continued to massacre and massacre her. When she was fifteen, her little brother was born, and his name was the Bolivarian Movement [the FARC's new political party].' I told them this story, and these guys said, 'We can't kick you out.'"

Other leftovers from the UP were also toiling in obscurity, looking for recognition for their deeds, or, as in the case of the hundreds of widows, indemnity from both the UP and the Communist Party and answers about their dead husbands. These women felt betrayed by the FARC and the Communist Party. Their husbands had died for the UP, and they got nothing but a life of misery and longing in return. Some sought revenge for the way the UP, the Communist Party, and the FARC had used their husbands. "I wish I could get the leaders of the FARC together," one of them told me. "I would sit them down and have a political trial."

If guilty, what would be their punishment? I asked.

"I would let them die like dogs," she said.

The city of Villavicencio was widow central. There was no formal network of widows as in other Latin American countries like Guatemala or Argentina. The only contact the women had with one another was through the party. When their husbands died, so did their connection to the UP and often with each other. But when they did meet by chance, they felt an immediate bond. They shared the same resentment toward the Communist Party and the UP. They also shared a struggle to understand.

"I don't know if it was his ideals," Cristina Cano told me about her husband when I visited with her and several other widows in the Villavicencio parish. "But he didn't want to leave Colombia. They told him, 'You're an idiot. You have to leave.' But he didn't want to." Cristina had soft skin and dark hair. Her husband had been a union organizer and UP militant. In 1988, he disappeared. His body was later found in a trash heap by one of the garbagemen has organized. Cristina was angry with him, but she was also disappointed with the Communist Party and the UP, who she said never took care of the families of the dead. "In public they talked about social welfare," she said. "But when someone died, they would never talk to you again."

It was the same for Marta Cecilia Garzón. Marta Cecilia's husband had been killed just a year earlier. "They [in the Communist Party] don't even know my name unless I identify myself as the widow of James," she said of her dead husband. James Barrera was thirty-seven when he died—a victim of his work in the FARC's new party, the Bolivarian Movement. He left Marta Cecilia, a plump woman in her mid-thirties, with two kids. "They don't help us at all," she said referring to the Communist Party and the FARC, "no work, nothing for the kids. We all have to find our own way to survive." Marta Cecilia was just barely making it by peddling small replicas of popular cartoon figures.

Some widows, however, had recovered from their financial losses. The same day I met with Cristina and Marta Cecilia, Gladys Fandino Grisales, the widow of slain senator Pedro Nel Jiménez, invited me to her house for a barbeque to celebrate her son's tenth birthday. Gladys was as jovial as a UP widow could be. She wore cakes of makeup and jewelry and she was sporting a T-shirt that read, "Happiness is being with someone you love." Unlike most of the other widows, she had succeeded in starting a new life after her husband's death. She had a second child, a new home, and a new job.

What was left for Gladys was the mental anguish. Pedro Nel's murder still followed Gladys wherever she went. Like so many before and after him, Pedro Nel was a willing martyr for the UP, and this tortured Gladys. Just after their daughter was born, Pedro Nel told Gladys that he didn't want to be a father "because I'm not going to be there for my child." The UP senator was shot in late 1986 while picking up his daughter from school. The incident left an indelible mark on the family, who'd sought refuge in the confines of a gated community. There was a twenty-four-hour guard at the front entrance, and Gladys was constantly worried that her daughter, who had witnessed the assassination of her father, might be next. "The Communist Party forgets that these people put their lives on the line," Gladys told me. "These orphans have been forgotten," she added, referring to her daughter. Not surprisingly, Gladys was averse to anything political. "I'd wash dishes if I could live in peace," she said.

Gladys's story mirrored Mariella Duarte's, the widow of Josué Giraldo. I went to Mariella's house shortly after speaking to Gladys. She lived on the outskirts of Villavicencio in the same two-story colonial house that she and Josué had shared with their two daughters. Mariella was a fair-skinned woman who dressed simply and wore very little makeup compared with her counterparts. She was working at a local hotel but still trying to figure out what had happened to her life, because, for so many years, Josué was her life.

On several occasions, Mariella told me, she had asked Josué to leave Colombia, but he had refused. "He said, 'You knew what you were getting involved with when we got married.' He never fully accepted that something would happen to him," she explained to me. "But when I saw that something had happened to someone from the UP, I got scared and would say to him, 'Let's go.' 'No,' he would say. 'That would be like being a coward. Calm down,' he would say. 'Nothing's going to happen.' I believed him. I didn't want to be the bitter one, and then make him bitter. I knew the situation he was in. Who am I to complain?"

Mariella's two daughters fidgeted on the couch next to her as she talked. They had pale skin and dark hair like their mother. Do you think he wanted to be a martyr? I asked her. Mariella paused, then looked at her daughters. The older one was a little chubbier than the younger, energetic one. They both looked back at their mother. "These guys loved their families," she began. "But they didn't think about what would happen once they died. This is like a martyr because nothing is more important than what you're fighting for."

Throughout my investigation, dozens of interviewees said it was the first time they had spoken about the UP. Theirs was a pain they kept tucked beneath a stern face or behind a demanding job. One woman said she hadn't even spoken to her husband of ten years about the party. Another former militant must have said to me a dozen times during our conversations that he had never told anyone what he was telling me. Other people insisted on seeing the book before it was published. They were scared. "You're too young to be handling this type of material," one UP militant told me. Most of them spent much of the time during the interview just holding back the tears, looking off into the distance, and softly recounting their tales.

One of the last times I met with former UP propaganda chief Álvaro Salazar, he seemed crossed between excited and sad about the possibility of a book: excited that someone remembered him and wanted to revive a bit of important Colombian history; sad at what he had seen, lived through, allowed to happen even. There was a twinge of guilt in Salazar's voice throughout our conversations, almost as if he wasn't yet liberated from the pain of having somehow participated in the massacre of the UP. "For me, Álvaro Salazar is a person who is very far away. Someone I had almost forgotten until you came along to revive him," he told me.

Salazar had taken on another name, which he didn't want me to publish. He had also tried to create another identity, reinvent himself. "When I went to Holland in exile, 'Álvaro Salazar' basically died," he said. "I wanted to forget this and start a new life; and get to know other societies and other models of government and reflect about a turbulent and very tragic time in my life during which many of my friends and colleagues were killed." He paused, then grumbled, "Agghh. There were so many useless deaths. A part of me feels responsible for the violence, and this hurts a lot. For a long time, I wanted to overcome this and forget it. So I moved farther and farther away, forgetting it little by little, leaving it behind and trying to create a new space."

But like so many others, Álvaro Salazar could not bury the UP. "I remember a phrase that Bernardo Jaramillo used: 'No idea, no matter how important, warranted war or killing someone.' Today there's no political project that justifies a war to take power. This no longer exists in the world. Today I can see that nothing justified killing so many people; or that so many people died in such a useless manner like all those who died during that time and continue to die today. They're still dying in this endless dirty war that we started in Colombia."

Salazar's feelings notwithstanding, for many people the UP experience had led them to the opposite conclusion. For them, the armed struggle remained an integral part of the larger political strategy. The Communist Party, for instance, continued advocating *la combinación de todas las formas de lucha*, the longtime strategy of combining all forms of legal and illegal struggles to topple the government. It was a strange, almost nostalgic argument Communist Party members gave me when I asked them about the strategy. "The Communist Party simply takes note of this reality," a withering and rough-edged party president Jaime Caycedo told me from his party office in a lower-middle-class Bogotá neighborhood. "It considers that these struggles are part of the people themselves: workers, peasants, civilians, city dwellers, academics, students, etc. But the guerrillas are also part of the people. Although it's difficult for us to understand and comprehend, for many people it's a reality. . . . There isn't a civil society here and an armed guerrilla society on the other side. They are two integral parts of the same society. You can't separate them. . . . The confusion comes more from the people who have bad intentions to begin with. . . . Some even say that our strategy is what causes the violence. But this has nothing to do with Colombian reality. The reality is that we've lost a lot of militants who didn't have a gun in their hands."

Sadly, for the Communist Party and what was left of the UP, it had only gotten harder. The party weekly, *Voz*, continued to be published, a few of its candidates did well at the polls, and militants attended homage after homage for its fallen leaders. But the risks remained the same. Communist Party and UP leaders were still being assassinated. And one day, paramilitary leader Carlos Castaño had his men hide a four-foot-long guided missile in a pickup truck full of fruit in front of *Voz*'s offices in central Bogotá. The missile didn't explode; Castaño later said it wasn't designed to. It was more of a message that he was still closely watching the Communists.

Meanwhile other former UP members, like the Communist stalwart Alberto Rojas Puyo, were flabbergasted by the Communist Party's continuing intransigence. When I met with him one time in his apartment, Rojas Puyo could barely hold back his emotions. "You can see communists all over the world reflecting, trying to find a new way to organize, looking for alternatives," he told me in a tizzy. "But here, they haven't changed at all. I don't understand anything. [Here] they're doing the same thing they've always done."

The Communists in Colombia aren't Marxist, Rojas Puyo said to me, they're Stalinists. "And Stalinism isn't Marxism," Rojas Puyo added. "In Marxism, you can't create the system to fit your theory. Your theory is an open one, and you have to permanently challenge it given the new realities. The principle of Marxism is that there is an incessant change; everything is in movement. . . . Marx said don't try to accommodate reality to the theory; do the opposite: Change the theory to accommodate the changes in real life. The revolutionary has to be aware of the scientific changes in the world. You can't have dogmas. Nothing is definitive. But Stalin, he decided to make Marx a religion. He worked against Marxism, against the dialectic thinking and criterion that is Marxism. And here in Colombia, they've stayed with those Stalinist dogmas."

When I asked him to give me an example, he went back to the heart of this story, to the cause of the destruction: *la combinación de todas las formas de lucha.* "I think this particular dogma has played a terrible role in the Left," he said, "this idea that you are in the armed struggle and legal struggle at the same time. What happened was that the armed struggle here became a dogma."

Are you angry with anyone in particular? I pressed him. "I don't mix my personal feelings with my political analyses," he explained. "I can't hate anyone; I don't hate anyone. Emotions can't interfere with my political analysis. You can be indignant when confronted with the injustice, but this indignation comes from certain principles, a conception of the world."

What have you learned then? I asked. "I understand the context in which [the destruction of the party] happens just like I understand the context in which the Communist guerrillas emerge: when the Communists have to decide whether they will die with their arms crossed or organize their own defense system," he said. "What happens, though, is that the violence has its own dynamic, it's own engine that can lead to the destruction of its very promoters. Violence escapes from the grasp of those who use it. It's like a snowball that ends up finishing off everything. That's why I'm decidedly against taking justice into your own hands. Even if the government's justice system is ineffective, it's better to trust in it. . . . And above all, bet on democracy to diminish the unavoidable social and political conflicts. There will always be conflict, and the only way to resolve it is through democracy. This is the lesson for me after what I've seen in Colombia and other parts of the world."

The official end of the UP happened subtly. The party's dwindling support became the subject of a formal investigation. Nearing two decades of existence, the government's election board declared that the UP no longer had the votes to maintain its legal status. The board then issued the death penalty, and the UP was stricken from the books. A few people protested the decision. The Communist Party, which had lost its legal status some years earlier for the same reason, assembled a team of lawyers. "How could they declare us illegal," one party member rightfully asked, "when they were the ones who killed us off in the first place?"

Others, like Mariella Barragán, the widow of slain UP leader Bernardo Jaramillo, promised legal action of her own. Few things made her as angry as the UP. She was bouncing from job to job and no longer wondering what her politics were. She had none. They were all the same, except for Bernardo and his dead party. "It would be a fight to calm my soul," she explained to me about trying to revive the UP's legal status.

But hardly anyone else seemed to notice. *El Tiempo*, the country's only national daily newspaper, buried a short story about the end of the UP. And only one major columnist, Antonio Caballero, took pity on the party. In the weekly magazine *Semana*, Caballero noted that the same day *El Tiempo* declared the UP dead, the paper also carried pages and pages of analysis about the possibility that the right-wing paramilitaries, under Carlos Castaño, would start a peace negotiation with the government. "And no one," Caballero boldly wrote, "not Colombia's only daily [*El Tiempo*], not the weekly magazines starting with the one I write for, says that it was these same paramilitaries—in collaboration with the armed forces and with the green light from successive governments—who assassinated, one after the other, all the candidates, the elected officials—the mayors, city councilmen, deputies, the representatives, its only senator, its presidential candidates—and the majority of [the UP's] voters."

Then, there was an apparent silence again. The UP was dead, and no one said anything. No one said that maybe the UP was the way to get the guerrillas out of the war; that maybe it was the chance to build a strong third party, an alternative to the ruling class in Colombia; that maybe the country could learn something from its past mistakes; that there was once hope, a time in which people dreamt of a peaceful Colombia. No one said a word.

Until, a few weeks later in a small run-down hotel in the red-light district of downtown Bogotá, there was a gathering. It was the launching of a book written by a Colombian Communist about the UP. The book had its problems: The author had gathered his material from one source, the Communist weekly, *Voz*; he had neglected to analyze the Communists' and FARC's own role in the destruction of the UP; he had written it as a book of lists rather than telling the story of the party as a narrative. But still, the people were there to support him and to remember the UP. Over a hundred of them—professors, students, politicians, unionists, and peasants—packed the stuffy hotel conference room to listen to a story they all knew by heart. They wanted to hear it again. They wanted to feel it again. They wanted to know that they weren't dead. And they weren't. When the author finished his presentation, one man, a dark-skinned peasant with worn shoes, a soiled shirt, and a five-o'clock shadow, shouted the UP's refrain, "For our dead, not a moment of silence, but a lifetime of struggle!"

The shout echoed through the red-light district.

EPILOGUE

Fear, I have come to believe, is relative. The further I am from a troubling situation, the more fear I have of that situation. When I am in those troubling situations, however, I feel in control, more secure. It is illogical, to say the least, but fear itself is illogical at times. As is illustrated repeatedly in this book, the protagonists of the UP approached their fears by facing up to them and, in some cases, challenging their would-be enemies head-on, even when their enemies had far superior firepower. Their strategy did not work, and I thought I understood this very well.

But I find myself repeating their mistakes — thinking myself invulnerable, facing an enemy with superior firepower. As I write this, I have been in Colombia for nearly eleven months and probably have several more years to go. My return to Bogotá may surprise some — I wrote in the preface many months ago that I could not return for fear of retribution. But I am here, covering the Andean region as the Bureau Chief for *The Miami Herald.*

That's not to say that I have had to face all my fears since my return. I am living here, but some of the things that caused me to be afraid remain far away. Angering left-wing guerrilla leaders was my biggest concern. Former FARC leaders like Jacobo Arenas — the man who devised the UP and then put his own life at risk for this same cause — has been elevated to near God-like status within rebel columns. Attacking him as I did is not advisable since the FARC doesn't easily forgive.

But I haven't seen the guerrillas since my return. They have been virtually inaccessible since the government launched an offensive, with the help of some $3 billion from the U.S. government, against the FARC and drove it into deeper reaches of the jungles and higher echelons of the mountains. The FARC, of course, will return, and has already shown signs of its old form by coordinating simultaneous assaults on various cities spread throughout the country.

Still, as the guerrillas go deeper into the hills, peace prospects go with them. The government has tried to squeeze them back to the negotiating table. But the FARC has responded with its usual patient approach. Time, remember, is on its side. While suffering some setbacks, the rebels have spent most of the last few years waiting for this government to leave. If they do not like the next government, there's a good chance they will do the same with it. There is no hurry in this revolution.

Politics, meanwhile, remains in the background for the FARC. Its efforts to create a clandestine political party, the Bolivarian Movement, have largely been failures. The guerrillas have not yet worked out a political angle. Their angle remains a military one. There is little reason to believe this will change.

The paramilitaries, I believe, might also have problems with the logic of this book. It pins them to the destruction of the party and asks the government to convict them and those who participated with them in those crimes. So far, only ten people have been convicted of crimes related to the UP and only two for masterminding any killing: Carlos and Fidel Castaño for coordinating the assassination of Bernardo Jaramillo chronicled in Chapter 12, "The *Suizo*." Cases like that of Josué Giraldo still languish in the archives. Amidst it all, the paramilitaries are negotiating with the government about how to end their war. They need a clean slate. The destruction of the UP is not a clean slate, as the country's leading daily, *El Tiempo*, reminded everyone in a recent three-page report on the death of the party and the impunity that has followed.

Still, my fears have abided, in part because some of the protagonists of the paramilitary part of the story are gone. Carlos Castaño, as predicted, has mysteriously disappeared; the location of his brother, Fidel, remains a mystery but his other brother, José Vicente, has emerged from the shadows to become the new leader of the paramilitaries. When I went to investigate Carlos's disappearance, his paramilitary cohorts assured me that he had simply gone missing. In an interview with the weekly magazine *Semana*, José Vicente hinted that Carlos may be in the United States working closely with the Drug Enforcement Administration (DEA). And Carlos's former attaché, who has since relocated to the United States, assured me that he was alive.

But few people believe these tales. Lawyers and paramilitary confidants told me that Carlos had a reputation as a snitch, and many of his colleagues suspected he was working with the DEA for years. In a way, he had already been working with the DEA, since he had helped protect many snitches over the years in a bid to gain favor in Washington so he could eventually escape his criminal past as illustrated in Chapter 15, "The Great Escape." But Carlos couldn't have it both ways: He couldn't be a snitch and work closely with the drug traffickers at the same time. His game as a double agent, it seems, may have caught up with him.

Most of the other protagonists in this book are still alive. Some, like Ivan Cepeda, continue to battle against impunity. When three paramilitary commanders gave speeches to Congress, Cepeda showed up with a large photo of his father, UP Senator Manuel Cepeda, killed by paramilitaries and military personnel in 1994. The pictures of Ivan with his father's photo in the balcony of Congress in the newspapers trumped the paramilitaries' show in Congress.

Others, like Mariella Barragán, the widow of Bernardo Jaramillo, are moving on in some ways. She has a serious boyfriend for the first time since Jaramillo was assassinated by the *suizo*, Andrés Arturo Gutiérrez, in the Bogotá airport. She is also working with the mayor, a former Communist Party and UP member.

In fact, leftist politics are enjoying a resurgence of sorts. The mayor and several leftist senators are playing prominent roles in the political discourse and debate. The Frente Social y Político has morphed into what is known as the Polo Democrático, which will probably ally with the Alternativa Política, a leftist coalition that includes the Communist Party, to present a single candidate for president. Even the Liberal Party has adopted a "Social Democrat" platform.

But Colombia remains Colombia, and politics remains its most dangerous sport. The FARC recently made clear that it was not going to participate in any elections when it attacked a city council session in the south of the country and shot a dozen unarmed councilmen, killing five. Paramilitaries, meanwhile, have said that they control a third of Congress and are seeking more control in the coming elections, which will certainly provide cannon fodder for anyone seeking to kill off a political enemy. And traditional political chieftains are seeking to retake their crowns. Semana calls it an "explosive cocktail."

However, as I know, the past doesn't matter, even when the future is certain. The candidates, especially from the left of the spectrum, will take enormous chances during their campaigns. The bullets, and probably bombs, will most likely come. Despite the violence, the politicians will celebrate their victories and their democracy, and prove yet again that fear and logic have no place in Colombia.

June 2005
Bogotá, Colombia

NOTES ON SOURCES

Prologue: The Martyrs

The foundation for this book came from my masters thesis, "Political Violence in Colombia: The Story of the Unión Patriótica," which can be found in the University of Texas at Austin library. Compared with other countries in Latin America, there are few history books on Colombia in English. Two of the ones used for this prologue were Pearce's *Colombia: Inside The Labyrinth* and Bushnell's *The Making of Modern Colombia*. One Spanish-language source was Gonzalo Sánchez and Mario Aguilera's *Memoria de un país en guerra* (Memories of a country at war). The material concerning the economic roots of *La Violencia* came mostly from Berquist et al. *Violence in Colombia*, in particular Charles Berquist's contribution. Accounts of the U.S. position vis-à-vis Gaitán came from *El saqueo de una ilusión*. Hobsbawm's quote was taken from an article he wrote in the *New York Review of Books* (November 20, 1986). Sánchez's analysis of *La Violencia* came from an article he wrote in the September 1990 issue of *Análisis Político*. The information concerning Communist Party strategy was drawn from interviews with Medófilo Medina and from his work in *Violence in Colombia*, and the two books he wrote on the history of the Colombian Communist Party. Accounts of the "self-defense" groups came from Communists themselves as well as from Matta's *Colombia y las FARC-EP: Origen de la lucha guerrillera; testimonio del comandante Jaime Guaraca*. Lenin's quote is taken from "Guerrilla Warfare" in Pomeroy's *Guerrilla Warfare and Marxism*. The concept of "armed colonialism" is taken from Alfredo Molano, who has compiled several masterful chronicles of the slow colonization process in the southeast of the country. The material for Josué's life came from his own account in *Ceder es más terrible que la muerte* (To give up is more terrible than death). The account of his death is drawn from interviews with Michael Lopez, an eyewitness to the murder, and Josué's widow, Mariella. More about Josué, as well as an excellent account of Colombia's war, can be found in Robin Kirk's *More Terrible than Death*.

Chapter 1: Fighting History

The profile of Betancur was taken from *Semana* magazine. Betancur himself refused to be interviewed and hasn't been interviewed for years. The estimates of the number of guerrillas came from interviews with political scientists such as Alejandro Reyes Posada and Alfredo Rangel, who has served as an adviser to the Colombian Defense Department. The accounts of Rojas Pinilla's repression came from Guzman et al. *La Violencia en Colombia, estudio de un proceso social*, Bushnell's *The Making of Modern Colombia*, and Serpa Erazo's *Rojas Pinilla: Una historia del siglo XX*. All the accounts of Betancur's management of the peace process were from interviews with participants in the process: John Agudelo Ríos, the government's chief representative, and delegates such as Alberto Rojas Puyo and Juan Sebastián Betancur, a representative of the business sector. Fallout because of Communist Party support for the Liberal Party hierarchy can be found in Sánchez's article in *Memoria de un país en guerra*. Concerning Communist Party support of the FARC, several ex-party and ex-FARC explained to me the means by which the party aided the rebels. Several others explained the hierarchy of the Communist Party and how people like Rojas Puyo were shut out from the debates on strategy. Rojas Puyo described for me the trek through Sumapaz to guerrilla headquarters. FARC specialists and members of the "movement," the rebels' name for themselves, explained to me the significance of being an "intellectual half-timer."

Chapter 2: The Desert Fox

The core of this chapter came from speaking with Landazábal and his family and from scouring through his voluminous writings. Accounts of Landazábal's plan to subvert the peace process came from government delegates as well as ex–military officers who participated in the process. Also helpful in reconstructing the U.S. National Security Doctrine and its significance were Lansdale's *In the Midst of Wars*, Linebarger's *Psychological Warfare*, McClintock's *Instruments of Statecraft*, Klare and Kornblugh's *Contrainsurgencia*, Gallón's *La república de las armas*, and Comblin's *El poder militar*, from which I drew citations. Blair's *Las fuerzas armadas: Una mirada civil* and Dávila's article "Ejército regular, conflictos irregulares: La institución militar en los últimos quince años" were helpful for explaining the idea that the military was weak and therefore turned to the paramilitaries for assistance. I also spoke to Dávila, Francisco Leal, Alejandro Reyes Posada, and Eduardo Pizarro, all of whom have studied Colombia's military in detail. Information about the repression under Julio César Turbay came from various sources, including *Tras los pasos perdidos de la guerra sucia* and interviews with Alejandro Reyes Posada and Eduardo Pizarro. Also useful were Luis Alberto Restrepo's article in Berquist el al. *Violence in Colombia*, FICA's *El libro negro de la represión, 1958–1980*, Grabe's *Razones de vida*, Lara's *Siembra vientos y recogeras tempestades*, and Leal's *El oficio de la guerra*. The training of Latin American military officers in the United States came from Black et al. *Garrison Guatemala* and Leal's *Estado y política en Colombia*. Numbers for Communist support throughout the hemisphere came from Smith's *Talons of the Eagle*. The figures on government spending on the Colombian military came from Dávila's "Ejército regular." There are several accounts of the first paramilitary meetings. I drew mostly from Smith's *Tras los pasos*. See also Kirk's *More Terrible than Death*. The violence in the Middle Magdalena Valley region was well documented at the time. I drew from Amnesty International reports as well U.S. embassy cables and *Proyecto Nunca Más* reports. For the number of deaths the military attributed to the paramilitaries, I drew from Colonel Orlando Zafra Galvis, "Conceptos sobre la inteligencia en la guerra subversiva," in *Revista de las Fuerzas Armadas*, No. 122, January–March 1987.

Chapter 3: The Master Plan

To reconstruct Arenas's younger life, I used Alape's classic and singular biography of Manuel Marulanda, *Tirofijo: Los sueños y las montañas*. Opinions of Arenas were diverse. He was a prickly character that few wanted to categorize as warmonger or politician. The FARC is useless on this subject since it takes the old Soviet line of glorifying all who have fought for the "movement." Arenas's battles with the Communist Party are well known. But his relationship with Communist leaders is less certain. There seemed to be a mutual respect, although Arenas believed he knew who needed to guide the Communists to power: the guerrillas. In this, he agreed with the M-19 guerrillas. Indeed, the creation of the M-19 came from Arenas's attempts to enter Bogotá. This material came from talking to ex-FARC and ex-M-19 members. Also helpful was Arenas's *Cese el fuego*. Information concerning the VII Conference is taken from documents obtained by the Colombian military on the conference. The part about kidnapping and illegal drugs came from interviews with ex-FARC. Additional information came from declassified U.S. intelligence reports on the guerrillas provided by the National Security Archives. Communist Party reaction to the FARC's proposal to set up the UP came from interviews with ex-party and ex-FARC. The poll concerning M-19 popularity is taken from Pearce's *Colombia: Inside the Labyrinth*. Details about Arenas's meeting with FARC commanders to explain his plan for the peace process came from interviews with ex-FARC and ex-UP.

Chapter 4: Guerrilla Politics

Information about Arenas's paranoia came from ex-guerrillas and was corroborated by people in the Communist Party who worked closely with him. The finest source on how the FARC organized its *Juntas Patrióticas* is the Communist Party weekly, *Voz*. The paper was the first to report it and had the best access to the camps where organizing was taking place. Other sources include ex-FARC and ex-Communist militants as well as newspaper accounts.

Chapter 5: Black Vladimir

Vladimir did not want to speak about his deeds; he said he was trying to sell his biography. His obstinance and ambition forced me to dig through the public records. There are a half-dozen Vladimir testimonies. He also spoke to a reporter for a local magazine, *VEA*, many years before he was famous. Information about Luis Rubio, Pablo Guarín, and Henry Pérez came from countless newspaper stories, government reports, and testimonies that I leafed through in the courthouse in Bogotá. I got access to the case against Victor Carranza and the case against the Castaño brothers for the murder of Bernardo Jaramillo. I also looked through declassified U.S. intelligence reports on the drug traffickers. The indispensable guide to the creation of the paramilitaries in the Middle Magdalena Valley is Medina Gallego's *Autodefensas, paramilitares y narcotráfico en Colombia: Origen, desarrollo y consolidación. El caso "Puerto Boyacá,"* from which I drew the Betancur quote supporting the Puerto Boyacá model. A useful supplement was *Las verdaderas intenciones de los paramilitares*, by Corporación Observatorio para la Paz, which has particularly good information on Henry Pérez. Additional information about Pablo Escobar and his ranch was gleaned from Cañón's *El Patrón: Vida y muerte de Pablo Escobar*. Kirk's *More Terrible than Death* was also very useful on all counts.

Chapter 6: Too Much Tic

Much of the part concerning buildup to the election was reconstructed using the Communist Party weekly, *Voz*, as well as countless interviews with former UP militants and supporters. Rojas Puyo told me of his worries with regard to the Communist strategy, and he wrote them in letters to Jacobo Arenas, which were published in Arenas's *Correspondencia secreta del proceso de paz: Recopilación, notas y comentarios*. The best account of the M-19's dramatic assault on the Supreme Court is Carrigan's *The Palace of Justice*. Accounts of Jaime Pardo Leal abound. He is as popular in death as he was alive, and most told countless stories of his escapades.

Chapter 7: The "Disposable Ones"

Much of this chapter came from reviewing the Communist Party newspaper, *Voz*. Matta's *Poder capitalista y violencia política en Colombia*, in which he chronicles the deaths of UP members using *Voz* as his source, was also extremely helpful. The notion that the FARC used the peace to promote war was shared by numerous ex-FARC, Communist Party insiders, and analysts. The army charted the rebels' growth. The FARC's expansion into coca-growing areas is detailed in Jaime Jaramillo's *Colonización, coca y guerrilla*. Accounts from *Semana* magazine and declassified U.S. intelligence documents were also helpful. Pieces of the story detailing Rodríguez Gacha's life, his drug business, and his commentary came from Cañón's *El Patrón: Vida y muerte de Pablo Escobar*. The foremost authority on the drug traffickers' massive land grab in the 1980s and 1990s is Alejandro Reyes Posada. In addition to looking closely at his work, I spoke to Reyes on several occasions. Rodríguez Gacha's relationship with the army and police was well known; it emerges in newspaper and magazine accounts of the paramilitaries. The fight between the FARC and Rodríguez Gacha was written about in *Semana* as well as in several books, including Castillo's *La coca nostra*. I corroborated this information with ex-FARC and paramilitaries. Álvaro Salazar told me of his trip to see Rodríguez Gacha in Medellín.

Chapter 8: A Moral Victory

Josué's connection to the rebels was nebulous, but numerous acquaintances verified that he had regular contact with the rebel group to talk strategy. It's harder to say whether that made him a criminal. For his enemies, it certainly did. The story of Julio Cañón came mostly from his widow, María Carmen, who furnished me with some documentation. I got additional information from *Voz*. Leah Carrol's studies on the UP were invaluable because she looked closely at the relationship between political and economic power, and political murder. Much of the information concerning the structure of the paramilitaries in Meta came from testimony of an ex-paramilitary, alias Travolta, who worked for Victor Carranza. Like many others under extreme pressure, Travolta later recanted much of what he had said. The number of people killed in Meta is taken from *Ceder es más terrible que la muerte*.

Chapter 9: The Return of Black Vladimir

Much of this chapter comes from Vladimir's own testimonies. Also instrumental in developing this chapter was *El camino de la niebla*, Volume III, in which the authors reconstruct the crime. Some of the same tireless human rights workers put together the extremely useful and well-documented *Colombia nunca más: Crímenes de lesa humanidad, zona 14 1966 ... tomo I*, of which there are three volumes. In addition, I visited Segovia on two occasions and compiled interviews with locals and witnesses to the massacre. A terrific account of the military offensive against the ELN in the region can be found in Joe Broderick's *El guerrillero invisible*, which is also the brilliant first volume of a biography of ELN leader Manuel "The Priest" Pérez. The information about the paramilitary training came from testimonies of ex-paramilitaries like Vladimir. There are also in-depth news reports concerning this subject, most importantly a groundbreaking report from *Semana* magazine called "The Paramilitary Dossier," which appeared in the issue dated April 11, 1989. I corroborated this information with the paramilitaries themselves.

Chapter 10: The *Perestroikas*

To write this chapter, I talked to a number of Jaramillo's friends, ex-lovers, and colleagues. I also used *Voz* and Vanegas's *Bernardo Jaramillo Ossa: "Es un soplo de la vida."* Sebastián himself told me about organizing security; former UP militants told me about the stresses of working in the party at that time. Several ex-FARC and ex-UP told me of Guillermo Banguero's odyssey in the hands of the FARC and of Braulio Herrera's paranoid trip into oblivion.

Chapter 11: The House of Castaño

Details of the meeting between Escobar and Jaramillo came from people close to Jaramillo as well as sworn testimony. Álvaro Salazar told me of his meeting with Escobar, which is corroborated in sworn testimony. Information about the Castaño family came from a hodgepodge of sources including Carlos Castaño in interviews, Aranguren Molina's biography *Mi confesión*, Castaño's paramilitary colleagues, attorney general investigations, testimony from other paramilitaries, military intelligence reports, and *Semana* magazine. Ronderos's *Retratos del poder* was also useful. The battles between the government and the "extraditables" are chronicled in many books, including Cañón's *El Patrón*, which was the source for the story about Fidel's nickname, "2000." *Semana* provided the details of the death of *El Mejicano*.

Chapter 12: The *Suizo*

Most of this chapter came from the voluminous case file on Bernardo Jaramillo's assassination. During the final proceedings the judge let me look through the file and discuss the case openly with him. In the file are testimonies from the teenage assassin, his family and acquaintances, ex-paramilitaries, and government agents. There are also government reports, newspaper accounts, television transcripts, photographs, and maps. I also spoke to Bernardo's widow and witness to the assassination, Mariella Barragán, on several occasions. A separate book was written about Pizarro's assassination, Roa Rojas's *El asasinato de Carlos Pizarro*. Carlos Castaño himself explained in detail how he trained Yerry, Pizarro's young assassin, in Aranguren Molina's *Mi confesión*. Information about the protests that followed the assassination of Jaramillo came mostly from newspaper accounts, in particular *Voz*. The story about the falling FARC magazines came from an eyewitness to the event. The growing alliance between the UP and the M-19 was well known at the time, and former members of both groups corroborated this information.

Chapter 13: FARC-*landia*

The estimates of FARC soldiers vary, but most calculate that the rebels have between 15,000 and 20,000 soldiers. A former guerrilla militant told me the FARC needs between two and three support people for every soldier it has. Reports of the Iranian meatpacking plant and the Grasso visit to FARC territory leaked into the local press immediately. I traveled through the northern and southern parts of the DMZ on several occasions to report on the peace talks and other matters like security, coca fields, and life in the zone. For a while, the zone became the journalists' second home.

Chapter 14: Justice as a Memory

Iván was kind enough to tell me about his father in detail. I also spoke to other militants about Manuel and his life. It was fairly common knowledge among these circles that Manuel was the Communist Party liaison with the FARC for many years. The Communists were never that secretive, even when the situation most required it. The lawyers collective, Colectivo de Abogados, provided me with the information about Manuel's case. I spoke to a representative of the Organization of American States (OAS) about the UP case. I also had several meetings with Jahel Quiroga, whose group, Reiniciar, furnished me with the figures on UP deaths, "disappearances," and threats. Lastly, I met with several investigators at the attorney general's office about the UP.

Chapter 15: The Great Escape

Material for this chapter was gathered during a six-month investigation into Fidel Castaño's disappearance, which was published by the *Washington Post Magazine* in November 2002. During that time I spoke to several fellow paramilitary leaders, including Carlos Castaño and some who worked closely with Fidel. I also leafed through much paramilitary testimony. Carlos's attempts to hand over drug traffickers to U.S. authorities were well documented at the time, in particular by Gerardo Reyes of *El Nuevo Herald*, the Spanish-language edition of the *Miami Herald*. Additional information about the attempted handover came from David Adams's accounts in the *St. Petersburg Times*, which appeared in early May 2003. And Mark Bowden's indispensable *Killing Pablo* helped deconstruct the role of the PEPES in the dirty war against Pablo Escobar.

Chapter 16: Shades of Jaime

Wilson's case is with the Colectivo de Abogados. The group also has Manuel Cepeda's case and is planning on publishing a book detailing the assassination of the UP leader. Both cases carry with them grave consequences. The Colectivo is under constant threat. Several of its lawyers have had to flee the country. Others continue to work under threat.

Chapter 17: Leftovers

The Communist Party did break from the FARC in 1993. But the rebels have slowly regained power within the party hierarchy, and the tenuous relationship continues in this ambiguous state.

Books and Reports

Alape, Arturo. *La paz, la violencia: Testigos de excepción*, Bogotá: Planeta, 1985.

Alape, Arturo. *Tirofijo: Los sueños y las montañas*. Bogotá: Planeta, 1994.

Amnesty International. *El panorama de los derechos humanos: ¿"Escuadrones de la muerte" a la defensiva?* London 1989.

Amnesty International. *Violencia política en Colombia: Mito y realidad*. London 1994.

Aranguren Molina, Mauricio. *Mi confesión: Carlos Castaño revela sus secretos*. Bogotá: Oveja Negra, 2001.

Arenas, Jacobo. *Cese el fuego*. Bogotá: Oveja Negra, 1985.

Arenas, Jacobo. *Correspondencia secreta del proceso de paz: Recopilación, notas y comentarios*. Bogotá: Oveja Negra, 1989.

Arenas, Jacobo. *Paz: Amigos y enemigos*. Bogotá: Oveja Negra, 1990.

Arrango, Carlos. *Guerrilleras FARC-EP*. Bogotá: ECOE, 1984.

Avila, Abel. *Proceso electoral y crisis en el sistema político*. Barranquilla: Grafitalia, 1981.

Bejarano Sandoval, Ana María. "El proceso de paz durante la administración Betancur (1982–1986): Resultados de un esfuerzo para ampliar el espacio de participación política en Colombia." Thesis for Universidad de los Andes. Bogotá, 1987.

Bernstein, Edward. *Evolutionary Socialism*. New York: B.W. Huebsch, 1912.

Bermúdez Rossi, Major Gonzalo. *Pronunciamiento, conspiraciones y golpes de Estado en Colombia: De la conspiración septembrina al Proceso 8000*. Bogotá: Ediciones Expresión, 1997.

Berquist, Charles, Ricardo Peñaranda, and Gonzalo Sánchez Gómez, editors. *Violence in Colombia: The Contemporary Crisis in Historical Perspective*. Wilmington, Delaware: Scholarly Resources, 1992.

Betancur, Belisario. *Una sola paz*. Bogotá: Talleres Editoriales, 1983.

Bethel, Leslie, editor. *The Cambridge History of Latin America, VIII*. Cambridge: Cambridge University Press, 1991.

Black, George, Milton Jamail, and Norma Stoltz Chinchilla. *Garrison Guatemala*. New York: Monthly Review Press, 1984.

Blair Trujillo, Elsa. *Las fuerzas armadas: Una mirada civil*. Bogotá: CINEP, 1993.

Bonilla, Guido. *La violencia contra la Unión Patriótica: Un crimen de lesa humanidad*. Bogotá: Centro de Estudios e Investigaciones Sociales (CEIS), 1990.

Bottomore, Tom, editor. *A Dictionary of Marxist Thought*. Cambridge, Massachusetts: Blackwell, 1996.

Bowden, Mark. *Killing Pablo*. New York: Atlantic Monthly Press, 2001.

Broderick, Joe. *El guerrillero invisible*. Bogotá: Intermedio, 2000.

Buenaventura, Nicolás. *Programa de los comunistas: Texto de estudio del programa del Partido Comunista Colombiano*. Bogotá: CEIS, 1981.

Buenaventura, Nicolás. *Izquierda y elecciones*. Bogotá: CEIS, 1983.

Buenaventura, Nicolás. *Tregua y Unión Patriótica*. Bogotá: CEIS, 1985.

Bushnell, David. *The Making of Modern Colombia: A Nation in Spite of Itself*. Berkeley: University of California Press, 1993.

Cañón, Luis M. *El Patrón: Vida y muerte de Pablo Escobar*. Bogotá: Planeta, 1994.

Carrigan, Ana. *The Palace of Justice: A Colombian Tragedy*. New York: Four Walls Eight Windows, 1993.

Carroll, Leah. "Backlash against Peasant Gains in Rural Democratization: The Experience of Leftist County Executives in Colombia, 1988–1990." *Berkeley Journal of Sociology*, 39, 1994–1995.

Carroll, Leah. "Pacted Peace or Escalated Violence: The Contrasting Effects of Democratizing in Rural Colombia." Paper for Washington D.C. LASA Congress, 1995.

Casas Aguilar, Justo. *La Violencia en los Llanos Orientales*. Bogotá: ECOE, 1986.

Castaño, Carlos. *Las autodefensas y la paz*. Talleres Colombia Libre, 1999.

Castillo, Fabio. *La coca nostra*. Bogotá: Editorial Documentos Periodísticos, 1991.

Castro Caycedo, Germán. *En secreto*. Bogotá: Planeta, 1996.

Centro Gáitán. *Once ensayos sobre la Violencia*. Bogotá: CEREC, 1985.

Cepeda Vargas, Manuel. *Cómo son las elecciones en Colombia*. Bogotá: Fescol, CEREC, and CIDER, 1986.

Chaliand, Gérard, editor. *Guerrilla Strategies: An Historical Anthology from the Long March to Afghanistan*. Berkeley: University of California Press, 1982.

Colectivo de Abogados. ASCODAS, Justicia y Paz, and ILSA, editors. *Ceder es más terrible que la muerte 1985–1996: Una década de violencia en el Meta*. Bogotá: Meta Civic Committee for Human Rights et al., 1997.

Colombia nunca más: Crímenes de lesa humanidad, zona 14 1966 . . . tomo I. Bogotá: Proyecto Nunca Más, 2000.

Comblin, Joseph. *El poder militar en América Latina*. Salamanca, Spain: Ediciones Sígueme, 1978.

Comisión Andina de Juristas-Seccional Colombiana. *Nordeste Antioqueño y Magdalena Medio*. Bogotá: Comisión Andina de Juristas, 1993.

Comisión Andina de Juristas-Seccional Colombiana. *Urabá*. Bogotá: Comisión Andina de Juristas, 1994.

Comisión de Estudios sobre la Violencia. *Colombia: Violencia y democracia*. Bogotá: Universidad Nacional de Colombia, 1987.

Comité Central del Partido Comunista. *Treinta años de lucha del partido comunista*. Bogotá: Ediciones Paz y Socialismo, 1960.

Córdoba Triviño, Jaime. *Informe para el Gobierno, el Congreso y el Procurador General de la Nacion: Recomendaciones del Defensor del Pueblo; estudio de casos de homocidio de miembros de la Unión Patriótica y Esperanza Paz y Libertad*. Bogotá: Ediciones Jurídicas, Gustavo Ibañez, 1992.

Corporación Observatorio para la Paz. *Las verdaderas intenciones de las FARC*. Bogotá: Intermedio, 1999.

Corporación Observatorio para la Paz. *Las verdaderas intenciones de los paramilitares*. Bogotá: Intermedio, 2002.

Cortés Arévalo, Fernando. *El asasinato de Galán*. Bogotá: Planeta, 1994.

Dávila Ladrón de Guevara, Andrés. "Ejército regular, conflictos irregulares: La institución militar en los últimos quince años." Article prepared for the Seminario de Estudios Estratégicos. Bogotá: Universidad de los Andes, March–October 1996.

Debray, Régis. *Revolution in the Revolution*. New York: Grove Press, 1967.

Dudley, Steven, "Political Violence in Colombia: The Story of the Unión Patriótica." Masters thesis for the University of Texas at Austin. Austin, 1998.

El camino de la niebla: Masacres en Colombia y su impunidad. volumes 1–3, Bogotá: Liga Internacional por los Derechos y la Liberación de los Pueblos-Sección Colombiana, 1990.

El saqueo de una ilusión: El 9 de abril: 50 años después. Photographs by Sady González. Bogotá: Ediciones Número, con el apoyo del Ministerio de Cultura y el Instituto Distrital de Cultura y Turismo, 1997.

Fundación Manuel Cepeda Vargas, editors. *La memoria frente a los crímenes de lesa humanidad*. Bogotá: La Imprenta Editores, 1996.

Fundación para la Investigación y la Cultura (FICA). *El libro negro de la represión, 1958–1980*. Bogotá: FICA, 1980.

Gaitán Pavía, Pilar, and Carlos Moreno Ospina. *Poder local: Realidad y utopía de la decentralización en Colombia*. Bogotá: Tercer Mundo, 1992.

Gallón Giraldo, Gustavo. *La república de las armas*. Bogotá: CINEP, 1983.

Gallón Giraldo, Gustavo, editor. *Entre movimientos y cuadillos*. Bogotá: CINEP and CEREC, 1989.

Giraldo, Fernando. *Democracia y discurso político en la Unión Patriótica*. Bogotá: Centro Editorial Javierana, 2001.

González Árias, José Jairo, and Elsy Marulanda Álvarez. *Historias de frontera: Colonización y guerras en el Sumapaz*. Bogotá: CINEP, 1990.

Grabe, Vera. *Razones de vida*, Bogotá: Planeta, 2000.

Guarín Bocanegra, Leonardo. *Pablo Guarín V.: El libertador del Magdalena Medio*. Editorial Magdalena Libre. (No date of publication given.)

Guevara, Ernesto. *Guerrilla Warfare*. Lincoln: University of Nebraska Press, 1985.

Guillén Martínez, Fernando. *El poder político en Colombia*. Bogotá: Planeta, 1996.

Guzman, Germán, Orlando Fals Borda, and Eduardo Umaña Luna. *La Violencia en Colombia, estudio de un proceso social*. Bogotá: Tercer Mundo/Colección "El Hombre," 1962.

Inés García, Clara. *Urabá: Región, actores y conflicto, 1960–1990*. Bogotá: CEREC, 1996.

Jaramillo, Bernardo. *Entrevista con la nueva izquierda: Bernardo Jaramillo (Unión Patriótica)*. Managua: Centro de Documentación y Ediciones Latinoamericanos, 1989.

Jaramillo, Jaime Eduardo, et al. *Colonización, coca y guerrilla*. 2nd edition. Bogotá: Alianza Editorial Colombiana, 1989.

Jiménez Gómez, Carlos. *Los documentos del procurador I*. Bogotá: Impreso Editorial Retina, 1987.

Jiménez Gómez, Carlos. *Los documentos del procurador IV*. Bogotá: Impreso Editorial Retina, 1987.

Kautsky, Karl. *Democracy versus Communism*. New York: Rand School Press, 1946.

Kirk, Robin. *More Terrible than Death: Massacres, Drugs, and America's War in Colombia*. New York: Public Affairs, 2003.

Klare, Micheal T., and Peter Kornbluh, coordinators. *Contrainsurgencia, proinsurgencia y antiterrorismo en los años 80: El arte de la guerra de baja intensidad*. México, D.F.: Editorial Grijalbo, 1988.

Landazábal, Fernando. *Estrategia de la subversión y su desarrollo en América Latina*. Bogotá: Editorial Pax, 1969.

Landazábal, Fernando. *La subversión y el conflicto social*. Bogotá: Ediciones Tercer Mundo, 1980.

Landsdale, Edward. *In the Midst of Wars*. New York: Harper and Row, 1972.

Laquer, Walter, editor. *The Guerrilla Reader: A Historical Anthology*. Philadelphia: Temple University Press, 1977.

Lara, Patricia. *Siembra vientos y recogeras tempestades*. Bogotá: Editorial Punto de Partida, 1992.

Lara Bonilla, Rodrigo. *Los partidos políticos colombianos: Presente y futuro*. Bogotá: Fundación Simón Bolívar, 1983.

Leal, Francisco. *Estado y política en Colombia*. Bogotá: Siglo Veintiuno Editores, 1984.

Leal, Francisco. *El oficio de la guerra*. Bogotá: Tercer Mundo Editores, 1994.

Leal, Francisco, editor. *Orden mundial y seguridad: Nuevos desafíos para Colombia y América Latina*. Bogotá: Tercer Mundo/Instituto de Estudios Políticos y Relaciones Internacionales–Universidad Nacional/Sociedad Internacional para el Desarrollo, 1994.

Leal, Francisco, and Andrés Dávila Ladrón de Guevara. *Clientelismo: El sistema político y su expresión regional*. 2nd edition. Bogotá: Tercer Mundo/IEPRI, 1991.

Leal, Francisco, and Leon Zamosc, editors. *Al filo del caos: Crisis política en Colombia de los años 80*. Bogotá: Tercer Mundo/IEPRI, 1991.

Lenin, V. I. *Marx, Engels, Marxism*. Moscow: Foreign Languages Publishing House, 1947.

Lenin, V. I. *Against Revisionism*. Moscow: Progress Publishers, 1966.

Linebarger, Paul. *Psychological Warfare*. Washington, D.C.: Infantry Journal Press, 1948.

Luxemburg, Rosa. *Reform or Revolution*. New York: Pathfinder Press, 1974.

Marulanda, Elsy. *Colonización y conflicto: Las lecciones del Sumapaz*. Bogotá: Tercer Mundo, 1991.

Marx, Karl, and Friedrich Engels. *The Communist Manifesto*. New York: Washington Square Press, 1967.

Matta Aldana, Luis Alberto. *Colombia y las FARC-EP: Origen de la lucha guerrillera; testimonio del comandante Jaime Guaraca*. Navarra, Spain: Txalaparta, 1999.

Matta Aldana, Luis Alberto. *Poder capitalista y violencia política en Colombia: Terrorismo de estado y genocidio contra la Unión Patriótica*. Bogotá: Ideas y Soluciones Gráficas, 2002.

McAleese, Peter, with Marc Bles. *No Mean Soldier: The Story of the Ultimate Professional Soldier in the SAS and Other Forces*. London: Orion, 1998.

McClintock, Michael. *Instruments of Statecraft*. New York: Pantheon Press, 1992.

Medina, Medófilo. *Historia del Partido Comunista de Colombia, tomo I*. Bogotá: CEIS, 1980.

Medina, Medófilo. *Historia del Partido Comunista de Colombia: Cuadernos de la historia del PCC, tomo II*. Bogotá: CEIS, 1989.

Medina Gallego, Carlos. *Autodefensas, paramilitares y narcotráfico en Colombia: Origen, desarrollo y consolidación. El caso "Puerto Boyacá."* Bogotá: Editorial Documentos Periodísticos, 1990.

Medina Gallego, Carlos, and Mireya Téllez Ardila. *La violencia parainstitucional: Paramilitar y parapolicial en Colombia*. Bogotá: Rodríguez Quito Editores, 1994.

Mendel, Arthur, editor. *Essential Works of Marxism*. New York: Bantam, 1961.

Molano, Alfredo. *Los años del tropel: Crónicas de las violencia*. Bogotá: CEREC/El Áncora Editores, 1985.

Molano, Alfredo. *Trochas y fusiles*. Bogotá: IEPRI/El Áncora Editores, 1994.

Motta, Hernán, editor. *Acción parlamentaria de la UP*. Bogotá: Korina, 1995.

Olmos, Victor. *Por un partido único Marxista-Leninista*. Medellín: Editorial 8 de junio, 1975.

Oquist, Paul. *Violence, Conflict, and Politics in Colombia*. New York: Academic Press, 1980.

Palacio, Germán, editor. *La irrupción del paraestado*. Bogotá: CEREC and ILSA. (No date of publication given.)

Pearce, Jenny. *Colombia: Inside the Labyrinth*. London: Latin American Bureau, 1990.

Pinzón de Lewin, Patricia. *Los partidos políticos Colombianos*. Bogotá: FESCOL, 1987.

Pinzón de Lewin, Patricia. *Pueblos, regiones y partidos: La regionalización electoral; atlas electoral colombiano*. Bogotá: CEREC, 1989.

Pizarro Leongómez, Eduardo. *Las Farc: 1949–1966*. Bogotá: Tercer Mundo, 1991.

Pomeroy, William J., editor. *Guerrilla Warfare and Marxism*. New York: International Publishers, 1978.

Restrepo, Luis Alberto. *Elección popular de alcaldes: Colombia y la experiencia internacional*. Bogotá: Tercer Mundo, 1988.

Reyes Posada, Alejandro, editor. *Pacificar la paz*. Bogotá: Comisión de Superación de la Violencia, 1992.

Róa Rojas, Mónica. *El asesinato de Carlos Pizarro*. Bogotá: Planeta, 1995.

Romero, Manuel, and Yira Castro. *La política de los comunistas colombianos: Texto de estudio de la táctica del Partido Comunista de Colombia*. Bogotá: Ediciones Suramérica, 1978.

Ronderos, María Teresa. *Retratos del poder: Vidas extremas en la Colombia contemporanea*. Bogotá: Planeta, 2002.

Rouquié, Alain. *The Military and the State in Latin America*. Berkeley: University of California Press, 1987.

Ruíz Novoa, Alberto. *El gran desafío*. Bogotá: Tercer Mundo, 1965.

Sánchez Gómez, Gonzalo. *Guerra y política en la sociedad colombiana*. Bogotá: El Áncora Editores, 1991.

Sánchez Gómez, Gonzalo, and Mario Aguilera, editors. *Memoria de un país en guerra: Los Mil Días 1899–1902*. Bogotá: Planeta, 2001.

Sánchez Gómez, Gonzalo, and Donny Meertens. *Bandoleros, gamonales y campesinos: El caso de la Violencia en Colombia*. Bogotá: El Áncora Editores, 1983.

Sánchez Gómez, Gonzalo, and Ricardo Peñarada, editors. *Pasado y presente de la Violencia en Colombia*, 1st and 2nd editions. Bogotá: CEREC, 1986 and 1991.

Serpa Erazo, Jorge. *Rojas Pinilla: Una historia del siglo XX, Rojas Pinilla*. Bogotá: Planeta, 1999.

Smith, Peter H. *Talons of the Eagle: Dynamics of U.S.-Latin American Relations*. Oxford: Oxford University Press, 1996.

Tras los pasos perdidos de la guerra sucia: Paramilitarismo y operaciones encubiertas en Colombia. Brussels: NCOS et al., 1995.

Trotsky, Leon. *Permanent Revolution*. New York: Pioneer Publishers, 1931.

Trotsky, Leon. *Terrorism and Communism: A Reply to Karl Kautsky*. Ann Arbor: University of Michigan Press, 1961.

Tse-tung, Mao. *Selected Works*, volumes 1 and 2. Beijing: Foreign Languages Press, 1965.

Tse-tung, Mao. *On Guerrilla Warfare*. Champaign: University of Illinois Press, 2000.

Valeriano, Napolean D., and Charles T. R. Bohannan. *Counter-Guerrilla Operations: The Philippine Experience*. New York: Frederick A. Praeger, 1966.

Vanegas, Napoleon. *Bernardo Jaramillo Ossa: "Es un soplo de la vida."* Bogotá: Foro Nacional por Colombia, 1991.

Vargas Meza, Ricardo. *Drogas, máscaras, y juegos: Narcotráfico y conflicto armado en Colombia*. Bogotá: Tercer Mundo, 1999.

Vargas Velásquez, Alejo. *Colonización y conflicto armado*. Bogotá: CINEP, 1992.

Vásquez, Álvaro. *Para la acción revolucionaria*. Bogotá: Fondo Editorial Suramérica, 1980.

Vélez Rodríguez, Claudia Patricia. "Estudio sobre un movimiento de oposición política en Colombia: Auge y decadencia de la Unión Patriótica, 1986–1990." Thesis for the Universidad de Los Andes. Bogotá, Colombia, June 1992.

Viera, Gilberto. *Política y revolución en Colombia*. Bogotá: Ediciones Armadillo, 1977.

Periodicals Consulted

Análisis Político (Universidad Nacional, Bogotá)
Associated Press
Berkeley Journal of Sociology
Colombia Hoy Informa
El Colombiano
El Espectador
El Mundo (Spain)
El País (Spain)
El Tiempo
Estrategia Económica y Financiera
Forbes
Foro Internacional
Fortune
The Guardian (London)
The Independent (London)
Justicia y Paz
La Prensa
London Times
Los Angeles Times
Margen Izquierda
Money
NACLA: Report on the Americas
New York Review of Books
New York Times
New York Times Magazine
Newsweek
Orlando Sentinel
Revista de las Fuerzas Armadas
St. Petersburg Times
Semana
Time
Vanguardia Liberal
Washington Post

INDEX